Evolution of a Movement

This publication is made possible in part by a subvention from the generous support of the Andrew W. Mellon Foundation.

The publisher and the University of California Press Foundation gratefully acknowledge the generous support of the Anne G. Lipow Endowment Fund in Social Justice and Human Rights.

Evolution of a Movement

*Four Decades of California Environmental
Justice Activism*

Tracy E. Perkins

UNIVERSITY OF CALIFORNIA PRESS

University of California Press
Oakland, California

Library of Congress Cataloging-in-Publication Data

Names: Perkins, Tracy E., 1980– author.
Title: Evolution of a movement : four decades of California
    environmental justice activism / Tracy E. Perkins.
Description: Oakland, California : University of California
    Press, [2022] | Includes bibliographical references and
    index.
Identifiers: LCCN 2021041063 (print) | LCCN 2021041064
    (ebook) | ISBN 9780520376977 (hardcover) |
    ISBN 9780520376984 (paperback) | ISBN 9780520976344
    (ebook)
Subjects: LCSH: Environmental justice—California—
    History. | Environmental justice—California—Case
    studies. | Environmentalism—California—Case studies. |
    Climatic changes—California. | California—Environmental
    conditions. | BISAC: POLITICAL SCIENCE / Public Policy /
    Environmental Policy | SOCIAL SCIENCE / Sociology /
    General
Classification: LCC GE235.C25 P47 2020 (print) |
    LCC GE235.C25 (ebook) | DDC 363.7/056109794—dc23
LC record available at https://lccn.loc.gov/2021041063
LC ebook record available at https://lccn.loc.gov/2021041064

Manufactured in the United States of America

28 27 26 25 24 23 22
10 9 8 7 6 5 4 3 2 1

This book is dedicated to the memories of

Judy Brady
Luke Cole
Teresa De Anda
Tessie Ester
Marie Harrison
Denny Larson
Mary Lou Mares
Emiliano Mataka
Nettie Morrison

*and to all other California environmental
justice activists, past and present*

Contents

Illustrations

Preface

As I revised this manuscript in the summer of 2020, the country was full of catastrophe. The COVID-19 pandemic was sweeping the globe, with the highest death toll in the United States. The long crisis of anti-Black police violence reached a new level of public awareness with the murder of George Floyd by a police officer, who kneeled on Floyd's neck for eight minutes and forty-six seconds while three fellow officers looked on. The scene was caught on video, sparking a summer of public protest, met with more police violence and more police killings of Black Americans. Californians suffered through another fire season, which yet again topped previous seasons as the worst on record.[1] The state's air quality, already poor in some regions, plummeted, and San Franciscans posted pictures to social media of their neighborhoods cast in the light of a sky orange with air pollution.

Police violence and the pandemic disproportionately killed people of color, showing how deeply ingrained racism remains in US society. The interwoven catastrophes of 2020 made brutally clear that environmental degradation is inseparable from racism and classism. COVID-19 hit particularly hard for people with preexisting health conditions, such as reduced lung capacity from living in areas with high air pollution levels—who are disproportionately people of color and the poor. They, like George Floyd in 2020, Eric Garner in 2014, and at least seventy others who died in police custody between 2010 and 2020, might also utter the piercing words "I can't breathe."[2] Indeed, some of the victims of police brutality were also victims of environmental racism: Eric Garner had asthma, and Freddie Gray had lead poisoning, both of which are more common in Black communities and other communities of color, which have some of the highest air pollution and lead exposure levels in the country.[3]

Similarly, the new language of "essential workers"—people whose jobs are so important to society that their workplaces were kept open during pandemic lockdowns—showcases the country's perverse social system: the people doing the work that society needs the most, such as growing and selling food, have the fewest protections. For example, farmworkers (who already are exposed to pesticides on the job, have poor access to health care, and are constantly under threat of deportation even though the country depends on their labor) were hit especially hard by COVID-19 and the California fires. While other, richer Californians sheltered in place in their homes to avoid exposure to coronavirus and to unhealthy smoky air, farmworkers continued on in the fields. The air pollution they breathed in worsened the impacts of the coronavirus, which ravages the lungs. This will only will only get worse: ongoing climate change means that future annual fire seasons will likely continue to intensify.

The movement for Black liberation, responding to anti-Black police violence, ramped up after George Floyd's murder and others that followed. Peaceful, law-abiding marches along designated routes were heavily policed, and Black protesters were subjected to tear gas, rubber bullets, and battery, while white supremacist counterprotesters were handled gently by police. (Indeed, some of those who later ransacked the nation's Capitol on January 6, 2021 *were* police, attempting to stop the official count of the vote that would make Joe Biden president.)[4] When Black people took their frustrations directly to the street, without waiting for marches to be planned and permits sought, a minority of protesters engaged in property destruction and roving confrontations with the police, which critics called riots. These critics, who declared that protesters should use established political channels, ignored the fact that those channels were not working; they had not stemmed the tide of racism leading to Black deaths.

I watched these events unfurl across the nation as I put the finishing touches on this book, which examines the political dynamics that play out around and in California environmental justice activism. Environmental justice activism has moved increasingly away from disruptive street protest and toward working through the more established channels: these days, many California environmental justice protests have permits and follow carefully scripted routes, rarely suffering police violence. This shift in movement strategy from working against "the system" to working within it is in part caused by changes in the larger racial context of the last four decades. Some racism has changed, gone underground; these forms appear on the surface to be less racist than prior forms. While I examine racism primarily in terms of the multiracial California environmental justice movement's tactics and aims, my observations also speak to racial justice activism more broadly. Although Governor Gavin Newsom has called California a "nation-state," positing a kind of Californian exceptionalism, California is also "of" the nation, and Californians struggle with racism, income inequality, and environmental degradation just as other US residents do. This book speaks to the deep problems—class, racial, environmental, social—that America has grappled with for centuries.

Most of the research for this book was completed during a time of Democrats' control of both California and national leadership, with the nation's first Black president serving at the top. But the Barack Obama presidency did not bring about the "post-racial society" touted by some observers (as if the election of a single Black man to the presidency could somehow solve over four hundred years of racism). The notion of a post-racial society is simply another form of the claim to "color blindness," which some have called "smiling" racism. The idea that our society no longer "sees race" in fact perpetuates racism by shrinking the space available to acknowledge that it continues as part of the fabric of American life, and thus also to address it. Indeed, any illusion that America had solved racism was broken by the 2016 election of Donald Trump, which relegitimized the public expression of overtly white supremacist attitudes. These two types of racism—the smiling "color-blind" and the more explicit and "spectacular" forms of racism—can and do exist side by side, and both help to maintain the racial status quo in America.[5]

During the Trump presidency, environmental justice activities in Democrat-led California continued much on the same path that they had been on during the previous presidential administration, with the exception of a more antagonistic relationship with the federal government. As a state, California opposed many Trump administration policies, from immigration to the environment. The Obama-era interactions between environmental justice activists and the California state government that I document here remained relevant during the Trump years, which affected California perhaps less than many other states whose leaders embraced Trumpism. This book's central concern remains relevant today: while opportunities for movement institutionalization—movement integration into formal organizational structures, in this case, nongovernmental organizations (NGOs) and government—wax and wane depending on political and social factors, the question of the value of movement institutionalization itself persists.

This book is also relevant to contemporary debates in other ways. It documents the intramovement dynamics of conflict between oppositional, disruptive activists and those who push for institutionalization within the California environmental justice movement: dynamics that are also visible among Black Lives Matter (BLM) activists. BLM's national, chapter-based organizational structure and its diverse approaches to political change reflect this same conflicted dynamic, as some of BLM's early organizers have moved into conventional politics and policy work, while others remain committed to more outsider tactics.

The challenges facing social movements are particularly visible when those in power are explicitly hostile to them, but they are not erased when those in power seem sympathetic and invite engagement. During these periods, they are simply blurred, swept out of sight under the smiling surface. I watched this dynamic play out from my chair in the faculty section of historically Black Howard University's 2016 commencement as President Obama addressed the graduates. After emphasizing the importance of compromise, he praised the one BLM activist who had participated in his police reform task force, implicitly chastising the many who chose not to participate in such institutional channels.[6] But activists have good reason to question whether institutional participation is the best way to influence the political process. I hope this book will help both academics and activists from all kinds of social movements grapple with the implications of social movement institutionalization by highlighting both its possibilities and its risks.

Acknowledgments

I did the research and writing of this book across a large swath of my adult life, beginning with my master's research at UC Davis and my doctoral work at UC Santa Cruz and continuing throughout my academic career: my first faculty appointment at Howard University, fellowships at the University of Arizona and the University of Maryland, Baltimore County, and my current position at Arizona State University. Along the way I explored much of California; drove across the country four times; lived in seven different homes; survived a global pandemic; lost my father; met countless wonderful activists, students, and colleagues; met my true love; and gave birth to a beautiful baby. To everyone who has been a fellow traveler along the way, thank you.

The threads that ultimately were woven into this book started early, during my time as a community development master's student at UC Davis from 2006 to 2008. Committee members Dave Campbell, Jonathan London, Julie Sze, and Natalia Deeb-Sossa guided my research on women's pathways into environmental justice activism in the San Joaquin Valley.[1] Julie Sze also supported me in turning some of the content from that project into the public-facing Voices from the Valley project, which featured interactive playback theater performances by Kairos Theater Ensemble, photo exhibits, oral history, teaching tools, a news feed/archive, and a website.[2] Conversations with Andy Szasz helped me select the topic of the changing environmental justice movement over time for my dissertation in the Sociology Department at UC Santa Cruz.

He also donated an old stack of EPA reports on hazardous waste from his own research (you can see the results on page 43). Andy, Jonathan Fox, and Miriam Greenberg guided this stage of my training generously.

Multiple sources provided funding to conduct interviews, attend conferences, and create public-facing projects from my research across my time as an MS student, PhD student, and early career faculty member. At Howard University, this includes the Advanced Summer Faculty Research Fellowship. From UC Santa Cruz, these include the Environmental Studies Department's Hammett Graduate Fellowship, the Center on Agroecology and Sustainable Food Systems' Research and Outreach Grant, the Graduate Student Association Travel Grant, and the Sociology Department Travel Award. From UC Davis, these include the Consortium for Women and Research Graduate Research Award, funds from the Humanities Institute, the Orville and Erna Thompson Travel Award, and the Henry A. Jastro and Peter J. Shields Graduate Research Scholarship. Thanks also go to the American Sociological Association's Spivack Program Community Action Research Initiative, the University of California's California Studies Consortium Graduate Research Travel Grant, the American Society for Environmental History's Travel Grant, and the American Studies Association's Community Partnership Grant.

Howard University also provided other forms of support. Okianer Dark, Rubin Patterson, Elka Stevens, Kehbuma Langmia, and Lenese Herbert provided community and time to write through the Jr. Faculty Writing and Creative Works Summer Academy, as did Sonya Smith through her organization of the ADVANCE writing retreat. Tony Smith, Ruth Rasby, and Angelique Carson ensured I had access to the library's resources. Marie Jipguep and Rebecca Reviere helped me navigate external fellowships. They also provided welcome encouragement, as did many other department colleagues; Ralph Gomes is much missed. I shared a wall and then an office with Christopher Gunderson over five years; I am grateful for his humor, keen intellect, and ready ear. To the rest of my departmental colleagues, thank you for the community you provided as I taught, researched, wrote, and settled into life in a new city. My newest colleagues at Arizona State have helped see me across the finish line with their goodwill and interest in the book.

Two semester-long fellowships during my time at Howard University provided space to think, research, and write. The University of Arizona's Agnese Nelms Haury Program in Environment and Social Justice hosted me as a visiting associate in the spring of 2018, with Tracey Osborne and Brian Mayer serving as my faculty sponsors. The University of Maryland, Baltimore County's Dresher Center for the Humanities hosted me as an Inclusion Imperative Visiting Faculty Fellow in the fall of 2019, where Jessica Berman, Rachel Brubaker, and Courtney Hobson provided a warm welcome.

Starting in my last year as a PhD student, I have been privileged to work with many different student research assistants who conducted background research, transcription, and coding. Thank you to Arizona State University undergraduate Alyssa Orozco; Howard University graduate students Jesse DiValli, Britany Gatewood, and Kemet Azubuike; Howard University undergraduates Amber Swain, Olivia Byrd, Sherille Bosfield, Aolani Aviles, Imani Bryant, and Lundyn Davis; and UC Santa Cruz undergraduates Savannah Coker, Zoe Stricker, Evelyn Torres Arrellano, Luis Morales, Alex Buck, and Amanda Bunnell. Research group meetings with these students and others working on other projects were a highlight of my week! Thank you also to Jay Driskell for your background research on hazardous waste.

I've also benefited from many other forms of community during the time I worked on this book. Manuel Vallée and Lauren Richter provided group check-ins over the years, as did Chan Thai, Greg Scontras, and Bharat Venkat. Until the pandemic, I spent lots of time writing in cafés by myself or with writing buddies, who provided companionship and energy to do the work. Thank you for writing with me, Annie Claus, Jordanna Matlon, Susan Shepler, Erin Collins, Brandi Thompson Summers, Michelle Glowa, Jeff Jenkins, Sandy Brown, Sarah Romano, and Jen Richter. Andy Couturier's book-writing group was another place where I found the companionship of other writers. Coauthors Aaron Soto-Karlin and Lindsey Dillon were part of my learning process around waste-to-energy/incineration facilities and international carbon offsets, both of which show up again in this book. Conference goers at the American Sociological Association, the American Association of Geographers, the American Society for Environmental History, and the North Carolina Environmental Justice Network asked helpful questions about early iterations of the book's content.

A number of people helped with the big lift of transforming my dissertation into this book. Thank you for reading and commenting on my book proposal, Alison Alkon, Andy Szasz, Karen Kelsky, David Meyer, Dvera Saxton, Laura Pulido, David Pellow, Jeff Jenkins, Lynette Perkins, and Jesse DiValli. Even more people read drafts of different pieces of the book along the way. In no particular order, thank you to these people from the environmental justice world: Leslie Fields, Caroline

Farrell, Jane Williams, John Mataka, Tom Helme, Maricela Mares Alatorre, Arsenio Mataka, Gladys Limón, Bill Gallego, Brent Newell, Strela
Cervas, Will Rostov, Jeff Conant, and Michele Prichard. Thank you also
to scholars Jonathan Fox, Laura-Anne Minkoff-Zern, Lauren Richter,
Patrick Bigger, Manuel Vallée, Danielle Purifoy, Michael Méndez, David
Meyer, Jill Harrison, Christopher Gunderson, Jonathan London, Ver-
non Morris, Michelle Glowa, Erin Collins, Kate Chandler, Annie Claus,
Jeff Jenkins, and Claudia Lopez. Thank you to Megan Carney for organizing a workshop on one of the book chapters (which, as it turns out,
I later cut) at the University of Arizona's Center for Regional Food
Studies. Thank you also to the undergraduate students in my Howard
University Environmental Inequality classes who read and discussed
drafts of this manuscript. Finally, thank you to the three anonymous
reviewers that UC Press solicited, who provided important feedback
that strengthened the quality of the finished product.

Other people on and off campus also supported my research process
in innumerable ways. Bernie Zaleha entertained me by phone with a narrative tour of my drive through the mountainous Cajon Pass and down
into San Bernardino on one memorable research trip. Court Lomax,
Trinidad Arredondo, Ryan Oprea, and Marla Pleyte provided places to
stay while on the road. Mateo Rutherford and Roy Rojas from Berkeley
Translation Interpreting and Transcription Services transcribed and then
translated my Spanish-language interviews.

As a first-time book author, I am grateful to everyone who showed
me the ropes and helped me cross the finish line. Ernesto Castaneda
and Alison Alkon shared their book proposals with me as I wrote my
own. Derek Musgrove, Susan Shepler, Annie Claus, and Sarah Romano
shared and talked through the letters they wrote in response to reviewer
feedback for their books. Heath Sledge and Petra Shenk's invaluable
editing taught me a lot about writing. Anya Paretskaya ensured the
citations are in good order. Ben Pease suffered through many rounds
of my revision requests while he made the map of successful anti-
incinerator battles in California, for which Jane Williams and Bradley
Angel provided key information based on their many long years fighting
these facilities. Ken Duckert edited my photographs into the beautiful
black-and-white versions included here, and Christina Rice provided
historical images from the Los Angeles Public Library archives. At the
University of California Press, Kate Marshall and then Stacy Eisenstark
handled the book's acquisition and review process, ably assisted by Naja
Pulliam Collins. Kate Hoffman was the production editor, and Teresa

Iafolla handled marketing communications. Jon Dertien at BookComp, Inc., managed the book's production, Sharon Langworthy provided excellent copyediting, Maureen Johnson created the index, and Robert Ludkey and Lynette Perkins provided fresh eyes for proofreading. Thank you all for showing me how a book gets made and for making mine the best it can be. All remaining mistakes are, of course, my own.

Most importantly, thank you to all the environmental justice activists who let me interview them over the years, in some cases multiple times. Learning about your work and hearing your stories has been a highlight of my career.

Last, thank you to my mother, who made me a better writer. And thank you to Vernon Morris and our son Teddy, for so many good things.

Introduction

Environmental Justice Activism
Then and Now

In the 1980s and early 1990s, environmental justice activists made headlines across California and the nation. Tribes, low-income communities, and communities of color faced serious environmental problems: agricultural poisons, incinerators that released toxic substances such as dioxin into the air, industrial accidents at oil refineries, and direct exposure to hazardous wastes, among others. But their pleas for help were typically ignored or stonewalled by public officials.[1] Many residents therefore turned to more confrontational tactics. Corporate representatives were run out of town by angry residents at raucous public hearings; roads were blockaded to prevent access to industrial sites; schoolchildren skipped school and set up their desks inside the halls of the state capitol; and Spanish-speaking residents of Kettleman City, told to "go to the back of the room" to hear a Spanish translation about a proposed hazardous waste incinerator, instead stormed the front.[2]

These kinds of disruptive "outsider" tactics are less common today. Now, many California environmental justice activists use "insider" tactics: they work *with* the government rather than disrupt routine government activities through protest. Many activists who now adopt insider political tactics had in the past been excluded from these institutional channels, and at least some of them had once seen these forms of activism as complicit rather than pragmatic. Nonetheless, environmental justice activists now sit on government advisory boards at the local, regional, state, and national levels. They are on staff in the governor's office, the Public Utilities Commission, and the California Environmental Protection Agency (CalEPA). Paid environmental justice professionals engage in politicking in the state capitol and train residents to lobby Congress. They write opinion editorials and host gala events that honor state regulators and local developers alongside the residents impacted by pollution and other environmental harms. Multiple groups endorse candidates seeking political office. People from the state governor to the largest waste management company in North America profess their commitment to environmental justice.

The shift from disruptive, demanding, and confrontational tactics to absorption into institutional structures was well underway by the 2000s. Many community groups had formalized into nonprofit organizations; later, their staff began to trickle into government. Increasingly, environmental justice nonprofits have professionalized, creating formal organizational and legal structures, focusing on fundraising, and hiring full-time paid staff to manage administrative work and community organizing. These days, when environmental justice street protests do occur, they are hardly disruptive at all; activists gain permits to hold marches and follow a predefined travel route, after which life quickly goes back to normal. This book documents this shift and examines how and why it took place. This history of the environmental justice movement in California analyzes how its members use "insider" tactics, "outsider" tactics, and the grey space in between—a project that is particularly important now, as California increasingly serves as a model of not just environmentalism but also environmental justice policy for the rest of the country.

DEBATING HOW TO MAKE CHANGE

The question of how to best bring about change is an old one, going back to even before the antislavery movement of the nineteenth century. Change-oriented groups seem to have always been internally divided over whether to push for improvements under existing forms of governance or to push for more radical, or even revolutionary changes intended to address the root causes of the problems. Noted abolitionist and orator Frederick Douglass grappled with these tensions in his own life, first pressing loudly the case for the Civil War and later trying to make improvements from within government. And like activists today, Douglass was critiqued by others for both modes of change.[3] Since then, the labor movement, the civil rights movement, Black Power, and many other movements have grappled with this central question.[4] In the environmental movement, this tactical split has played out in a messy, public fashion. Some environmentalists tried to directly disrupt business as usual, chasing down whaling boats at sea to block their harpoons, sinking illegal whaling vessels, or chaining themselves to trees and conducting long-term "tree-sits" high above the ground to protect redwood forests from being cut down.[5] Others worked to reduce harm through regulatory change, lawsuits, public education, and collaboration with industry or government.

These two poles are sometimes loosely, if imprecisely, referred to as "revolution" and "reform." Reformists tend to focus on improving existing forms of governance in incremental ways through insider tactics: ways of working within the current system, such as electoral politics and policy advocacy.[6] This approach to social change has remained fairly constant across time. Revolutionaries, on the other hand, have seen peaks and troughs in their numbers and popularity throughout US history. Their efforts encompass activities ranging from (infrequent) efforts to actually overthrow the state to cultural revolution to rhetoric. Today, revolutionary rhetoric has largely been replaced by calls for deep structural change in existing forms of governance. Although these calls often do not specify how such transformative changes are to be achieved, they are associated with more disruptive, outsider political tactics, engaged in by those shut out of or averse to participating in government.

However, the boundaries between "insider" and "outsider" tactics are not always clear. Some groups use outsider tactics in support of incremental policy change; some of those working for change in political insider spaces find themselves still treated as outsiders; others pursue "inside-outside" strategies by attempting to use multiple sets of tactics at different times and places; and still others continue to use the time-honored outsider practices of protests and marches, although (as I show in chapters 2 and 3) many of these once-outsider tactics have become so routinized that they have lost some of their disruptive punch.

Very few environmental justice activists today embrace the explicitly revolutionary language or ideology that was said to be "in the air" in the United States during the 1960s and 1970s, but which had waned by the time people began to organize under the banner of environmental justice activism in the 1980s. In the 1980s and early 1990s, environmental justice activists frequently used disruptive practices, but this was as often because they were shut out of traditional formal government processes as because their political perspectives were particularly radical. The early environmental justice movement was made up of people with a wide array of political ideologies, and as a movement it was never explicitly revolutionary. Some activists simply wanted particular polluting industries not to be located where they lived, others brought with them personal experiences with more radical movements, and still others were politicized to varying degrees through their experiences with environmental justice activism.[7] This internal diversity of political perspectives was somewhat occluded by the unifying force of being "against something" (often the construction of new polluting facilities) and being shut out of government decision-making about the thing the activists were against. As more opportunities to work in or with the state have emerged over time, much environmental justice activism has moved to institutional spaces and tactics. However, there is still much continuity between the early environmental justice movement and its contemporary form.[8]

To make matters more complicated, the labeling of activist groups as revolutionary or reformist, insiders or outsiders, institutionalized or grassroots is value laden, and sometimes such labeling is used rhetorically in attempts to discredit activists. For example, one activist pointed out that she was called "radical" by local opponents as a way to paint her as "over the top," or unreasonable. What were her radical demands? Nontoxic, potable water in residents' homes. This is hardly radical, for the provision of potable water is widely considered to be a basic obligation of government in the United States. Perhaps the most controversial value attribution within activist work is labeling a particular person, organization, or movement as having been co-opted: induced to change its actions through provision of funds or status, or otherwise incorporated into an existing structure or process in ways that minimize the impact of activism.[9] These allegations are particularly divisive when levied from within movements.[10]

Although few scholars have directly focused on internal tactical debates among environmental justice activists, much scholarship implicitly engages these debates.[11] Much early environmental justice scholarship celebrated the disruptive actions and potential of the environmental justice movement, although scholars did not necessarily focus on analyzing these tactics. Another thread of scholarship analyzes reformist approaches, with particular attention to environmental justice policy implementation.[12] Today, the latter thread of scholarship predominates in research on efforts to solve environmental injustices—unsurprising, since reformism currently makes up the dominant wing of environmental justice activism.[13]

FIGURE 1. Tap water samples from San Joaquin Valley towns, labeled with their contaminants, November 10, 2007. Photo by author, previously published in Perkins and Sze, "Images from the Central Valley"; and London, Huang, and Zagofsky, "Land of Risk/Land of Opportunity."

A handful of scholars attending to the movement's changing politics have begun to criticize its shift to insider tactics and reformist goals; these scholars argue that the environmental problems facing residents in poor communities and communities of color cannot be addressed by "tinkering with policies."[14] Indeed, Laura Pulido and Juan De Lara write that the emphasis on "rights-based strategies that seek recognition and redress from the liberal state only validate the underlying injustice of racial capitalism and colonialism."[15] Such scholars perhaps carry on the firebrand legacy of portions of the early environmental justice movement; their calls for deep transformation that fundamentally alters the balance of power in society echo the 1960s- and 1970s-era appeals for revolution.

The environmental justice movement responds to the fact that the burden of modern environmental harms—toxins, polluted air and water, pesticides—is disproportionately borne by people in poor communities and communities of color. As some environmental justice activists and scholars see it, in order to do away with environmental racism and other forms of environmental inequality, we must fundamentally remake society and the state. And yet how is such a transformation to be achieved? Many contemporary scholars and activists do not see a path to achieving such deep changes, and they turn to reformism to try to make what improvements they can.

This is the first book-length treatment to examine the changing politics and tactics of environmental justice activism along these lines over time, as well as the intramovement tensions that these changes have produced. While I am not dismissive of reformist policy work, I take critiques of it seriously. Ultimately, I focus less on what I think environmental justice activists *ought* to do and instead on what they *have been* doing, why they have been doing it, and how well it is working. I also examine how environmental justice activists struggle to balance *ought* with *is*, ideals and pragmatism; I attend to both radical scholars' critiques of state-centered policy reform efforts and the changes that such efforts have achieved so far. In other words, this book embraces the messy middle ground where many activists spend their time, trying to make change as best they can within the powerful structural constraints that limit their efforts, facing a state that is both a cause of their problems and, at times, at least a partial solution to them—a source of countervailing pressure that could be made to rein in the worst excesses of capitalism.

The constraints on activism, which affect what forms it takes, are often underanalyzed. Environmental justice activists are not completely free actors making decisions independent of the larger world in which they are enmeshed. Therefore, this book locates activists within the complexity of the society that shapes their tactics, following the tradition of social movement scholarship that analyzes political constraints and opportunities.[16] For example, scholars in the political process school of the study of social movements show how political opportunities appear when governments reduce repression, elect a new leader, or see existing leadership destabilized. Political opportunities can also be influenced by formal and informal mobilizing structures into which people are already organized, such as the Black churches and colleges that helped mobilize people into the American civil rights movement.[17] I do not examine in detail how these existing social institutions funnel people into activism; instead, I focus on the interlocking matrix of racial politics, economic neoliberalism, and social constraints in the United States. These form the context in which activists must work.

This does not mean I believe activists have no agency. I draw on individual interviews to share activists' perceptions of their political options, their successes and failures, and the rationale that informs the tactics they use. I also show how arguments about tactics are based on value judgments regarding what constitutes victory and failure. Some activists see in the history of environmental justice activism a string of successes, with many polluting facilities having been closed or prevented from opening. These groups tend to value the movement's disruptive roots and see them as valuable tactics to be retained. Other activists look at the same history and see failure, for low-income communities and communities of color continue to experience disproportionately high levels of pollution. Some of these activists have moved away from early disruptive tactics and focused on institutional approaches to change instead.

WHAT IS THE ENVIRONMENTAL JUSTICE MOVEMENT?

The environmental justice movement is a form of environmental activism that seeks specifically to redress the disproportionate effects of environmental harms on people in poor communities and communities of color, which are often the sites of industrial facilities, landfills, pesticide drift, and more, and the acute and chronic exposures to toxins that result. It also addresses the lack of environmental amenities such as parks in the same places. These are daunting tasks; the unequal distribution of environmental harms and benefits seems almost unavoidable, for industries and the state have actively fostered and maintained the long histories of racism, classism, and violence that underpin capitalism. Over fifty years after the legal high-water marks of the civil rights movement, white supremacy continues to be a structuring principle of the US political and economic system, as evidenced by police violence, the outsized incarceration of people of color, the underfunding of public education systems, voter disenfranchisement, and the unequal distribution of pollution that undermines life in communities of color.[18] At the same time, income inequality is skyrocketing, with parts of the former middle class getting pushed into the working class and the poor. These persistent, entrenched inequalities are not accidental and certainly are not produced by any cultural, intellectual, or personal failings of the poor or of people of color. Rather, these inequalities are the result of long-standing efforts by many whites and the wealthy to gain or preserve their access to profits, resources, and psychological benefits at the expense of people of color and the poor. Such practices are entangled with the broader economic system of capitalism, which both helps create and extracts profits from social systems that devalue some people's

FIGURE 2. Buttonwillow Park, January 30, 2009. Photo by author, previously published in Perkins and Sze, "Images from the Central Valley"; and Wells, *Environmental Justice in Postwar America.*

FIGURE 3. Teresa De Anda standing across from her home, into which pesticides regularly drifted from agricultural fields, Earlimart, March 7, 2008. Photo by author, previously published in Perkins and Sze, "Images from the Central Valley"; Harrison, *Pesticide Drift and the Pursuit of Environmental Justice*; and London, Huang, and Zagofsky, "Land of Risk/Land of Opportunity."

lives (i.e., people of color, women, and the poor) in favor of others (i.e., whites, men, and the wealthy).

Patterns of social inequality align with contemporary patterns of environmental inequality. For example, the disproportionate exposure to air pollution experienced by people of color has a great deal to do with histories of legal and extralegal housing segregation, urban redevelopment that regularly built freeways through communities of color, and city planning that zoned these neighborhoods for industrial land uses.[19] Contemporary disasters such as the lead poisoning of residents in Flint, Michigan (through contaminated drinking water) come from this same long history of housing segregation, combined with deindustrialization, lack of maintenance of public infrastructure, and a privileging of profits over the well-being of the predominantly Black and poor residents of the city.[20] Concepts such as the racial state, racial liberalism, racial neoliberalism, racial capitalism, and a racialized "treadmill of production" highlight how the racialized political economic processes of capitalism create and sustain environmental inequality through both racism and classism.[21] Environmental inequality is deeply rooted in the structures of modern society—perhaps even a cornerstone of modernity itself.[22]

Historical accounts of US environmentalism have long perpetuated racism and classism, ignoring the contributions of people of color and the poor to the environmental movement.[23] Even as late as 2018, David Vogel's *California Greenin': How the Golden State Became an Environmental Leader* ignored the contributions of Latinx, Black, and Indigenous people and Asian Pacific Americans. Their contributions to environmentalism first received widespread attention during the early 1990s, when journalists began to attend to environmental activism in communities of color that were living with more than their "fair share" of pollution. These activists, and low-income whites, adopted a new label, environmental *justice* activism, to distinguish themselves from the broader environmental movement, which was populated largely by white, middle- and upper-class Americans who sought broad protections for air, water, animals and wild places. In contrast, environmental justice activists typically lived in the polluted, low-income communities and communities of color that they sought to protect, and their work often proceeded site by site as they sought to prevent the construction of polluting facilities near their homes and to clean up those already in existence.[24]

It is difficult to write about environmental justice, because the term is applied very broadly. *Environmental justice* might refer to (1) activism

FIGURE 4. Los Angeles skyline, November 20, 2013. Photo by author, previously published in Perkins, "Research Trip to Los Angeles."

or a social movement; (2) a goal, ideal, or form of justice; (3) "environmental justice communities," or the disproportionately polluted places that environmental justice activists seek to protect; (4) environmental justice activists, or people who work in the environmental justice movement; and/or (5) an analytic lens. Scholars, politicians, and activists all use the term environmental justice for their own purposes, expanding the term's meaning in multiple and sometimes contradictory ways.[25] Some of these uses undercut the intentions of the activists who coined the term. For example, to some regulatory actors, environmental justice simply means including residents in environmental decision-making via advisory boards or public hearings, whether or not the decisions made follow the residents' recommendations.[26]

When I write about environmental justice activism in this book, I am referencing a historically, geographically specific social movement. The intersection of social inequality and the environment has a long history, which in the United States goes back all the way to colonization, as does engagement with the environment by Latinx, Black, and Indigenous people, Asian Pacific Americans, and the poor.[27] However, I define the environmental justice *movement* more narrowly, as the US social movement whose participants began to self-identify as environmental justice activists in the 1980s. Their origins overlap with the antitoxics movement and multiple anti-racist movements. (California's environmental justice activists draw on a rich array of social movement traditions, including civil rights, Black Power, the farmworkers' movement, the Chicano movement, Red Power and the American Indian movement, and multiple Asian Pacific American organizing traditions.)[28] However, even within this bounded category, the term environmental justice is used in different ways by different people. Some activists wholeheartedly embrace the term to describe their work, while others use environmental justice framing in some political contexts but not in others.[29] The term is used to cover an increasingly diverse array of activism, including efforts that focus not just on redressing environmental problems, such as pollution and toxicity, but also on adding environmental benefits, such as parks and community gardens. This, too, is part of the story of the ongoing political evolution of environmental justice activism.

The environmental justice activists of the 1980s and early 1990s sought to clearly distinguish themselves from the broader environmental movement represented by organizations such as the Sierra Club and the World Wildlife Foundation. (Such organizations are part of what is often called the "mainstream" environmental movement, a convention I follow here to distinguish it from the environmental justice movement, though such borders are messy.) But the separation between the environmental justice movement and the grassroots antitoxics movement was much less clear. The antitoxics movement was a low-income, multiracial movement that had, since the late 1970s, been working to fight toxic spills, hazardous chemicals, water poisoned by industrial runoff, and so on. This movement specifically focused on stopping the release of toxins into the environment and cleaning up existing hazards. The antitoxics movement's understanding of where pollution was located, and thus who needed to be helped, was largely class- rather than race-based: they worked for and with poor and working-class people of all racial backgrounds.

The overlap between the antitoxics movement and what would later become the environmental justice movement is visible in the late 1970s Love Canal campaign, which some see as an early campaign of the antitoxics movement and others see as an origin point for the environmental justice movement. In the Love Canal campaign, white woman Lois Gibbs became the highly visible spokesperson for a working-class community in Love Canal, New York. Love Canal was built on top of liquid hazardous waste that oozed up into residents' basements and backyards, causing severe health problems. Eventually, more than eight hundred Love Canal residents were relocated, and the federal Superfund system for cleaning up highly toxic sites was created.

My own research confirms that the antitoxics and environmental justice movements had significant overlap and, in some cases, no clear-cut boundaries. The environmental justice movement did not "begin" with Love Canal. Rather, Love Canal is part of the origin story of the low-income, multiracial, but often white-dominated antitoxics movement. As racial tensions grew within antitoxics activism, and as it became increasingly evident that not only class but also race and indigeneity shapes where pollution ends up, the environmental justice movement gradually emerged from the antitoxics movement and activism taking place around the country that drew on other regional, racialized social movements.[30]

Contrary to some scholars' assertions that the antitoxics movement was predominantly white, my research shows that people of all racial backgrounds participated in antitoxics activism before the creation of the environmental justice frame, though some of the most visible antitoxics groups with national reach were predominantly white. Over time, some groups that began as predominantly white antitoxics groups became more oriented around activism by and for people of color. Other antitoxics groups whose members were already predominantly people of color switched to an explicit environmental justice framing of their work. Still other predominantly white antitoxics groups collapsed. With these changes, low-income whites became less and less a focus of activists' efforts.

Where some see the environmental justice movement originating with the Love Canal protests, others say it began in the Warren County protests of 1982, in which protesters lay down on the road to block trucks from transporting soil contaminated with polychlorinated biphenyls (PCBs).[31] The PCBs had been illegally dumped along North Carolina roadsides to evade new federal laws governing the disposal of hazardous waste. The toxic soil removed from the roadsides was slated to be placed in a landfill located near the predominantly Black town of Afton in Warren County, North Carolina. Local activists came together with regional and national civil rights leaders to stage twenty-five days of protest over seven weeks, during which 523 people were arrested.[32] Despite the protests, the contaminated soil was eventually located in Afton, but the evocative photo of Black residents lying down in the road to block the trucks became an iconic image of early environmental justice activism. While it is overly simplistic to say that the environmental justice movement "began" in Warren County when so many other people were confronting similar problems in other places, the protests there did give birth to the powerful concept of "environmental racism," as well as key reports documenting the relationship between race and waste disposal.[33] They also linked the leadership and framing of the Black civil rights movement to environmental activism, as it was bubbling up in low-income communities and communities of color.

Because the histories of the environmental justice and antitoxics movements overlap, the story I tell about early environmental justice activism in California includes activists and low-income communities of all racial and ethnic backgrounds. As the book progresses through the evolution of the movement, my focus switches primarily to low-income communities of color. The book's emphasis thus reflects the shift away from class-based antitoxics framing and toward a racialized, classed environmental justice frame, which in California eventually became associated primarily with low-income communities of color.

WHY MORE ENVIRONMENTAL JUSTICE RESEARCH?

Environmental justice research is now a strong subfield in academia, though it still lacks the level of institutional support allocated to broader environmental research. With so many excellent papers and books available on this subject, why add another? Mostly because scholarship about the environmental justice movement is only recently beginning to trace the movement's evolution.[34] The studies that do examine how environmental justice activism has changed over time tend to focus not on activist tactics themselves but on the expanding discourse and framing of environmental justice, especially as it is used by scholars.[35] As a result, in some cases the early shape of the movement—grassroots activists fighting local battles in their hometowns—continues to be the framework used to interpret today's more institutionalized activism.[36] Alternately, other studies primarily focus on insider tactics, such as policy advocacy from activists working inside the government.[37] This book connects these two sets of scholarship by describing the changes in environmental justice activism over time, analyzing the reasons behind the changes, and reflecting on the strengths and risks they pose.

Evolution of a Movement traces California environmental justice activists' efforts from the 1980s to today, showing the double bind that results when the same institutional structures that create environmental inequality in the first place also constrain activists' efforts to address those inequalities. The book also bridges scholarship that calls for radical social change with scholarship that documents efforts toward incremental improvement through existing political mechanisms. What follows, therefore, is not a feel-good success story in which a local movement was able to scale up and become a significant statewide power through institutionalization. Nor is it a story of the co-optation and blunting of grassroots power over time. It is instead a complicated story of political trade-offs rooted in the experiences of environmental justice activists who have struggled for decades to obtain clean air to breathe, clean water to drink, and safe, healthy communities in which to live. The book provides a close-up and personal view of activism, complete with activists' aspirations, disappointments, and internal conflicts.

I also offer a novel synthetic account of the environmental justice movement in California. Existing scholarship on California environmental justice activism has typically focused on case studies of places, agencies, or policies without linking them into a coherent whole. Analyzing California's historical and contemporary environmental justice activism as a single, internally diverse unit illustrates the depth and breadth of activism happening there. However, the scope of the movement prevents this book from being a comprehensive history. Many struggles, organizations, and individuals go unmentioned, but not for lack of recognition of their importance. Nevertheless, I hope the historical approach of this book will be useful and perhaps inspire more comprehensive historical documentation of the environmental justice movement in California and elsewhere. As one activist I interviewed put it, "When you win, there's an immediate effort to make sure that that win is minimized. As an activist, you have to stay at the table. You can't take your eye off the ball, because it'll just disappear. And if the people that come in after you don't know the history . . . they don't know what to keep an eye on." Her comments are applicable not just to activists but also to scholars, who need to continue to document and analyze long-standing problems even as we watch for changes in the ways activists respond to them.

METHODS

This work is informed by participant observation in California environmental justice activism from 2007 to 2015. Of course, participant observation in activism happening over such a large geographical area and with so many groups includes more contact with some groups than with others. I therefore had more exposure to some activists' analyses of contemporary environmental justice activism than to others'.[38] This is significant given the fragmented nature of environmental justice activism across the state. To counteract this, I conducted interviews with a broad swath of environmental justice activists with a variety of perspectives on the issues I examine here, and the case studies I include fall both within and outside my primary group affiliations.

The in-depth interviews on which this book is based use activists' own words and experiences to bring the dynamics of the movement to the fore. I draw on interviews that took place between 2007 and 2018. I conducted interviews specifically for this project from 2013 through 2015 with fifty-five environmental justice activists from across the state, ranging from Sacramento in the north to the California-Mexico border in the south. I also draw on interviews conducted from 2007 through 2011 with thirty-nine San Joaquin Valley environmental justice activists, nine interviews conducted in 2016 with pesticides activists in the Salinas Valley, and twenty-two interviews conducted in 2017 and 2018 with participants in the 1990s-era Ward Valley antinuclear waste landfill campaign along the lower Colorado River.[39] All unattributed quotes are drawn from these interviews.[40] Some attributed quotes are also included; either I was given permission to include the speakers' names for other articles and websites I have published, or they are drawn from other scholars' work. Either way, the citations are provided.

In addition to interview data, I use press coverage as well as policy and legal research to support my analysis of two case studies. One case study analyzes thirty-plus years of environmental justice activism in the San Joaquin Valley's Kettleman City, which hosts the largest hazardous waste landfill west of the Mississippi. The other analyzes environmental justice activists' involvement with policy advocacy on the 2006 California Global Warming Solutions Act and its ongoing politics.

My choice of activists to interview was informed by my definition of environmental justice activism, which I see as a historically specific form of political action that originated in the United States, rather than as a broad analytic category that describes any activism at the intersection of environmentalism with social justice concerns. I therefore interviewed people who self-identified as environmental justice activists or who were identified by their peers as such. This approach emphasizes core groups that have long been active in the world of environmental justice activism, as well as groups that entered that network later. Conducting my interviews through this densely networked group of activists means that activists from outside of this network, or at its periphery, are largely excluded from my analysis. This approach unfortunately gives short shrift to Indigenous activists in Northern California, as their advocacy networks have not been well integrated into many of the rest of California environmental justice activist networks.[41] This research approach also reveals that the question of who "counts" as an environmental justice activist has become more contentious as the meaning of the term expands and as more people use the language of environmental justice activism to describe (and secure funding for) their work.

These methods—participant observation and the many interviews I conducted over the years—allow me to highlight activists' own intellectual engagement with the themes of this book. Environmental justice scholarship that does not draw from interview or participant observation data often underestimates activists' intellectual engagement with the themes about which scholars write. The lack of intersection between these two sets of conversations impoverishes all our analyses. Therefore, I quote extensively from my interviews with activists, showcasing and building on their reflections on decades of work. While my own analysis does not always align with that of the interviewees, in all cases, my own intellectual contributions are indebted to theirs.

WHY CALIFORNIA?

The disruptive activism of the 1980s and parts of the 1990s was not exclusive to the California environmental justice movement. As mentioned, in Warren County, North Carolina, protesters lay down in the street to block the progress of trucks loaded with PCB-contaminated soil.[42] In Louisiana, activists walked eighty miles from Baton Rouge to New Orleans to publicize the problems of "Cancer Alley," a strip of toxic industries along the Mississippi River.[43] In Love Canal, New York, activists took a government official hostage. On the Southeast Side of Chicago, activists chained themselves to vehicles that blocked trucks carrying hazardous waste to be incinerated.[44] Given the many places where people have pursued environmental justice activism for many decades, why locate this study in California?

California stands out from the rest of the United States in many ways. It is the fifth largest economy in the world (calculated as if it were a country) and an economic engine of the United States. The state's level of income inequality is among the highest in the nation, and it is a leading source of pollution and greenhouse gases in the country. California preceded much of the nation in becoming a majority people of color state, and in 2014 Latinxs surpassed whites to become the single largest racialized group in the state. Recent census data show that the United States is on track to become a majority people of color country by 2044, and California is often seen as a bellwether for how the changing demographics of the United States will affect electoral politics. Because of its demographics, California's relationship to environmentalism is particularly important. Although Latinx, Black, and Indigenous people and Asian Pacific Americans have diverse political affiliations and relationships to environmentalism, recent polls show that many people of color voters, and Latinx voters in particular, are more likely than whites to believe in the science of climate change and are more in favor of environmental legislation to slow it down.[45] This suggests that the racial politics of environmental and environmental justice activism in California—particularly the relationship between environmental justice activists and the Latino Legislative Caucus in the state capitol—could be a sign of things to come in other parts of the country.

California has also long been an environmental policy trendsetter. Some California state standards initially surpass federal standards and are adopted later more widely across the country.[46] Accordingly, environmental justice activists and policymakers across the country pay attention to what happens in California. One Washington, D.C.–based environmental justice activist puts it this way:

> The great thing about the Californians is they've got great state and federal leadership. You've got Boxer and Pelosi and Waxman and Maxine [Waters] and Barbara Lee. I mean, the delegation is the best. So, we're always counting on them to lead the way on every issue. . . . They're an extremely important flank in the environmental justice movement. . . . [T]hey have the right convergence of progressive leadership, resources, and the diverse communities who have this fabulous gumbo of activity going on. . . . So, it's a very special place. I always tell my California friends, don't send us any bad stuff, keep being the model for the rest of the country, because really, seriously, it's very important.

While California is something of a national outlier in its approach to environmental policy, it remains part of the nation and shares the national struggles with problems such as poverty, education, mass incarceration, racism, and environmental degradation. (Even this vaunted environmental state continues to be influenced by powerful pressures to continue oil drilling and limit regulations on air quality and pesticides.) California's successes thus offer one possible model for other blue states as people of color become majority populations. As Manuel

Pastor notes in *State of Resistance: What California's Dizzying Descent and Remarkable Resurgence Mean for America's Future*, California recovered from its own mid-1990s, anti-immigrant "Trump moment" to emerge later as the leader of the anti-Trump resistance. If Pastor's argument that "California is America fast-forward" is true, we would all do well to understand California's political and environmental trajectory.[47] I am less optimistic than Pastor about the state of California politics. However, California is widely seen as a "best case scenario" for progressive American politics, and the state's mixed experience shows the opportunities and limitations of what can be achieved through contemporary activist practices.

As I show here, the professionalization of California's environmental justice movement and the ensuing changes in tactics came with significant trade-offs. This discussion is relevant to activists in other states who are located at different points along the spectrum of professionalization and protest. I hope my analysis of California will model ways to explore the successes and constraints of activism in other places. I build on the careful case studies of activist campaigns and policy advocacy conducted by other scholars of environmental justice activism in California, while also drawing on cases and theories from other places to elucidate my arguments and show the commonalities of activist experiences across locations. I seek to answer the following questions: How has the California environmental justice movement evolved over time? How has the agency of environmental justice activists combined with broader political, demographic, and social trends to shape activist strategy and outcomes? What are the opportunities and limitations engendered by such changes?

Evolution of a Movement tells the story of the changes in the environmental justice movement across four decades of struggle by California activists. It offers a broad overview of the environmental justice movement's history and ties together a range of campaigns across regional, topical, and organizational divides. It also puts divergent activist reflections in dialogue with one another in ways not always easily done within movement spaces. Furthermore, the book situates the daily concerns of activism within broader political trends, providing a tool for reflection for those who make it their daily business to think tactically about environmental injustice. It offers uninitiated readers an invitation to learn from those activists who have gone before and to take up the pressing work that remains. And for scholars and activists alike, it offers insight into how California environmental justice activism changed over time, why it changed in the ways that it did, and what risks and rewards that pathway offers.

ROAD MAP

The rest of this book proceeds as follows. Chapter 1 describes the environmental justice movement in the 1980s and early 1990s, when activists often responded to environmental threats with local action, using tactics such as disrupting permit hearings for the construction of new polluting facilities. This period reveals early environmental justice activists as being sometimes more (and sometimes less) radical than is now widely remembered. It explains why activism of that time so often relied on disruptive, outsider tactics, and what the outcomes of such activism were.

Chapter 2 describes the process of environmental justice activists' adoption of insider politics. Many activists took seats on government advisory committees, were elected or appointed to public office, or worked with legislators to pass new state laws. Some also found new common ground with former opponents in industry. At the same time, activists' use of disruptive tactics declined, in part due to the increasing reliance on foundation funding and in part on the "negotiated management" practice of policing protest. Not everyone was happy about these changes; activists less predisposed to collaborate with the state and industry sometimes viewed them as co-optation—and as I show, institutionalized tactics had many drawbacks.

Chapter 3 further explains the reasons behind these changes in environmental justice activism tactics. It shows that activists worked to "scale up" their work into the policy realm in order to proactively address problems at the root, rather than reacting individually to each new pollution problem. It historically situates these changes within the broad social and political context of California environmental justice activism, showing how activists are influenced by external political currents. In particular, I focus on the effects of three sets of overlapping changes: California's shifting racial politics, the ongoing pressures of neoliberal governing ideologies, and the normalization of risk. I also show how activists are influenced by the history of their own movements; environmental justice activism from the 1980s and 1990s shaped the political terrain in ways that facilitated the trend toward insider politics for later generations of activists.

Chapter 4, the first case study, tells the story of Kettleman City, a small, primarily Latinx town set alongside vast fields of industrial agriculture, an interstate highway, and the largest hazardous waste landfill west of the Mississippi. This chapter traces how the changes in the environmental justice movement (itself responding to economic and political changes) played out on the ground, documenting the overlaps and intersections between the multiple forces acting on low-income, majority people of color places. The town's anti-incinerator campaign of the 1980s and early 1990s was described at the time as a David versus Goliath battle from which the residents emerged victorious.[48] It was a beacon of hope for others fighting similar battles across the country, and the Kettleman City success story shows the effectiveness of early, disruptive environmental justice protest tactics paired with legal action. The story also shows the limitations of these early site-based strategies, for after the incinerator permit was denied, Kettleman City still had more conflicts ahead of it. Activists have continued to fight the landfill and other sources of environmental risk since then; the story of the town's tragic 2008 birth defect cluster makes clear both the ongoing nature of harm and how government and industry perpetuate it. Finally, I examine the effects of the broader environmental justice movement's policy advocacy efforts on hazardous waste landfills in California. Kettleman City's story thus underscores the successes and limitations of both site-based protest and policy advocacy in the context of long-established patterns of pollution and social disenfranchisement.

Chapter 5 offers another detailed case study, this time of the environmental justice movement's use of institutional tactics, exemplified by activists' attempts to shape the California Global Warming Solutions Act of 2006 (AB 32) and its implementation. Activists sought to undergird the policy with an environmental justice framework, insisting that global warming policies should also attend to effects at the local level to ensure that low-income communities and communities of color would get relief from their crushing pollution levels. A central component of their efforts was to stop the state from using a market-based cap-and-trade approach to regulate industrial greenhouse gas emissions, but against the activists' recommendations, cap-and-trade was adopted. This chapter also traces a short-lived conflict within the environmental justice movement itself, which arose as a result of the internal debate over implementation of AB 32: in addition to those environmental justice activists trying to stop the state from using a cap-and-trade system, there were others who instead backed legislation that would divert cap-and-trade revenues into their own communities. This chapter of the story of AB 32 again raises the eternal question about how much to compromise policy goals and whether and when to work within the existing political system. Overall, this story helps explain why activists scaled up their work to the level of state policy advocacy and what the limitations of this approach are.

The book's conclusion describes the current political dilemmas facing environmental justice activists as they navigate the tensions between institutionalized environmental justice groups' increasingly collaborative relationship with the state (both a cause and a product of their shift to insider tactics) and the parallel decline in disruptive environmental justice protest. Should activists participate in time-consuming stakeholder engagement processes, or should they boycott them? Should they protest at the California EPA offices or get activists appointed to roles on the inside, or do both? Analyses of social movement institutionalization often polarize over such questions, coming down on one side or the other rather than presenting a description of the strengths and limitations of each. Instead, this chapter—and this book as a whole—highlights the trade-offs inherent in each of these sets of tactics. Ultimately, I show that institutional tactics have helped environmental justice activists make incremental progress toward their goals, at the risk of a slow slide into increasingly centrist goals and tactics that limit the movement's accomplishments. When activists embed themselves within racist, profit-driven state structures that are fundamentally at odds with their goals, they must be ever alert to the possibility of being used to forward goals not of their own making.

CHAPTER I

Emergence of the Disruptive Environmental Justice Movement

On November 12, 1988, activists from fourteen California communities traveled to East Los Angeles to march with residents who sought to block the construction of two large-scale commercial incinerators. The incinerators would be the first of their kind in the state to burn hazardous waste. Growing resistance to living near landfills meant industry and government officials had difficulty siting new ones to manage growing waste production.[1] As a result, proposals to build incinerators skyrocketed; the East Los Angeles incinerators were part of a wave of at least thirty-four proposed in the state during the early to mid-1980s.[2] The waste industry hoped to avoid the opposition that plagued landfills by depicting incinerators as a new technology that was clean and safe. Some industry representatives even claimed that incinerators could make waste disappear. Industry proponents also argued that incinerators could help supply electricity to energy-hungry urban areas—a compelling argument after the 1970s energy crises. Accordingly, state and federal governments favored the incinerator industry with tax breaks and guaranteed electricity sales.[3] Activists, however, contested industry claims that such facilities could effectively generate significant amounts of electricity. And, they pointed out, waste incineration does not make waste disappear. It converts it into toxic ash and health-threatening air emissions, such as dioxins and furans, which can cause hormonal changes, reproductive and immunological problems, and cancer.[4]

FIGURE 5. Residents and supporters marching in protest against proposed Vernon hazardous waste incinerators, November 12, 1988. Photo by Mike Sergieff, Herald Examiner Collection, Los Angeles Public Library.

The East Los Angeles incinerators were to be sited in Vernon, a small industrial town that bordered the low-income, predominantly Latinx residential areas of Maywood, Bell, Boyle Heights, and East Los Angeles, in general.[5] They would be built and run by California Thermal Treatment Systems, whose parent company, Security Environmental, had been repeatedly cited for violating pollution rules at its other nearby sites in Long Beach and Garden Grove, cities that were in transition from majority white to majority people of color populations during the 1980s. Although the new incinerators were projected to create nineteen thousand tons of toxic ash, dust, and other hazardous waste per year, adding a significant new source of air pollution to the most polluted air basin in the country, regulators green-lighted the project without even requiring that an environmental impact report first be conducted. As community members learned more about the project, their opposition grew. But they faced an uphill battle. As their lawyer remembers, "Before opponents knew what hit them, the thirty-day statute of limitations under CEQA [California Environmental Quality Act] had expired. With construction permits already issued by the South Coast Air Quality Management District and EPA [Environmental Protection

Agency], and with the support of the California Department of Health Services, and the City of Vernon assured, the project looked unstoppable."[6] Nonetheless, angry residents and their supporters forcefully voiced their opposition. As one participant recalls:

> There was a series of meetings that the government did, as part of their process for rubberstamping this hazardous waste incinerator proposal. . . . Then they announced the hearing. . . . They thought a lot of people weren't going to show up, after all, "It's East LA." It was awesome because 600 people showed up. . . . So the place is packed . . . hundreds marched in. It was awesome. And again, just a massive crowd. The hearing's in English, and the crowd starts asking for translation. They say no. So, the entire crowd is on its feet, at the top of their lungs for probably 45 minutes: "*En español, en español!*" It was mass civil disobedience, right? You are not going to have this hearing in English in East LA! . . . Then a state official . . . announced, "We'd really like to be able to translate this for you." Of course, they're saying this in English, "But state law prohibits us from translating this meeting."
>   The crowd is going nuts, right? Young people unfurled a banner behind the stage, and the place is rocking. And then mysteriously after a really long time, half hour, 45 minutes, the law must have changed, because the state official gets up and says, "Well, I guess we can translate, but we don't have anybody who could do that." And so, a young Latina with Greenpeace, she offered to go translate. So, the hearing starts. But moments later, the fire department curiously showed up and announced that half the crowd had to leave. And the massive crowd is on its feet chanting in English and Spanish, "Rent the Coliseum, rent the Coliseum!" And nobody would leave. . . . They stopped the hearing and said they would have to reschedule it in a bigger place. So, it was a big victory. And then the next hearing, as I recall, there was like 1,000 people.

Residents, led by Las Madres del Este de Los Angeles (Mothers of East Los Angeles), built support to block the construction of the incinerators through community organizing, lawsuits, and protests. They built partnerships with politicians, nonprofits, and community groups near and far, including other California grassroots environmental justice activists; on the November day in 1988 when community groups around the state came to march with them, the visiting activists were mostly residents of other low-income communities and communities of color who were fighting off waste threats of their own. The tone of the day was boisterous, in keeping with a campaign that had already extended for years and sometimes spilled over into rowdy and disruptive activism. As one participant remembers:

> One of the things people were learning . . . was that the government is totally in bed with the polluters, and that if you follow their way of doing it and,

you know, "behave," [laughter] you will lose. . . . When the march started, we didn't have permits, we just poured into the street. And the rally, after the mile-long march or whatever it was, in front of the proposed site on Bandini Boulevard, we didn't rally on the sidewalk. It was smack in the middle of Bandini Boulevard. That was really intentional. It was to up the spirit of the people and show defiance, that people aren't going to take this lying down, literally.

Ultimately, the anti-incinerator campaign in Vernon was successful, and it became a central event in the coalescence of disparate groups into the statewide environmental justice movement. The company proposing to build the incinerators abandoned the project in 1991 after an unfavorable ruling in court and unceasing local opposition that led key political leaders, including Tom Bradley, the first Black mayor of Los Angeles, to withdraw their support.

While the campaign started with local Latinx residents and their political representatives, it eventually pulled in a multiracial group of people and organizations from across the state. When the network of people from places facing similar proposals came to East Los Angeles in November 1988, they gathered at the Santa Isabel Church in East LA to meet one another and march together. The next day, activists in Northern California got together in the San Francisco Bay Area town of Martinez for the same purpose. These back-to-back gatherings helped create the first statewide, grassroots alliance to formally link communities facing environmental justice threats: California Communities Against Toxics (CCAT).[7]

EMERGENCE OF THE ENVIRONMENTAL JUSTICE MOVEMENT

CCAT helped connect and provide support for communities across the state, but by the time it was created in 1988, California activists had already been pursuing overlapping antitoxics and environmental justice campaigns for over a decade. Some of these are well known in certain activist circles. One such fight was the successful campaign against the LANCER waste incinerators. The first of three incinerators proposed under this project was to be built in South Central Los Angeles. Robin Cannon, Charlotte Bullock, and the predominantly Black Concerned Citizens of South Central Los Angeles (CCSCLA) organized against the incinerator beginning in 1985.[8] CCSCLA's efforts, and those of the others opposed to the South Central incinerator, prevented a new source of air pollution from being added to what was then the most heavily polluted air basin in the country. These efforts also prevented the associated, localized negative health impacts of that air pollution, which would have been disproportionately born by the largely Black residents of South-Central.

Farther inland from East Los Angeles, another high-profile California case took place at the Stringfellow Acid Pits and the town below; resistance to the acid pits came from the predominantly white working-class residents of Glen Avon. These residents had been complaining about fumes from the liquid hazardous waste storage site above their homes since 1963. In 1969, some of these residents called the police because fumes were so thick it was difficult to breathe, and liquid hazardous waste was flowing down from the Stringfellow Acid Pits into the city streets. In 1978, in anticipation of heavy rains that might breach the dam holding back the liquid hazardous waste, the Santa Ana Regional Water Quality Control Board authorized a "controlled release" into the ravine below. The liquid hazardous waste combined with floodwaters to flow down the ravine and onto the roads and sidewalks of Glen Avon, where children played in the foam it created. Residents organized into the neighborhood group Mothers of Glen Avon, later Concerned Neighbors in Action. They worked for years to address the problems stemming from the site. Activists engaged in a protracted campaign to clean up the site that continues to this day.[9]

Other toxics threats across the state—threats to both communities of color and low-income majority-white communities—also catalyzed local antitoxics and proto-environmental justice residents' groups and NGOs. In the small San Joaquin Valley town of McFarland, predominantly working-class Latinx residents spent a decade fighting for redress for a childhood cancer cluster discovered in the early 1980s that may have been caused by the heavy use of carcinogenic pesticides in the nearby fields. The town's children developed a variety of cancers, such as neuroblastoma and lymphatic cancer, and between 1981 and 1983 residents also suffered through heightened rates of birth defects, miscarriages, and fetal and infant deaths.[10]

In the San Francisco Bay Area in the 1980s, the then predominantly white Silicon Valley Toxics Coalition organized against the Silicon Valley semiconductor factories. The factories were exposing their workers, many Asian Pacific American, to hazardous chemicals. The factories also polluted local groundwater. In December 1981, it was discovered that a well that provided the drinking water to 16,500 homes in South

San Jose—an area predominantly inhabited by people of color—was contaminated with trichloroethane (TCA), a solvent used to remove grease from microchips and printed circuit boards as part of the semi-conductor manufacturing process.[11] Officials estimated that fourteen thousand gallons of TCA and another forty-four thousand gallons of other toxic waste had been leaking from an underground storage tank for at least a year and a half.

Also in the San Francisco Bay Area, a multiracial array of activist groups—the predominantly Black West County Toxics Coalition, the then predominantly white Citizens for a Better Environment (later, the multiracial Communities for a Better Environment), and the predominantly white National Toxics Coalition—all organized residents in the 1980s to oppose Chevron's day-to-day refinery operations, which created pollution and industrial accidents that impacted a predominantly Black area of Richmond. Black resident and activist Henry Clark recalls what it was like to live in Richmond at that time:

> We lived next to the oil refinery, next to the Chevron Refinery. Next to it in the sense that the refinery is located on the mountain range, and in between the refinery and our house there's a field which I understand is owned by Chevron. So as you leave from the refinery on the hills and look there to the first streets in the residential area, the first house is our house. So that's why we say that North Richmond is on the front line of the chemical assault because whenever there was any fires and explosions, that would rock the houses like they were caught in an earthquake. . . . I would be hit first and people on that street, because we were the first street there. . . . I can remember clearly waking up many mornings and finding the leaves on the tree burnt crisp overnight from chemical exposure, or going outside and the air would be so foul that you would literally have to grab your nose and try to not breath [sic] the air and go back in the house and wait until it was cleared up. Those types of situations, you know, were a common experience.[12]

The geographically separate but roughly contemporaneous activist campaigns in McFarland, Glen Avon, Silicon Valley, Kettleman City, Vernon, South Central Los Angeles, and Richmond have been well documented individually (though they are rarely written into a single narrative of California activist history). Other antitoxics and environmental justice campaigns of the 1980s and 1990s that took place both before and after the formation of CCAT are less well documented and risk being lost to history altogether. For example, in the open desert above Los Angeles County, activists led by white resident "Stormy" Williams prevented the construction of a hazardous waste landfill in Rosamond. And in 1989, after years of organizing, others closed the hazardous waste landfill in the coastal town of Casmalia, where landfill managers had been spraying liquid hazardous waste onto the hillsides in order to speed evaporation, sending overpowering toxic fumes into the local school.[13]

There was also a slew of campaigns from Indigenous organizers that tied together earlier activism with the emerging environmental justice movement. In the late 1970s, Latinx and Chemehuevi activist Alfredo Figueroa worked to defeat the proposed Sundesert Nuclear Plant. It was to be built in the Mojave Desert, part of the greater US Southwest that has long been burdened with toxins from the long-term impacts of the nuclear life cycle. Southwest deserts have been used for everything from uranium mining to nuclear bomb testing and are consistently proposed for various nuclear waste storage plans. Other Indigenous activists in the area conducted different campaigns, fighting to prevent the dumping of sewage sludge on land owned by the Torres Martinez Desert Cahuilla Indians and working against numerous other proposals to site toxic infrastructure on reservations—proposals that spiked in the late 1980s and early 1990s.[14] In the 1990s, other Indigenous and white activists worked to prevent the construction of a nuclear waste landfill in the Mojave Desert's Ward Valley. The dump would have marred culturally and spiritually significant landforms and threatened to contaminate the Colorado River. The project was proposed not long after the Fort Mojave Indian Tribe had finally won an extensive legal battle to regain access to water from the Colorado River that the tribe had used long before Europeans colonized the area.

Finally, in neighborhoods, towns, and reservations across the state almost too numerous to list, activists prevented the construction of incinerator after incinerator. Since the mid-1980s, only three commercial, municipal solid waste incinerators have been built on new sites, all between 1987 and 1989: one in the San Joaquin Valley town of Crow's Landing and two in the Los Angeles region, in Commerce and Long Beach.[15] In contrast, so many incinerators were proposed that it is unlikely I have documented them all. The following map 1 shows the forty-five successful anti-incinerator battles that the activists I interviewed could confirm, all against incinerators proposed since the mid-1980s. (These include incinerators never built; incinerators prevented from adding a new waste stream; cement kilns that were prevented from being used to incinerate waste; commercial and noncommercial incinerators; and both the older generations of incinerators and the modern facilities that use technologies such as pyrolysis, gasification, and plasma arc, which opponents call "incinerators in disguise." If built, the facilities depicted would have incinerated multiple waste streams, including municipal waste, solid and liquid hazardous waste, radioactive waste, and medical waste.) However, many more incinerators were proposed than the forty-five shown here, by my count likely upward of seventy-five.[16] Many of these were proposed by what veteran incinerator fighter Bradley Angel called "fly-by-night operators hoping to get rich quick" in what appeared for a time to be a booming new industry.[17] And even seventy-five is a low estimate of the total number of incinerators proposed in California since the early 1980s, as it does not include biomass facilities designed to process agricultural waste or sewage sludge.

These cases of the 1980s and 1990s took place in the early overlap between the antitoxics movement, which tended to favor class-based analysis and activism, and the emerging environmental justice movement, which incorporated racism as an explanation for the distribution of pollutants across the United States. The environmental justice movement grew out of the multiracial antitoxics movement combined with the racial justice concerns of the Black civil rights movement and other movements that attended to racism and classism, such as the farmworkers' movement, the Chicano movement, Black Power, and the activist traditions of Asian Pacific Americans and Indigenous peoples.[18] But as environmental racism became better documented and more widely publicized, the environmental justice movement increasingly moved away from some of the original antitoxics groups. Some white antitoxics activists resisted the environmental racism frame, continuing to emphasize class-based forms of environmental oppression that spoke to their experiences living next to toxic facilities and landfills. Some predominantly white antitoxics organizations closed. Other multiracial or predominantly white antitoxics organizations continued their work and adopted the framing of environmental justice. Still other predominantly white antitoxics organizations slowly transformed into environmental justice organizations with multiracial staffs largely serving communities of color.[19]

While the overlapping antitoxics and environmental justice movements experienced tension, the relationship between environmental justice activists and much of the broader environmental movement was even more fraught. The latter two groups had differences across race, class, gender, education levels, funding levels, tactics, and even goals, and these differences produced conflict. The year 1990, in which incineration proposals peaked, was also the twentieth anniversary of the

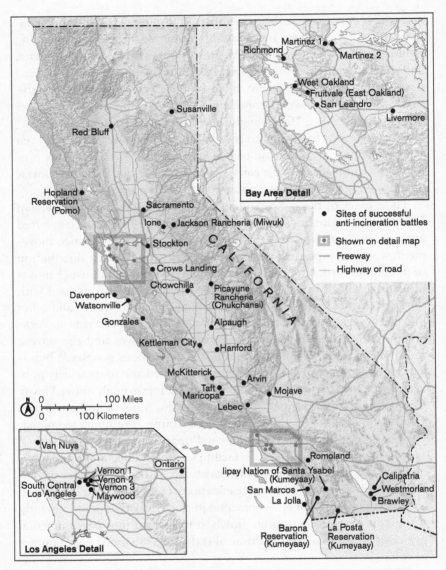

MAP 1. Locations of some of the successful California anti-incinerator battles since the mid-1980s. Map by Ben Pease.

first Earth Day.[20] In this watershed year, activists and scholars of color directly challenged the existing environmental movement. They sent a series of letters to federal environmental agencies and to national environmental organizations, levying several charges: a lack of attention to the environmental problems impacting communities of color, racism within their predominantly white staffs, and the misappropriation of Indigenous peoples' lands in the United States and abroad.

The first letters to national environmental organizations were sent to "The Group of Ten," overwhelmingly white groups that organized themselves into a coalition when Ronald Reagan was elected to the presidency in 1980. When the group was established, each organization's CEO was white, and most were male; it was not until 2005 that one of the organizations appointed the first Black person as chair.[21] As Gottlieb writes, "there were no African-Americans or Asian-Americans and only 1 Hispanic among the Sierra Club's 250 professional staff. At the [Natural Resources Defense Council] there were only 5 people of color among 140 professional staff, and the Audubon Society had only 3 African-Americans among its 315 staff members. Even Friends of the Earth had only 5 people of color among a 40-person staff and 1 person of color on a 27-member board."[22]

The protest letters were followed by action. Activists organized the First National People of Color Environmental Leadership Summit to support alternative environmental organizing with social justice–oriented values led by Latinx, Black, and Indigenous people and Asian Pacific Americans. It took place the next year (1991) in Washington, D.C. Together, the letters and the summit brought environmental justice activists attention on the national stage. Attendees at the summit created the "Principles of Environmental Justice" document, which solidified "environmental justice" as the core framing of the movement and produced a bold set of core values that challenged much of the American economy and social life. The letters and the summit also served to knit California activism, along with activism from other places, more tightly into an increasingly networked national movement.

GRASSROOTS STRUCTURES AND DISRUPTIVE ACTIVISM

Early antitoxics and environmental justice activists drew on both existing and newly created organizing structures. A hallmark of early antitoxics and environmental justice activism was the looseness of the umbrella "movements"; both were primarily made up of small community groups working to address toxicity problems on a local scale. These loosely organized community groups had in common a shared residence in the same town or neighborhood and, typically, an opposition to some kind of discrete, "point-source" toxic threat, such as a landfill or an incinerator—though some groups addressed more diffuse problems, such as pesticide exposure through agricultural field work or through its drift into residential areas. Their leadership and decision-making structures were usually informal, without elections or other formal decision-making mechanisms. Activists volunteered their time, and membership was free and came without any particular requirements. For the most part, if you wanted to participate, you did. Many of these groups were short-lived, forming around a particular toxic threat and disbanding soon after the campaign was won or lost. Others lasted longer, with a few key actors staying involved over long periods of time while broader community involvement waxed and waned with the perception of local threats.

Some community groups became nonprofits and moved into a longer life, gaining paid staff and financial support from philanthropic and government grants. The movement drew on a variety of other organizing structures, including unions and tribal governments, and to a lesser extent, churches, student groups, and affinity groups, but nonprofits ultimately became the dominant organizing structure. This has been an important shift, for the way that activists are organized impacts the types of activism they undertake. Antitoxics and environmental justice activists of the 1980s and early 1990s understood this. Indeed, some looked to the organizational form of the mainstream environmental movement as part of the problem: they were seen as big, memberless, top-down organizations led by professionals that used what many environmental justice activists saw as excessively centrist, insider tactics. As Eileen McGurtry writes, "Perhaps most troubling to critics of mainstream environmentalism was the use of professional tactics such as lobbying and negotiating. These tactics made them part of the same system that produced environmental injustices and prevented mainstreamers from fully understanding and embracing diverse communities. As critics from environmental justice circles saw it, the mainstreamers had abandoned their roots as a social movement and embraced interest group politics."[23]

The mainstream environmental organizations had been rapidly professionalizing during the 1980s. Some were simultaneously embracing "third wave" environmentalism, partnering with business and promoting market-based environmentalism during the environmentally hostile Reagan presidency and George Deukmejian governorship of California. Antitoxics and environmental justice activists were emerging as a grassroots force to be reckoned with, in part because they intentionally moved in the opposite direction.[24] The Madres del Este de Los Angeles, for example, were proud that they "did their own lobbying" by visiting legislators at the state capitol in Sacramento. At first, they preferred to remain a grassroots, community organization based on volunteer labor, deciding against incorporating as a nonprofit (although, like many of the community groups with long lifespans, they eventually did so). Erlinda Robles described the limitations of incorporation and the impact of pursuing grants that would accompany it: "We should not take money from anybody so that we won't be dictated to by anybody."[25] They understood that relying on philanthropic donations and government grants might constrain the kind of work they undertook and the way they did it.

Others, such as the Silicon Valley Toxics Coalition (SVTC), pursued local initiatives and direct-action tactics because their leaders did not think they had the funds or the influence to be successful in the state capitol, where their corporate opponents held sway. Republican governors controlled the state capitol from 1983 to 1999, which limited the political opportunities for antitoxics and environmental justice activists to successfully engage in policy work there. SVTC's logic was that if it could make changes at the local level in enough places, these changes would eventually filter upward to the state government.[26]

The antitoxics movement and the early environmental justice movement, which were often hostile toward state agencies after being treated poorly by them, often took deliberately disruptive action to pressure government regulators; street protests, rallies, occupations, blockades, and disruption of public hearings were all common tactics. Public hearings, in particular, were frequently raucous events, as we saw with the LA meeting at which the Madres protested the proposed East LA incinerator. According to *Work on Waste,* North Carolina's Davidson County was listed in the *Guinness Book of World Records* for the largest turnout at a public hearing, with fifteen thousand people showing up for a 1987 meeting about a waste incinerator. The overwhelming number of would-be participants meant the hearing never happened: "The state's Hazardous Waste Treatment Commission had to be escorted out of the county by the Highway Patrol for their own safety. The Commission never came back."[27] In California's Kettleman City, when the Spanish-speaking residents were told to "go to the back of the room" if they wanted to hear a translation of the proceedings about a proposed

FIGURE 6. Demonstrators protesting the planned construction of a hazardous waste treatment plant less than 1,000 feet from Huntington Park High School, August 26, 1988. Photo by Mike Mullen, Herald Examiner Collection, Los Angeles Public Library.

hazardous waste incinerator, they instead stormed to the front. Similarly, hearings about the proposed incinerators in Vernon were interrupted by residents chanting, "*en español, en español*," and "rent the coliseum," which succeeded in getting translation, delaying the hearing, and sending a strong signal to local politicians about the unpopularity of the project. In other cases, as in North Carolina's Davidson County, hearings once disrupted never resumed. A longtime California activist tells one such story set in the high desert lands between Los Angeles and the San Joaquin Valley:

[They're going to] burn hazardous waste at this plant. . . . [A] bunch of the folks in Rosamond, because we're downwind of the plant, put on this public meeting, and had a big hearing, and Bradley [Angel, an organizer with Greenpeace] came down for it, and Pat Costner [a scientist with Greenpeace] was here.[28] And I remember my mom—she told this story many times—Bradley told [Pat], "Now listen, Pat, I don't care what happens. You just got to get the mic. You've got to get the mic. You've got to get the mic." She weighs like—tiny. Tiny! Maybe eighty pounds, at most. And looks like a librarian. She's got the little hair in the little bun, and the glasses, and the little dress on. . . . And so this guy gets up there, and he's from the company that's going to burn the waste, and he's talking. So, Bradley's telling her, "Now, listen. Your sole objective. Now, get the mic, get the mic!"

So the guy's up there from the company talking about how it's fingernail polish remover that they're going to burn. It's your unused chemicals from underneath your sink that they're going to burn. . . . It's no problem. The air is going to be cleaner coming out than it was when it went in. And, "We're going to clean the air by burning this hazardous waste." And he is just up there laying out a line of crapola that you just can't even believe . . . and it's just one lie after another. And so, one guy stands up, a big huge burly guy, and he's saying, "Well, it doesn't sound to me like you're telling the truth on some of this stuff. This doesn't make any sense. Why the hell would you have to spend so many millions of dollars to retrofit the kiln, if all you're going to burn is nail polish remover?" And the crowd is just getting all uptight . . . and yelling, and people had a bunch of signs, and Bradley's like, "Now, Pat, now! Just go up there, Pat. Pat, now, now, now!"

And Pat walks up there, you know . . . all eighty pounds of her . . . and the guy is still talking. . . . And she's standing there. "Hello. I'm Dr. Pat Costner from Greenpeace, and I would like a chance to talk into the microphone." And I mean, there was just all this noise, so finally she just reaches up, and the guy's yelling in the mic—she just reaches up and snatches it right out of his hand. Snatches it! And then, there she is. "Hello, I'm Pat Costner from Greenpeace, and I'm an expert on the emissions from these types of facilities, and you came—" And it was all over! The town was just in an uproar. And thank goodness there was a side door to the gymnasium, so when the guy finally gave up and left, he didn't have to walk through the crowd.

This same activist has many such stories about public hearings. Here's one from an anti-incinerator fight in the San Joaquin Valley town of Alpaugh:

My mom kept this whistle on her windowsill for fifteen years. They handed out whistles when they went into the big meeting at Alpaugh, right? . . . [T]hey started banging the chairs. That's why they always have to tie the chairs together now. . . . So they would pick up the chairs that were steel, and they would bang them on the floor of the meeting hall. And then they had the whistles. And then kids, actually, some of the high school kids went up, and when the guys—they had this huge podium, and they had all these white guys up there, and each one was going to come up and give his story. One was from the state, one was from the county, one was from the facility, or whatever. There's like six of them, right. Well, some of the teenage boys went around back behind the stage, and when the guy would get up to talk, they'd fold his chair up and take it away. So he couldn't sit back down again. And so, pretty soon these guys didn't have any place to sit, and people were becoming extremely agitated. They started throwing the chairs, and then they finally fled out the side door. Got in their cars and drove off.

These disruptions put sand in the gears of government to keep it from rolling over residents' wishes. These tactics were sometimes a by-product of anger and impatience, as some of these stories show. But these tactics were also used intentionally by some activists. For example, one organizer recalls his interactions with the residents before the Alpaugh hearing and the press coverage of it afterward:

> [We] said, "If you're really serious, and if the town's united, they're going to have this meeting. Make sure it's the first and the last." And we talked about how to do that. . . . [Afterward], this article starts by saying "State and county government officials and attorney working for Bakersfield hazardous waste company were run out of town Monday night by citizens of Alpaugh. They probably felt lucky not to have been tarred and feathered." That pretty much summed up what happened.

During this period, the national mood over toxics was tense, and in some of these disruptive protests—in California and in other states, where similar threats were occurring—violence and property destruction threatened.[29] Though it is usually left out of the story of the protests in Warren County, North Carolina, the campaign there nearly turned violent, as Dolly Burwell recalls:

> I was hearing talk of violence from people in the community, including my own brother. In fact, my brother was like, "I'm not gonna let anybody come in here and destroy my life. And if I have to get my gun, I'm going to shoot the first truck [carrying the PCB-contaminated soil]"—it was that kind of talk. Both white and Black people that I had heard make statements in meetings that we had in the courthouse made me think that there would be some violence if we didn't bring the faith of the community into it. . . . Someone— I don't know how they got over in that landfill, but they got over in the landfill, and they just cut up the liner. They cut it all up; and people were saying that that was indicative of what was going to happen to a truck driver. Somebody was going to take action against the truck drivers the same way they took action against the landfill itself.[30]

As she notes here, Burwell ultimately helped bring the faith community into the fight in Warren County, hoping it would help direct tensions into nonviolent protest rather than violence. Indeed, contacts in the church helped attract nationally known Black civil rights leaders to the Warren County fight. They trained residents to respond to police through nonviolent means such as going limp while being taken from their road blockade to waiting police cars.[31] But threats were not only, or even primarily, aimed at polluters. Some activists risked a great deal. For example, arsonists burned down the home of Pat Costner, the national director of the Greenpeace Toxics Program who spoke at the public hearing in Alpaugh described previously. While the fire destroyed her extensive library of technical documents and interviews, it did not silence her.[32]

These examples speak to the national mood, but the same anger was in the air in California. Here, two Greenpeace organizers narrate their recollections of the blockade of the sewage sludge dump on the Torres Martinez Cahuilla Reservation near San Diego in 1994:

> White environmental groups, to their credit, stopped the dumping of sewage sludge into the ocean, but they then washed their hands of it. These unscrupulous companies illegally dumped it on this reservation, and created what was called Mount San Diego . . . the government wouldn't follow their own laws and shut it down at the request of the tribe . . . it was completely illegal, and it was backed by gun thugs, literally gun thugs helping the company scare off even the tribal government. . . .
>
> It started as a non-violent blockade. Federal marshals came and then left, and the police all left, and when nobody would do anything, EPA wouldn't do anything, the BIA [Bureau of Indian Affairs] and the company put out a death list, and brought in AK-47s to break up our blockade. The blockade turned, at least for a night, from a peaceful blockade with fences and barricades, and railroad ties, and trenches we dug, and rumor has it, some people poured sand into the tanks of the sludge trucks. Not rumor has it, that's exactly what happened. The tribal members decided, "Well, we've got to get weapons." And it was an armed standoff, people almost got killed. It was pretty scary. You just didn't know what was going to happen next. . . .
>
> And we're out in this rural place, and it was pretty heavy. So there was this huge rally of hundreds and hundreds of people, where [people were singing] farmworker, union songs. You had the Native people, everybody, singing. And you had the farmworkers and everybody else doing the Cahuilla bird dance, to the traditional songs. And then it was decided that only the warriors would stay. And the chairwoman and myself, and others, were put into hiding for the night, and so instead of hundreds of people, it went down to a few dozen. We put spotlights on the trailer where the gun thugs were, and it was an armed standoff all night. Oh, and during the day, they tried crashing the barricades. I mean, it was wild stuff. . . . We shut that place down.[33]

The thirteen-day blockade drew support from not only local farmworkers and Greenpeace but also the American Indian Movement, the Indigenous Environmental Network, and the Southwest Network for Environmental and Economic Justice. Together they stopped the illegal dumping, but other similarly tense standoffs took place elsewhere. In 1998, well into what became a 113-day occupation of federally owned land in protest against the impending construction of a low-level nuclear waste landfill in the Mojave Desert's Ward Valley, activists were faced with similar threats of state violence in support of corporate pollution; federal Bureau of Land Management rangers came to the site in riot gear and armed with M16s. The weapons were never fired, but activists experienced a long night when anything seemed possible, and some resolved to die for the cause. One Fort Mojave Indian Tribe member remembers the moment at which she saw one of the federal law enforcement agents pointing his gun at her younger brother while the group was performing spiritual ceremonies at the front of the blockade. Her memories echo those of many others at the scene:

> My brother was singing, and the singer was singing . . . and they were both singing, and dancing, and I was dancing with them. And I saw—like I don't know if it was a police officer, or a soldier, it looked like a soldier, point a gun at my brother. . . . And when I saw that, and I saw that person aim at my brother, it made everything real, you know, and it made it serious to all of us that we really—that night, it was us, and they—if they were going to shoot us, then we have to be okay that we were doing it, and someone would know about it. And if no one knew about it, then that's just what we had to say yes to. . . . It was a really pivotal point for me on how I understand the world, and how I believe in our traditional beliefs, and why I believe in them so strongly today. My grandma gave us the gift to know that, you know, we were different, and that we were strong, and that we were okay, when her whole life, there were a number of people telling her she couldn't be Mojave, she couldn't speak her language, she couldn't do this, or she had to go here. And to be 12 and 13 years old, and be strong, I felt like, you know, we made her proud, that we made our family proud that night.

In general, these kinds of disruptive tactics and threats of violence in the environmental justice movement diminished over time, as I show in the next two chapters; increasing reliance on the nonprofit form bound many activist groups more tightly to tactics such as lobbying, fundraising, and policy reform. But not all nonprofits embraced institutional, nondisruptive tactics. Some nonprofits instead facilitated the use of confrontational direct-action tactics by community groups. Greenpeace, for example, encouraged activists to put their bodies in the way of an unwanted action, such as the transport of waste to a landfill, in order to draw attention to it by disrupting business practices as usual, and supported local activists who were already doing so. Similarly, the Center for Health and Environmental Justice (formerly the Citizen's Clearinghouse for Hazardous Waste, which grew out of the Love Canal struggle) published a booklet titled *How to Win at Public Hearings*, which described techniques for how to disrupt public processes when other methods had failed.[34]

Not all activists of the period easily embraced direct-action and disruptive tactics. Some were afraid of retribution and potential job loss. A white activist from Alpaugh describes her ambivalence about participating in a blockade of a hazardous waste landfill in Kettleman City:

They decided they were going to have this hearing in Hanford [the county seat] about the incinerator and they wanted to draw attention to the hearing. So the day before the hearing they were going to blockade the dump [where the incinerator would be built] with a bus and they were going to have people in the bus and they were going to have one guy chained underneath, under the bus, once they parked it crossways in the entrance. And they asked me if I would be in the bus. And at the time I thought, OK, well, there's going to be plenty of people from Kettleman there. I was substitute teaching at the high school, or at the whole entire school, K–12th grade. I was only substituting in Alpaugh, but the superintendent happened to live in Kettleman City. But anyway they said, "Will you be in the bus?" and I said, "Sure." I was thinking there would be so many people I won't be noticed. They were expecting everybody to be arrested, you know, but they said, "We'll get you out, we'll pay your bail," and I'm like, "OK, I think I'll do it." And then I found out I was going to be the only local person. There weren't going to be any from Kettleman, because nobody from Kettleman wanted to do it. Activists from LA and San Francisco, yeah, a bunch of college students, but I'd be the only local person. I said, "I'm going to hear a lot of attention and I'm afraid that they will never hire me again if I get arrested," you know. It's just a reality. So I had to tell them no, I felt really bad. . . . Nobody was arrested, so I could have gotten away with it. . . .
    [At the hearing the next day] I was astounded by how many people from Kettleman were participating. They bussed them in—Greenpeace had hired a big bus [and] got the people there. The people in Kettleman were fabulous. I guess they didn't feel like they could take the chance of getting arrested, that's why they weren't going to go on that bus and I didn't feel I could either. It's sad though, but I—God, I should have done it. Because they didn't get arrested. But that would have been pretty hard on me, I think, being arrested. Although if I hadn't had that specific job that I felt like would have been threatened and that was meaningful, you know, that point that money was important, family. I would have done it, I would have done it.

As this activist's experience shows, participation in direct-action tactics can have consequences, and economically vulnerable people and communities must balance their desire to protest things that threaten their well-being with the need to protect themselves from the potential consequences of protest itself. In the following, a Latina activist describes her predominantly Latinx neighbors' fears about participating in the public permitting process for a new hazardous waste incinerator:

> Every time that people appeared at meetings, they would call the police. Of course that intimidates people. You're going to be scared. Most of the people in Buttonwillow are not radical—they're just working families who want to raise a family. They're not wanting to be troublemakers or having trouble with the police. But I kept telling them "They're just intimidating. They're going to try to intimidate us. Nothing is going to happen to you." Nothing really happened. They would just stand there and try to intimidate people. They said they would never translate the meetings and we got them to translate them. They said they would never translate the EPA report and they translated a big portion of it. It took them a long time so if we had not been at that meeting and we had not gone and started asking questions . . .

Concerns about participating in protests, or even in public hearings, can be particularly salient for Latinx living in the United States without legal documentation and at risk of deportation.

While many of the previous stories show the anger that many activists felt toward the polluters who sought to profit by harming their communities, not all environmental justice activists were motivated only by personal anger. Some were motivated by deep political critiques of the existing political system, sometimes bringing radical ideologies into the environmental justice movement. For example, Pam Tau Lee entered into activism through student politics, Chinese American activism, and multiracial ethnic solidarity movements of the 1970s, and she brought relatively radical political investments with her when she cofounded the Asian Pacific Environmental Network in 1993. Similarly, Richard Moore, a New Mexico–based activist who led the Southwest Network for Environmental and Economic Justice (a group in which many Californians participated) held preexisting radical political ideologies; his interviews touch on capitalism, colonialism, Chicano and Black nationalism, and third world socialism.[35] There were ideological differences and motivations between these radical activists who sought to remake existing political and economic structures and the people who simply did not want toxic facilities in their backyards, though some of the latter quickly developed such broader political critiques. While the fights against specific local threats held together diverse coalitions who could agree on what they did *not* want, this agreement would later fracture as some activists moved toward broader political goals, as shown in the following chapters.[36]

CAUSES OF DISRUPTIVE ACTIVISM

What led the many activists who were not politically radical to use confrontational tactics that put their lives and livelihoods at risk? The widespread adoption of these tactics was a product of a particular historical moment: a convergence of factors that set the stage for furious public outcry about hazardous waste dumping and other toxic, polluting enterprises being located in their backyards. This desperate, angry response came from a combination of a new public consciousness about the dangers of hazardous waste, a lack of trust in the government's ability to regulate or manage hazardous waste dumps safely, and a concern for the safety and economic health of the places they called home.

During the late 1970s and 1980s, hazardous waste took on a new and terrifying importance in the public imagination.[37] Until the mid-1970s, hazardous waste had been a poorly understood issue. Regulators did not know how much of it there was, where it was located, how it was being disposed of, or what its potential environmental and health impacts might be. As Szasz writes, a 1973 survey showed that in the early 1970s the public had been

> remarkably unruffled by the prospect of having a hazardous waste disposal facility for a neighbor: 60 percent of respondents favored or strongly favored placement of [a national disposal site] facility in their own county; 58 percent thought that such siting would either leave property values unchanged or actually increase those values . . . [and] almost 60 percent of the sample were willing to live within five miles of a hazardous waste disposal facility.[38]

Until 1976, when the Resource Conservation and Recovery Act (RCRA) was passed, hazardous waste was a largely unregulated industry; in 1978, Penny Newman, who lived downhill from the Stringfellow Acid Pits that stored liquid hazardous waste, still had trouble convincing regulators of the severity of the threat the pits posed. She said:

> In '78, there were very few people who even knew what toxic chemicals were, so we'd go to talk with some of our legislators and Congress people and have to, basically, explain what we were talking about. It's kind of hard in these days to realize how ignorant we were about these things. I think it underscores why the Water Board didn't see a big problem, if you mixed [the liquid hazardous waste] in with rain water, it couldn't possibly be a problem after it traveled 200 feet. You know, kind of that old mentality. . . . So over a five-day period they were doing this pumping, releasing it into, in the reports they always called it "a controlled release," but it was into a little dirt wash that ran down the canyon and into the community on Pyrite Street, right

where our elementary school is, and other houses that were along there. During that five-day period, nobody bothered to tell any of us what was going on, so myself and many of my friends were sending our kids off to school without any idea what they were being subjected to. So my kids, like the others in the community, were playing in the puddles. They were making beards out of the foam that they found. It was very intriguing to them. They were splashing around in these pools of toxic chemicals. It wasn't until that five days had passed that we really found out what was going on.[39]

In that same year, hazardous waste would suddenly become intensely salient in the minds of the American public, for it was in 1978 that Love Canal suddenly made horrifyingly visible the public health threat posed by hazardous waste. Public opinion about hazardous waste facilities changed dramatically in the wake of this widely publicized disaster. Whereas in 1976 a US Environmental Protection Agency (EPA) survey had found that only 42 percent of owners and operators of hazardous waste treatment, storage, and disposal facilities felt that "public opposition was a constraint in obtaining new sites or expanding old ones," by 1979 a General Accounting Office survey found that "virtually all of the disposal industry officials interviewed indicated that public opposition was a major problem."[40]

Nationally, concern about the health impacts of hazardous waste was peaking in the early 1980s, when the Warren County protests took place. According to Dolly Burwell, local opposition to the proposed Afton hazardous waste landfill grew out of residents' intense fear for their health, stoked by news reports about Love Canal and other disasters:

> The whole community was coming to the meetings at the courthouse. Because of the images that people saw on TV about how dangerous the PCBs were or how they perceived it, people—including my own child Kim—actually thought that once the PCBs were put in Warren County that people would immediately start dying from cancer. That's the way they perceived it on TV, they saw the men dressed up in these space suits, they just really thought that people would die immediately—it was almost like anthrax.[41]

The perception was that hazardous waste would cause immediate, catastrophic harm, and residents were willing to use disruptive tactics to protect themselves and their families.

The public was deeply concerned about government corruption and mismanagement in addressing hazardous waste dumps. The lack of regulation of hazardous waste disposal meant that the government did not even know the location of all the hazardous waste sites in the country.

In California, a 1979 study of abandoned deposits of hazardous waste listed 25,000 potential sites; 1,904 were identified as likely problem sites. By 1985, the EPA had 19,400 potential hazardous waste sites listed in its national inventory but stressed that the list was incomplete, estimating that an additional 130,000 to over 378,000 "undiscovered" hazardous waste sites likely existed.[42] In the same year, public polls reported that 79 percent of Americans thought that not enough had been done to clean up toxic waste sites, 64 percent were willing to pay higher taxes to fund cleanup in their area, 63 percent thought existing protections weren't being adequately enforced, and 45 percent said they did not think current laws went far enough to protect them.[43]

As a result of this intensifying public concern, some existing hazardous waste landfills were closed, and new ones were increasingly difficult to build in the face of public opposition. As we saw in Los Angeles, government and industry therefore turned increasingly to the prospect of burning waste in incinerators rather than landfilling it; these were the incinerators that many Californians banded together to fight. Some incinerators were proposed in small, rural towns that did not already have an existing industrial base into which a new facility could blend. Many of these rural communities saw themselves as being clean, natural, and unspoiled. The proposal of a facility to burn hazardous waste thus ran against these towns' prevailing self-concept. As one activist told me, they moved to the rural San Joaquin Valley precisely because it seemed clean and healthy, before its air pollution and pesticide drift problems were widely known:

> We moved to the Central Valley because we were living in Los Angeles and we wanted to be in the country, to get out of the chaos in Los Angeles. We wanted a healthier, cleaner environment. Socially and environmentally, we thought it would be better for the kids. We moved to Alpaugh in '84, but in '89 we heard that there was a company proposing to build a toxic waste incinerator in town.

In these cases, the shock of an industrial facility being proposed for what residents had perceived as a "clean" town resulted in angry, disruptive activism. In other cases, communities already suffering from various forms of pollution were identified as places in which to put new incinerators, leading residents to protest the additional new threats that incinerators posed to their health.

Residents were also concerned about their property values being lowered by the siting of toxic or polluting enterprises nearby. Although many of the poor and working-class people who were most exposed to hazardous waste rented, for those who did own their own homes, fear about the impact of toxins on their health was compounded by the concern that local hazardous waste sites would reduce the economic value of their homes. For example, activists in North Carolina were motivated to act in part to protect their homes. As Dolly Burwell recollects from the Warren County campaign:

> Many people in the Afton community were poor, but they owned their own little home, the piece of property that had been left to them by their family and that was the only thing they had. I knew folks who worked in the cotton mills. They owned their own little home, and they thought that, if they brought the chemicals here, that was going to destroy the value of the little property that they owned. They had to try to stop somebody from destroying their livelihood.[44]

In the face of this multilayered public opposition to siting waste disposal enterprises near people's homes, in 1984 the California Waste Management Board commissioned a report to provide advice on where and how to locate new incinerators. Known infamously as the "Cerrell report" (named for the consulting company that wrote it), the report advised the state on which locations would be least likely—or least able—to resist the nearby siting of incinerators. While previous studies had described rural communities as being less likely to resist incinerators, the Cerrell report noted that in California, both rural and urban communities frequently opposed them. The Cerrell report instead recommended that incinerators be located in places with low education and income levels. The report's blatant recommendation to burden the poor (and, indirectly, communities of color, though the authors did not explicitly mention race) with health-threatening incinerators angered residents of these communities when it was leaked to the public, facilitating their willingness to participate in disruptive political tactics.

Many early activists got involved in protest-based, disruptive actions after other tactics had failed. Indeed, local government officials were rarely sympathetic. They often lived outside of the area affected by the pollution, had personal or financial connections to the industry, or wanted to keep or acquire the taxes that the industry might provide. Residents' concerns were met with hostility shot through with racism, classism, and sexism.[45] Activists during this period remember these experiences vividly:

> Along the way, we got insulted a lot about not having education and not knowing what we're talking about. Actually, we weren't talking just to talk,

you know, we were reading and we were listening to people that would bring us information. I think that helped us win, not only seeing how we were discriminated against not only for our color, but for not having the education.

This poor treatment by agency officials and industry representatives served to politicize early environmental justice activism. In some cases, the dismissive treatment they received at the hands of those with power angered them almost more than the environmental hazard itself. One environmental justice activist describes her motivation during the 1980s and early 1990s this way:

> The anger in me was what drove me for a lot of years because I don't like for people to be prejudiced against Mexican people because of whatever—not just color but I think because of the language, because of class, because of lack of education, because you're poor and all that. You could see in the faces of these people when we go to these meetings because the majority of people that went to the meetings were farmworkers like my husband.

Environmental justice activists of this period were outsiders to the political establishment, and many had no ambitions to join it. This reduced any inhibitions they might otherwise have felt about engaging in disruptive behavior. As Richard Moore reflected in 1998, "Another reason we are a threat to the EPA is that we have nothing to lose. We are not looking for positions in the Clinton administration or funds from the U.S. government, so we cannot be bribed."[46] As a result of the heightened sense of the risk of environmental toxins, the stark visibility of the inequality between activists and officials, and the exclusion of residents from institutional and political modes of redress, disruptive action was a frequent outcome.

OUTCOMES

The early, disruptive years of the environmental justice movement successfully prevented the construction of a rash of new polluting industries across the state. The successes that came through disruptive public action at hearings worked in two ways. Sometimes the action convinced the company proposing the polluting facility to withdraw its proposal. Often the companies had already invested significant time and money in the proposal before ever getting to the stage where public hearings happen. Unanticipated delays in the process ran up their expenditures even further, and strong public protest often convinced them that their plans would become ever more expensive as public opposition and lawsuits further dragged out the process. In other cases, strong displays of public opposition got key local politicians to withdraw support they had previously given to proposed incinerators. For example, Los Angeles mayor Tom Bradley reversed his previous support for the LANCER incinerators in 1987 after sustained public opposition, and this was a key turning point in the defeat of the proposals.[47]

These early environmental justice activists were sometimes criticized as "not in my backyard" (NIMBY) activists, concerned solely with protecting their own neighborhoods. It is true that many of the early campaigns were place based, and that immediate threats to their health and homes galvanized residents in ways that more remote threats perhaps did not. But it is also true that many activists put considerable effort into sharing information with people in other parts of the state, country, and world and traveled to support each other when possible. The impact of local campaigns scaled up when they were replicated across the state and the country—a fact that many of those charging NIMBY-ism overlook. As one participant said, activist responses to the slew of incinerator proposals springing up in the 1980s and 1990s built on each success: "After that big march on Vernon, [activists] killed all those twelve [incinerator] proposals. Then they started shutting down the existing ones." Indeed, "by 1989, of the 34 major waste-to-energy plants that had been proposed, 28 had been terminated or put on hold," and "of the other six facilities, only *one* was operating."[48] This trend would ultimately continue into the 1990s and 2000s, and not just in California. Although more than seventy-five new or expanded incinerators have been proposed in California since the early 1980s, no new commercial municipal solid waste incinerators have been built there since 1989, and none have been built on a new site in the entire country since 1995.[49]

In other cases, the coalitions built to defeat single polluting facilities impacted local politics far beyond that single siting battle. Blumberg and Gottlieb write that the success of Concerned Citizens of South Central Los Angeles at defeating the LANCER incinerators in South Central Los Angeles ultimately pushed the city to invest more in waste reduction through recycling.[50] Consistent local opposition to incinerators led to less favorable government policies for incinerator projects across the board. Antitoxics and environmental justice activists' efforts contributed to the passage of local, statewide, and national "right-to-know" laws that required the public release of information about what chemicals were in use in workplaces and what pollutants were being released by

FIGURE 7. Incinerator in Crows Landing, one of only three new commercial municipal solid waste incinerators built in California since the mid-1980s, January 13, 2009. All three were built in predominantly Latinx areas. Only two are still functioning. Photo by author.

industrial facilities into the surrounding communities. They also helped win improvements to Superfund law and hazardous materials storage.

Despite these successes, California and US environmental justice victories intersected with the global "race to the bottom" to locate industry in the cheapest places with the least restrictive environmental and labor regulations. This is why polluting high-tech manufacturers began relocating from the Silicon Valley in California's San Francisco Bay Area to the Southwest in the 1990s, and then to the Global South. Activist networks worked together to combat these environmental threats wherever they appeared. Silicon Valley–based activist groups worked with activists in the Southwest to try to limit the damage when the factories moved the first time, and globally networked activists in the Global Anti-Incinerator Alliance and other transnational activist networks worked together to fight the growth of the incinerator industry in the Global South.[51] But defeating the construction of new polluting industries is extremely difficult for activists with limited time and budgets to address on a global scale: these industries often pop up elsewhere.

Although California activists had great success preventing the construction of new polluting facilities in particular locales, these individual successes did not, in general, translate to large-scale change. The towns and neighborhoods targeted as host communities remained vulnerable to future threats. There was little meaningful response to environmental justice activists' concerns about the systematic racialized distribution of pollution and enforcement of environmental regulations. Indeed, some of the broader environmental successes of the period may have helped to redistribute risk from wealthier, white communities to poorer communities of color. For example, Wang and colleagues suggest that the creation of the Toxic Release Inventory, which required certain polluting industries to publicly report their air pollution emissions, encouraged some companies to move facilities out of privileged communities (which they saw as being able to leverage the new data source to force compliance) and into poorer communities with lower education levels.[52]

CHAPTER 2

The Institutionalization of the Environmental Justice Movement

Three decades after the beginning of the environmental justice movement, much remains the same, and much has changed. Take, for example, a 2013 protest outside the headquarters of the California Environmental Protection Agency (CalEPA) in the state capital. It was a familiar scene: protesters chanted, held placards, and made speeches. They even brought an actual bed to make the point that environmental regulators were "in bed with polluters," a tactic that had been used in the earlier years of the environmental justice movement.

But the familiar scene was also changed. While protesters included activists from the early days of the movement, a new generation of activists were also present. Brothers Emiliano and Arsenio Mataka were part of this new generation. Their parents, John and Rosenda Mataka, are longtime environmental justice activists from the San Joaquin Valley town of Grayson who spent their early years with the Chicano rights movement. Emiliano and Arsenio grew up in a household immersed in the environmental justice movement, fighting air pollution, pesticide drift, a nearby incinerator, and a giant tire fire. But the two brothers had very different experiences at this particular protest. Emiliano stood outside the CalEPA building with the other protesters, while his brother Arsenio, the assistant secretary for environmental justice and tribal affairs, was on the inside looking out.

Arsenio and Emiliano represent two strands of the environmental justice movement. Emiliano's approach retained much of the grassroots flavor of the early years, with a modern twist. He and some politically like-minded friends ran a group called Valley Improvement Projects that tackled a wide variety of issues in their area, including pollution and police violence. During my visit in 2013, they had rented a building they used as a community space, which they staffed in shifts. It included a shop for fixing bikes, a small activist-oriented library, and meeting space. The coffee table in the front room held political magazines and a bowl of free condoms, and the walls were covered with flyers, graffiti, and framed renderings of Malcolm X and other political leaders. They provided free rides to the grocery store for low-income people without easy access to healthy food and conducted "know your rights" workshops to respond to police abuses of power. They also attended phone conferences on air pollution and goods transportation with activists around the state. Funds were hard to come by; later, they closed the community space but continued their work together. Valley Improvement Projects functioned largely as a volunteer collective, inspired by both the environmental justice activism of Emiliano's parents' generation of activists and by contemporary horizontal, direct-action movements, including the anti-globalization movement and Occupy Wall Street. Emiliano continued his work with Valley Improvement Projects until his tragic death in a car accident in 2015.[1]

Emiliano's brother Arsenio was also influenced by his parents' activism, but he put it to work in a different way. Arsenio went to law school, then worked for Antonio Villaraigosa, the first Mexican American mayor of Los Angeles in over 130 years. Eventually, he became the directing attorney for California Rural Legal Assistance (CRLA), an organization with environmental justice roots. CRLA, with Ralph Abascal, led many key pesticide-related lawsuits on behalf of farmworkers starting in 1969.[2] In the late 1980s and early 1990s, CRLA also helped a young lawyer named Luke Cole get started in the work that would lead to the creation of the Center for Race, Poverty and the Environment, now a core organization of the California environmental justice movement. Arsenio worked at CRLA until control of the governor's office shifted from Republican Arnold Schwarzenegger to Democrat Jerry Brown in 2011, when he was appointed to a position inside the California EPA, taking over as the assistant secretary for environmental justice and tribal affairs. The position had been created in 2000 in response to the efforts of previous generations of environmental justice activism. Arsenio served in that role for six years before becoming the state's special assistant attorney general for the environment. In 2021 he moved

FIGURE 8. Emiliano Mataka speaking at the People's Earth Day protest at the Region 9 (Pacific Southwest) headquarters of the EPA in San Francisco, April 22, 2013. Photo by author.

FIGURE 9. Arsenio Mataka speaking with residents at a public workshop for CalEnviro-Screen 2.0., a government tool to identify places most affected by multiple sources of pollution, Fresno, May 6, 2014. Photo by author.

on to a role in the nation's capital as the senior adviser for health equity and climate at the US Department of Health and Human Services.

The brothers' diverging paths eventually placed them on opposite sides of the thick glass windows at the CalEPA protest, one on the inside looking out, the other on the outside looking in. In some ways, their story represents the larger trajectory of the environmental justice movement. Some activists continue with practices of disruptive protest and "outsider" politics, while others have increasingly moved within the state apparatus or engaged it through traditional forms of political influence, such as policy advocacy, lobbying, electoral politics, and participation in public decision-making mechanisms such as advisory committees. The two approaches are not mutually exclusive; the 1990s, in particular, saw both strands happening in parallel. But today the bulk of the movement's activities have shifted away from the disruptive outsider approaches that dominated the early years.

THE PATH TO INSTITUTIONALIZATION

Arsenio Mataka's role in CalEPA, like the roles of other environmental justice activists working in government, was made possible by the work of the activists who came before him. While much activism of the 1980s and 1990s was locally focused, some activists during this period were also pressing for broader regulatory changes. Some antitoxics activists of the 1980s, for example, were heavily invested in toxics legislation at the federal and state levels, particularly the Superfund legislation and right-to-know measures making pollution data available to the public. These efforts continued into the 1990s and beyond. However, after the First National People of Color Environmental Leadership Summit in 1991, the emerging strand of activism instead emphasized environmental racism and the cumulative health impacts of multiple pollution sources to which individual communities, particularly communities of color, were exposed. Policy mechanisms were poorly equipped to address these problems. As this chapter shows, both strands of activism eventually facilitated the partial institutionalization of activism and advocacy within both state and federal governments.

For example, the Southwest Network for Environmental and Economic Justice (SNEEJ) used protests, rallies, and contact with existing political representatives to crack open doors that had long been closed to them within environmental regulatory agencies—cracks that later activists would continue to pry open. Gaining this access was not easy.

SNEEJ applied multiple points of pressure to finally get the US Environmental Protection Agency (EPA) to sit down with them. In 1990, SNEEJ sent a letter to the EPA charging them with racism in their ranks and received an unsatisfactory response. SNEEJ therefore leaked to the press an internal memo that detailed how the EPA planned to respond to the critique and the protests that accompanied it. As Richard Moore describes, the resulting negative press was what brought the EPA to the table:

> The Network chose to confront the EPA publicly because it had rarely if ever opened its doors to people of color or their organizations in the past. Demonstrations and press conferences in Dallas, San Francisco, and Albuquerque, New Mexico, accompanied the submission of the letter. When the EPA refused to respond, another round of demonstrations was held, including the occupation of the San Francisco EPA Region IX office. While EPA continued to give little public response to these events, top-level EPA officials prepared a lengthy confidential plan to use the national media to paint a positive image of the EPA's record on environmental equity. The memo termed environmental racism to be "one of the most polemically explosive environmental issues yet to emerge." Action needed to be taken, it was claimed, before resentment against the EPA reached a flashpoint at which "grass-roots groups finally succeed in persuading more mainstream (sic) groups to take ill-advised actions." When the Network leaked the memo to the public via Congressman Henry Waxman (D-CA), the EPA began to seriously discuss the Network's concerns with the organization and other environmental justice leaders.[3]

As this quote makes clear, multiple tactics were at work here. SNEEJ used outsider protest tactics at first, but ultimately gained access to the EPA through pressure on a formal political representative (a nondisruptive tactic working through existing channels of power), though that pressure was brought to bear through leaking the EPA memo (arguably an outsider tactic), which itself responded to the original protests.

Environmental justice activists often had to fight to be included in spaces already occupied by the mainstream, whiter environmental movement. Latinx Richard Moore described his continuing frustration with environmental organizations in the mid-1990s, which appeared to have learned nothing from the letters that environmental justice groups had sent to them in 1990, or from the subsequent summit in 1991:

> They still treat us in an extremely paternalistic fashion. In some ways, it's worse than it was three years ago. National environmental organizations send us memos that are so bad they should be used as examples in anti-racism workshops. We heard about a meeting in November 1992 where the

national environmental organizations were going to get together and form their own environmental transition team for the incoming Clinton administration, without any environmental justice organizations being invited. We then sent them a memo asking if they had learned anything. We asked if there were any environmental justice representatives that were invited to this meeting. I don't know if we can have any relations with these groups because of their deep lack of respect for our movement.

Eventually, Black environmental justice activist and scholar Dr. Robert Bullard was appointed to the Bill Clinton administration's environmental transition team. However, the fact that the mainstream organizations initially completely overlooked the environmental justice movement in building this team says much about their priorities at that time.

During and after the 1990s, environmental justice groups tried to enact new policies via all three branches of federal government. Multiple environmental justice bills and one amendment to the Constitution were put forth in the 1990s and 2000s, sponsored by civil rights leaders John Lewis and Jesse Jackson, as well as future vice president Al Gore, Minnesotans Max Baucus and Paul Wellstone, and California legislators Barbara Boxer and Hilda Solis. However, these federal legislative efforts all failed.[4]

Some initial progress was made in the courts, but it was largely stymied by a 2001 Supreme Court ruling that Title VI of the Civil Rights Act only applied to racialized outcomes that were proven to be intentional. Although this case was not about environmental concerns, it undermined court cases related to the racist distribution of pollution, because it is much more difficult to legally prove intentional racism than racist outcomes. The courts also limited the application of the Equal Protection Clause of the Fourteenth Amendment of the US Constitution, the National Environmental Policy Act (NEPA), and the ability of the EPA's Office of Civil Rights to accept Title VI complaints, making it more difficult to use the legal system to directly curtail environmental racism.[5]

Administrative action within the executive branch and agencies, however, got more traction. In 1990, the US EPA created the Office of Environmental Equity (which later became the Office of Environmental Justice), and in 1993 the National Environmental Justice Advisory Council (NEJAC) was put in place. NEJAC members pressed the Clinton administration to take executive action on environmental justice. In 1994, Clinton signed Executive Order 12898, which required all federal agencies to "make achieving environmental justice part of its mission by identifying and addressing, as appropriate, disproportionately high and adverse human health or environmental effects of its programs, policies, and activities on minority populations and low-income populations in the United States and its territories and possessions."[6] At the time, many activists saw this as a breakthrough—a chance to have their concerns taken seriously at the federal level. Rita Harris, a longtime environmental justice activist, describes the day she heard about the executive order as a joyful one:

> I remember where I was on that day in 1994 clearly. I was attending a conference at the Crystal City Marriott being hosted by NIEHS (National Institute for Environmental Health Sciences). There was a horrible snow storm and government offices in Washington, D.C. were all closed. However, word was quickly passing around the crowds of people at the conference that a select group of activists from our ranks had been called over to the White House. There was so much excitement among the attendees, and it grew even wilder once the group returned and told us why they went to the White House. We were told that President Clinton had signed an Executive Order that would mandate all federal agencies develop strategic plans to address environmental justice (EJ). This was groundbreaking and historic! Many of the activists that were present at the conference and at the signing felt like this was just the one-two punch that was needed to help us with our many EJ fights and help communities across the country. "EJ will finally be recognized now that we have the President in our corner," is what some said.[7]

The executive order required federal agencies to attend to the problem of environmental justice after years of obstructionism. Richard Moore of SNEEJ describes their long fight to get the administrator for the federal EPA unit responsible for the Pacific Southwest, Region 9, to visit nine of the communities of color in which SNEEJ members were working in the 1990s: "We finally saw some movement. After up to ten years of struggle in some of these communities, people finally saw the EPA begin to move. Medite here in New Mexico, for example, was cited with fifteen or sixteen citations after the regional administrator visited."[8] SNEEJ began to have quarterly meetings with the EPA chief administrator and got much of its desired language included in an Earth Day statement made by President Clinton.

Despite the executive order, activists knew that they still faced an uphill battle to get the federal government to take significant action on environmental justice issues. According to Moore, activists believed that the federal government remained more allied with industry than with environmental justice causes. As he wryly put it, "We are taking Clinton up on his offer of an 'open door policy.' Maybe he was just talking about corporations; if so, he should have said so at the beginning."[9] And indeed, the actions of the federal government on environmental justice issues proved to be small concessions, in no small part because of industry lobbying. Polluters pushed back hard against environmental justice efforts, saying that the EPA and the Clinton administration had created a "monster," and that they wanted "nothing short of shutting down all business activity."[10] States claimed that the federal government's environmental justice efforts infringed on states' rights, using the concept of states' rights as cover for the right to be racist. Black activist Florence Robinson from Alsen, Louisiana, drew parallels to state responses to federal action in the earlier civil rights movement: "They said the same thing in the civil rights movement. 'Our darkies are happy. Why are they coming in, stirring things up?'"[11] Anti-environmental justice interests sought to discredit the very existence of environmental racism by cultivating select Black leaders, including Black business leaders such as Detroit mayor Dennis Archer and the president of the National Black Chamber of Commerce, Harry Alford, to argue against environmental justice legislation. Alford wrote that "environmental racism is a claim that has been lingering around since the late '70s. As a strategy, Green Peace [sic], the Sierra Club and others have decided to fuel (fund) the concept and enlist newly recruited activists. These activists are quickly indoctrinated into thinking that this is a continuation of the successful Civil Rights Movement. The truth is a poor fake."[12] Alford attempted to undercut claims of environmental racism by attributing them to the predominantly white, middle-class organizations Sierra Club and Greenpeace, rather than the predominantly low-income communities and communities of color that generated them.

In 1998, industry representatives managed to have their allies in Congress enact a moratorium on the EPA's ability to accept Title VI complaints.[13] Under the George W. Bush administration, from 2001 to 2008, the EPA moved backward, erasing the limited progress it had made during the Clinton administration, and reframed its efforts on environmental justice using an earlier version of today's "All Lives Matter" framing: it billed itself as "working to secure environmental justice for *all* communities" and stressed that "environmental justice is not necessarily limited to low-income and/or minority populations only."[14] This shifted the emphasis away from the people who suffered the most: low income communities and communities of color that the environmental justice movement had emerged to protect.

But let us return to the 1990s, the period when the federal government was making some slow progress on environmental justice concerns under Clinton. During this same period, California legislators were also forging ahead on environmental justice efforts in the state government, with mixed success. California state legislators passed five different environmental justice bills between 1991 and 1998, but all were vetoed by Republican governor Pete Wilson.[15] Many of the bills required only that various sorts of demographic data be submitted as part of permitting processes, land use in the state's General Plan, and the CA Environmental Quality Act.[16] When Democrat Gray Davis took over the governorship in 1999, environmental justice priorities began actually making it into law. A series of successful bills obliged the governor's Office of Planning and Research and CalEPA to take up environmental justice initiatives, including the creation of model environmental justice mission statements, advisory committees, and a new assistant secretary position for environmental justice—the same position that was held by Arsenio Mataka between 2011 and 2017.[17]

Environmental justice activism in California both influenced and was influenced by Clinton's Executive Order 12898. For example, Kettleman City activists' legal battle to get Spanish translations of key documents related to the incinerator proposed to be built at the nearby landfill was designed to enable the city's many monolingual Spanish-speaking residents to meaningfully participate in the decision-making process. This influenced President Clinton to include a recommendation for the same in EO 12898.[18] At the same time, much of the early work by CalEPA and its assistant secretaries for environmental justice was modeled on environmental justice efforts at the federal level: the work done by the EPA, the Office of Environmental Justice, the National Environmental Justice Advisory Committee, and President Clinton's Executive Order 12898.

Neither the federal nor the California legislation specified the exact meaning of environmental justice or required specific action that agencies should undertake to achieve it. Both also provided little to no funds for implementation. Legislators left it up to the agencies to create plans for achieving environmental justice, supplying only some procedural guidelines. The one clear mandate in these 1990s and early 2000s efforts at both the federal and state levels was that decision-making processes must be transparent and residents of the impacted communities should have input into the process. Accordingly, mechanisms for increasing participation in environmental decision-making became the key way that environmental justice concerns were integrated into governance. These new opportunities for activist and community participation in policymaking and legislation had both advantages and disadvantages (as I explore later in this chapter and in chapter 3). Among these, it contributed to the institutionalization—and, some would argue, co-optation—of the environmental justice movement.

INSTITUTIONALIZATION ARRIVES

The drive in the 1990s to integrate environmental justice principles into environmental policy and administration changed the way that future activists—both in California and across the nation—would pursue their agendas. As the 1990s became the 2000s, much activism shifted away from disruptive "outsider tactics" and toward institutional means and "insider tactics." Activists sought to make their voices heard using three key institutional modalities: electoral politics, public office, and policy advocacy; collaboration with state and industry; and participation in decision-making processes through public hearings and advisory committees. The next section examines each of these modalities in some detail, describing the institutionalized contexts in which much of California environmental justice work is done today. The chapter's final section offers a preliminary account of how the environmental justice movement got where it is today, examining the "processes of routinization" that have pushed the movement away from disruptive tactics and direct action and toward incremental reform, accomplished through institutional channels using established political tactics.

Electoral Politics, Public Office, and Policy Advocacy

Environmental justice activists increasingly use electoral politics, positions within government, and policy advocacy to work toward their goals.[19] Politicians are accountable to those constituents who will help decide future elections, and some environmental justice organizations therefore endorse particular candidates and work to increase the turnout of voters who care about environmental justice issues. For example, Richard Moore explained why in the 1990s SNEEJ and its affiliates planned to promote voter registration drives:

> Many of our organizations don't believe that the system totally works for them, but they want to make sure that politicians in their communities represent their constituency. In the 1960s and 1970s, when we marched into city halls, county buildings, and commission meetings, the politicians would ask how many of us were registered voters and only about five percent of us would raise our hands. We saw that politicians were not accountable to the

people they perceived as not voting. So we will be pressing for more account-ability by elected officials in the coming years as a focus of our movement.[20]

Environmental justice activists have increasingly engaged in electoral politics since the 1990s, and their organizational structures reflect this focus: many environmental justice groups have created or participated in 501(c)(4) organizations, which are nonprofits that are explicitly designed to engage in the political process through lobbying and campaigning for particular candidates. Both 501(c)(4) and 501(c)(3) organizations are nonprofits, but unlike "c3s," "c4s" trade their tax-exempt status for the ability to endorse political candidates and donate time and money directly to political campaigns.

In addition to politicking on behalf of particular candidates, environmental justice activists have themselves been increasingly seeking election or appointment to public office. Especially after Democrat Jerry Brown became governor in 2011, a number of environmental justice activists and sympathizers were appointed to key roles in his office and in state agencies. The trend continued under Democrat Gavin Newsom, who succeeded him as governor in 2019.

These electoral tactics aim at implementing environmental justice goals in broad, systematic ways, and they require activists to connect with decision-makers outside the environmental justice world. As one activist put it, "[We realized] that we have to get political. Yeah, we need to address the board of supervisors, but we really need to have a voting bloc that cares about this. If you have a facility issue or whatever, that only impacts 300 people, and that district is elected by 100,000, you have to form some partnerships." Building these broader connections also brings with it a new set of challenges, as activists decide where to compromise and where to hold their ground, both with their new allies and with other activists within the movement.

These trade-offs and the tensions they can cause are also seen in policy advocacy, which expanded significantly during the transitions from Republican to Democratic governors in 1999 and again in 2011. Nonprofits such as the Community Water Center, the Environmental Justice Coalition for Water, Californians for Pesticide Reform, and the California Environmental Justice Alliance (CEJA), to name just a few, have all contributed to the increasing focus on policy reform. Since passage of the first wave of policy measures that set up California's environmental justice infrastructure within CalEPA in the late 1990s and early 2000s, their efforts have focused on tightening environmental regulations, prioritizing environmental enforcement while promoting investment in the most polluted and vulnerable communities, promoting alternative energy and associated "green-collar jobs" in low-income communities of color, establishing a human right to clean drinking water, funding drinking water treatment to reduce contamination, and assorted efforts to improve public participation in environmental decision-making and access to information.

While the increasing attention to policy advocacy is widespread among California environmental justice activists, CEJA has played a particularly strong role by coordinating the statewide policy efforts of six environmental justice organizations and four organizational partners.[21] Beginning in 2013, CEJA published annual environmental justice scorecards that grade how California legislators vote on the bills CEJA advocates for and against, and in 2016 it began releasing scorecards for California environmental agencies. These reports make CEJA's policy and administrative reform efforts more visible, and they pressure the people and agencies being graded to do better. Much of this pressure hinges on CEJA's ability to join with other coalitions to influence the now majority demographic of voters of color in favor of or against specific politicians—or at least to make credible the threat that they can do so. CEJA staff therefore track the legislative process for their members, organize lobby days for participants to come to the capital, write op-eds, and engage in the policy process. CEJA describes its work as a necessary way to push back against the better financed lobbying efforts of its opponents. This CEJA member describes its origins:

> A bunch of these organizations [current CEJA members] are like 30-plus years old. . . . So they're well established organizations, pretty large, considering they're non-profits. Some of the member organizations had done work together prior to 2001 on different campaigns and issue areas, but in 2001 they really felt like there was a need to form a statewide coalition, because there was such a gap in strong environmental justice policy. . . . Each of the organizations does incredible local work, and they thought that they needed a statewide formation to lead on environmental justice policy from the ground up, from the grassroots perspective. And so that's how CEJA formed, and the intention behind it.

As this quote shows, CEJA has deep roots in the environmental justice movement. It seeks to link the traditional methods of the environmental justice movement—direct connection with low-income communities and communities of color's daily lived experiences in polluted environments—with attempts to improve people's lives through policy advocacy that will affect the environmental decisions being made in the state capitol. Indeed, CEJA explicitly tries to balance these two modes of activism: while member groups coordinate policy activities in the state capitol, they all also undertake more localized action and "base building." CEJA has also been part of larger efforts to organize protests such as the People's Climate March in 2018, which took place in San Francisco and linked to protests around the world.

Nonetheless, CEJA's attempts to unify the policy voices of its members in a way that represents their grassroots constituents show the challenges of scaling up to engage the state on its own terrain—challenges that many other environmental justice groups also face. First, CEJA's structure and membership are under critique. Forming a coalition or network of groups, as CEJA did, requires deciding which groups are "in" and which groups are "out." CEJA originally included only six environmental justice organizations (later adding five more partner organizations), leaving out the rest of the state's many environmental justice groups. This exclusion created tension that at times made it difficult for CEJA groups to work with non-CEJA groups, and impeded coordination of policy advocacy efforts. A similar concern about inclusion and exclusion was raised by the change in the network's name, from the original Environmental Justice Working Group to the California Environmental Justice Alliance. Despite CEJA's arguments to the contrary, a number of groups outside the organization saw the new name as implying that CEJA spoke for the statewide environmental justice movement, in spite of the fact that it excluded many groups and voices. The charge of exclusivity also carries more specific complaints, with multiple excluded groups critiquing CEJA as made up of relatively large, institutionalized nonprofits rather than small grassroots community groups and having no Indigenous representation.

Second, and related to the first critique, CEJA is also sometimes accused of being too willing to compromise on environmental justice priorities in its work with legislators and state agencies, a criticism that has been levied against many, perhaps all, social movement groups that work through state political mechanisms. One activist told me the following story about a legislator with whom CEJA was working. The story shows how shifting and instrumental alliances with politicians complicate, and sometimes erode, intramovement solidarity:

I think there are some real policy problems exemplified, for example, by the recent *Congreso* in Sacramento about a month ago, where [CEJA] invited and featured Senator Ricardo Lara, and wrote a glowing bio of him in the conference packet that, honestly, could have made me puke. And you can quote me, because Lara sponsored one of the worst pro-polluter bills in the state legislature this year. And that information was censored by CEJA. When I tried to raise it in their meeting, in a discussion about renewable energy, I was literally cut off. And he was invited to speak at an environmental justice rally at the exact same time a lot of EJ communities . . . were fighting it. So it's like night and day, compared to, I think, real social justice movements.

This quote shows the tensions that result when legislators are seen as compromised, as working for both sides, on the one hand working with movement partners to accomplish movement goals, while on the other hand working with industry and other opponents in ways that impede movement goals. Lara partnered with environmental justice activists on some issues, but he also supported a bill that would have allowed the electricity created from burning waste at the state's three existing incinerators to qualify as renewable energy.[22] If passed, this would have not only legitimized the inherently toxic practice of incineration by classing it as a producer of renewable energy (a term reserved in most people's minds for "clean" energy sources such as solar and wind) but also would have undermined ongoing efforts to prevent a new incinerator from being constructed in the Salinas Valley town of Gonzales.[23] These kinds of alliances with politicians who are not fully committed to movement goals across the board are divisive: while some activists view relationships with particular legislators as extending only as far as their interests coincide, others see these inherently compromised partnerships as signaling the breakdown of movement solidarity.

As such critiques show, working with partners outside the movement proper—integrating the movement into existing institutions in hopes of advancing environmental justice causes—is a double-edged sword. (I discuss the benefits and drawbacks of collaboration with the state more fully in the next section of this chapter.) Movement institutionalization can help achieve policy victories and enshrine policies into law rather than fighting each individual battle in an ad hoc fashion. At the same time, it can create or deepen rifts within the movement itself, as some activists adopt the incremental reformism typical to working within the state apparatus and others are either left behind or refuse to play along, sticking to an oppositional vision of the environmental justice movement. In the case of CEJA, this ideological division was materialized, as some of the groups left out of the alliance created an alternate statewide network, the California Environmental Justice Coalition (CEJC), that is open to all environmental justice activist groups in California. CEJC convened its first statewide gathering in 2014.

Collaboration with State and Industry

As the environmental justice movement has institutionalized and professionalized, it has sought to make its voice heard through existing political channels. As the previous section showed, one of these channels is electoral politics. By helping elect politicians who share their goals and values, environmental justice activists believe they can make a difference through legislative and policy means. Another of these channels is collaboration with the state and even at times with industry. Newly cordial and collaborative relationships with such entities—the environmental justice movement's original opponents—have in some cases replaced the more contentious relationships that early movement groups had with these groups.

Collaboration with groups that were once seen as the "bad guys"— polluting industries—was originally a tactic of last resort. This is apparent in Richmond resident Henry Clark's account of how he helped negotiate the first good neighbor agreement with the neighboring Chevron refinery. Good neighbor agreements create legally binding documents between an individual facility's owners and organizations representing the local community. Typically, the industry agrees to some improvements in its industrial processes designed to lower risk to residents and provide some local financial investments in exchange for the community groups' agreement not to sue them. Such agreements were not easily won. Chevron would not even come to the negotiating table until 1990, after the West County Toxics Coalition had done substantial local organizing against it and brought nationally visible political leaders and recent presidential contender Reverend Jesse Jackson to one of their meetings. The first good neighbor agreement was signed in 1992, after two years of negotiations. Richmond activist Ahmadia Thomas recounts the difficulty of getting Chevron to the negotiating table and expresses a notable lack of enthusiasm for the outcome:

> It was a hard time to sit down at the table with them. They wouldn't do it at first. They was angry. It took a while. Then they finally said, "Yes, we will meet you." . . . I know it worked out finally, but it was hard negotiating as a good neighbor. When they mention that "good neighbor" and the "right to know," that was a long road, [to the] good neighbor [agreement]. But I guess they consider themselves a good neighbor now.[24]

Henry Clark counted the signing of the agreement as one of the movement's successes, despite the drawbacks to such a deal. Chevron made some concessions to the town (including the relocation of ammonium storage tanks that Clark mentions in the next quote; the tanks were originally located near the North Richmond side of the industrial property near people's homes, and Chevron agreed to move them to a more distant part of the property to minimize the impact in case of an industrial disaster). But as Clark notes, there are limitations inherent in the good neighbor approach:

> Well, it's like I said, it's project by project. Say, for instance, when the company agreed to relocate the ammonia storage tanks, you know, on that particular issue and concern, that would be a good neighbor agreement because they sat down with their neighbor and the neighbor sits down and discusses an issue and concern about those ammonia storage tanks being too close to the North Richmond community. We were successful in getting the company to relocate them, so that was a good neighbor agreement on that particular project. But as you can see, a good neighbor agreement does not necessarily mean that you're a good neighbor all the way around. I mean, on the next particular issue or concern, they may not necessarily be so receptive.[25]

Good neighbor agreements are often divisive, as some activists favor signing them (in service of incremental change or immediate harm reduction), but others want to hold out for better solutions (in service of real fundamental change that addresses the root problems). As many activists have learned, these agreements, and the town/industry collaborative relationships they purport to encode, can potentially subvert and depoliticize activism.[26]

This process is visible in Chevron's history in Richmond. Initially, relations were hostile on both sides, with Chevron opposed to any negotiation and residents angry with Chevron's actions in their town. Later, though, the relationship took on at least the appearance of good neighborliness, with Chevron conducting community outreach and efforts designed to present a kinder face to its neighbors. These public relations efforts were fairly extensive. By 2017, Chevron was publishing the glossy English/Spanish *Richmond Refinery Newsletter*, which glowingly covered its own facility's many good deeds and presented Chevron as part of the community, a good neighbor working with residents for the town's benefit. The December issue, for example, included a "community corner" feature written by the owner of a local Mexican food truck, who expressed heartfelt thanks to Chevron for letting him serve food at the Richmond refinery. The same issue also included a glossy full-page photo

FIGURE 10. Jared Blumenthal, regional administrator of EPA Region 9 (Pacific Southwest), addressing the crowd at the People's Earth Day protest, San Francisco, April 22, 2013. Environmental justice activists Tessie Ester and Henry Clark, from Bayview-Hunters Point and Richmond, on right. Photo by author, previously published in Perkins, "Slideshow: Happy People's Earth Day!"

and Q and A with a longtime local Black environmental justice activist.[27] This activist had been present at the very beginning of the California environmental justice movement in the 1980s and spent much of his activist career fighting Chevron. This opposition slowly shaded into collaboration, which eventually turned into what looks like co-optation: he spent much of his activist career fighting Chevron, then negotiated with the company, and at the very end, sang its praises in its corporate newsletter. His appearance in the newsletter led to a serious rift with other environmental justice activists with whom he had long worked. Whatever his reasons for agreeing to the feature, the support he expressed for the refinery after so many years of opposition helped Chevron to paint itself as reformed, as no longer in need of watchdogs such as activists or regulators. Further, his appearance in the newsletter also provided cover for the corporation, helping Chevron defuse decades of claims of environmental racism from its neighbors.

Collaborations are not always so divisive, especially when they are with state entities. At one protest I attended, Jared Blumenthal, the San Francisco–based head of EPA Region 9, took a meeting with a select group of activists immediately before protests scheduled in front of his workplace. He later come out to address the rest of the protesters. In this case, activists were pursuing a variation of an "inside-outside" strategy, literally. First they went inside the EPA building to talk with its most high-ranking leader, and later they came back outside the building to hold his agency's feet to the fire with other protesters. Blumenthal's willingness to come out to address the protesters showed a new level of receptiveness to environmental justice concerns within the EPA after the election of Democratic president Barack Obama.

Many environmental justice groups also now hold annual award ceremonies to recognize state agencies and sometimes corporate actors for their support. During my fieldwork, I attended several such ceremonies. At the twenty-fifth anniversary celebration of the Center for Community Action and Environmental Justice and a fundraiser organized by Pacoima Beautiful, the organizations gave awards to state and business representatives, in one case accompanied by wry comments about their formerly antagonistic relationship. Sometimes these ceremonies can paint a picture of multiple different stakeholders working in harmony toward shared goals: the original vision of some activists who sought institutionalization and work as state employees and politicians. For example, in 2015 the Community Water Center (CWC) began holding an annual Water Justice Leadership Award ceremony. At the 2015 event it honored two grassroots activists, an Assembly member, a senator, a staffer from the governor's office, and a staffer from a related water nonprofit, with the chair of the State Water Resources Control Board serving as master of ceremonies. Such gatherings are material representations of the collaborations and partnerships among activists, nonprofits, politicians, and sometimes industry, which can produce meaningful changes in leadership. CWC's deepening engagement with the state ultimately resulted in cofounder Laurel Firestone leaving her codirectorship there and accepting an appointment to the State Water Board, where she continues to press for clean drinking water for all Californians from inside the state apparatus.

However, the picture is not always so rosy. These kinds of collaborations, whether with corporations or the state, often require compromise from activists who have historically defined themselves in opposition to these entities. As we saw in the story of CEJA's partnership with Lara, activists often find themselves working with people or industries whom other activists oppose.

FIGURE 11. Ivanpah Solar Electric Generating System, Mojave Desert, April 1, 2018. Photo by author.

In another example, at one point CEJA sought to promote its rooftop solar agenda through partnerships with the solar industry, which is primarily oriented around the construction of large, utility-scale solar farms in the California desert. Other environmental justice activists oppose such solar farms, for they are often located on traditional Indigenous lands that are no longer under the tribes' legal control, and as a result may destroy sacred areas and uproot artifacts from their resting places in the earth. Solar farms may also be built on publicly owned desert lands that previous generations of environmentalists went to great lengths to protect and do not want to see bulldozed to accommodate the construction of solar panels. In place of these utility-scale solar farms, environmental justice groups typically promote distributed solar infrastructure built on existing rooftops instead. For its distributed rooftop solar project, CEJA partnered with the Solar Energy Industries Association; this group supports the Ivanpah solar project in the Mojave Desert, which was sued by a local organization dedicated to preserving Indigenous sacred sites and cultural artifacts in the area. Here, one person from a CEJA member organization describes the conflicts inherent in partnerships like these; even though CEJA's focus is on distributed (local) solar, it considered acquiescing to some utility-scale solar in order to gain a local labor union's cooperation:

> Our focus has been pretty much on local solar. But I would take it kind of closer to home. We're working at the LA Department of Water and Power [DWP]. We want them to adopt a comprehensive clean energy program. So, they're saying, well, we're getting off of coal. By 2020 to 2025, we're going to end our contracts with folks in Utah and Arizona. But we're going to replace them with natural gas. They're talking about San Onofre [the nuclear power plant], and we replace that with natural gas. . . . Technically, we can show how they can adopt a comprehensive clean energy program, and it's cost effective, it's reliable and so on. But we had to get the union on board. We had to get IBEW Local 18 [International Brotherhood of Electrical Workers], they're the big union in LA DWP. So, the question we're having is, will we have to support some utility scaled solar? And if we did, what would be the conditions under which we would support that?
>
> So, part of that would be, what do the folks where these [utility-scale solar] projects are happening, what do they say, what are their demands? So, we're looking at that. Our preference is for total local solar, but we don't know if we have the strength to achieve that. And if we don't, is labor going to fight us, and then we end up with natural gas? Because right now, their thing is, "Let them build natural gas, we get the jobs." So, we said, "You can get the jobs, but you've got to support X amount of [utility scale] solar and most importantly, X amount of [local] solar." I don't know. It's a discussion that is going on, but it hasn't been resolved yet.

Such reflections represent the difficulties of fully entering the formal political sphere. This discussion of the concessions and trade-offs involved in getting things done is not just happening around solar; the same tensions are present around all kinds of environmental justice goals, and indeed around social movement goals in general. Here, the speaker is weighing the benefits of one highly valued outcome, local solar, against the costs that would be incurred by compromising on another outcome, utility solar. The basic problem here is that progress toward one fundamental goal (local solar) could compromise others (strong relationships with other politically marginalized peoples and the protection of Indigenous lands and artifacts). This is why participation in the formal political sphere and collaborations with industry are so fraught.

CEJA's dilemma with solar exemplifies both the benefits and drawbacks of working through insider channels in partnership with the state or industry.[28] Of course, as I have reiterated, the increase in scaled-up tactics that use policy advocacy, lobbying, and participation in electoral politics at the level of the region or state has not entirely replaced the original strain of locally directed or oppositional activism. For some groups, this means continuing to oppose the construction of new polluting facilities and trying to reduce pollution from existing sources through local government or direct protest against the polluting industry. However, other, newer expressions of localism in environmental justice activism have also emerged. There is a growing interest in creating community gardens, bicycle shops, and worker cooperatives to improve health, create jobs, and build community in low-income communities of color. These community gardens and worker-owned cooperatives fit into the increasing popularity of DIY activities as a form of political action; they also help to build community and create grassroots coalitions of people who can then be integrated into other types of political action. In some cases, these efforts flow out of the Occupy culture and anarchism in which some of the more recent generations of activists are steeped. In other cases, these new efforts respond to the increasing availability of foundation funds to support such programming. These efforts largely sidestep the issue of oppositional versus institutionalized tactics; they are typically neither disruptive nor part of established political channels. Although they are seen as generally less political than other environmental justice activities, they meet the service goals of environmental justice groups and often serve their political goals as well in indirect ways (as explored in chapter 3).

Participation

As the environmental justice movement has evolved, activists have sought to make their concerns heard in more professional and more institutional ways. I have already discussed electoral politics and collaboration with state and industry. The third institutional channel through which activists seek to make their voices heard is one set up by the state itself, though often as a response to public pressure to do so: participation in public environmental decision-making processes.

Many of the federal environmental laws that still dominate national environmental policy were created in the 1970s and include numerous mechanisms for public participation. The year 1970 alone saw the creation of the Environmental Protection Agency, the National Atmospheric and Oceanic Administration, the Clean Air Act, the Water Quality Improvement Act, and the first Earth Day. The Clean Water Act, the Endangered Species Act, and the Safe Drinking Water Act followed soon afterward. By 1980, two more landmark bills had been passed: the

Resource Conservation and Recovery Act (RCRA), which regulates hazardous waste, and the Comprehensive Environmental Response, Compensation and Liability Act (CERCLA), which created the Superfund program to clean up sites contaminated by hazardous waste.

These 1970s-era environmental laws require government hearings, which are legally required to take place before regulatory decisions are made, be open to the public. They also require that the public be allowed to submit comments to government bodies and set aside scheduled times for that purpose. Perhaps most important, these statutes, unlike most federal regulatory statutes, give the public recourse through the law: members of the public are explicitly allowed to sue government environmental agencies that are not meeting their own regulatory timelines and standards, as well as companies that are breaking environmental laws. By the late 1970s, these participatory practices included members of the general public in a wide array of decision-making in government, science, and the private sector. However, the outcomes of these public participation processes are limited by the fact that they often take place well into the formal planning period of siting a new polluting facility.[29] In these cases, the company has already made considerable investment and built political momentum, and the responsible government agencies are typically already on board. This makes it difficult to stop or fundamentally transform the nature of the action being considered. Other problems that impede meaningful public participation in such hearings include the technocratic language that dominates; the time of day and week at which they are offered (often when much of the public is at work); their location, which can be difficult to reach when hearings are not held in the immediate vicinity of the impacted neighborhoods; a lack of interpreting for people who do not speak English; and in some cases police intimidation. Environmental justice activists have worked hard to improve these legally mandated forms of participation, focusing in particular on the provision of simultaneous interpreting for participants who do not speak English, as well as the translation of key documents into Spanish. Improving public participation in spaces where it is already mandated by law has been one of the activist demands that has gained the most support in government environmental agencies.

In addition to these 1970s-era mandated mechanisms, another form of public participation in decision-making has emerged: the advisory committee. These committees often follow what Edward Walker, Michael McQuarrie, and Caroline Lee call the "new public participation": stakeholder engagement processes that are managed by paid pro-

FIGURE 12. South Coast Air Quality Public Management District hearing about the Exide Technologies battery recycling plant, Los Angeles, December 14, 2013. Participants are using headphones to hear the Spanish-language interpretation of the proceedings. Photo by author, previously published in Perkins, "Slideshow: The Faces of Public Participation."

fessional facilitators.[30] These types of committees typically rely on consensus-based processes of deliberation and are voluntarily undertaken by government agencies, industry, and the military in order to incorporate multiple public viewpoints and goals into their planning and decision-making.

Environmental justice activists have long pressed for a "seat at the table" in governmental decision-making spaces, hoping to have their concerns and solutions heard and acted upon. However, the recommendations of these advisory committees are not binding, and the array of solutions up for debate in these spaces is often limited. I witnessed this firsthand during my own brief tenure on one such advisory committee. The committee was to create a plan for improving the drinking water quality and sanitation in a low-income, agricultural region of the state. The process was designed to include an array of stakeholders. At the first meeting, other attendees included a representative of the environmental justice group that had been hired to manage the process, other NGO representatives, government representatives, and one lone "community member," who was working to improve drinking water where he lived and therefore a potential beneficiary of any plans the group might design.

In that first meeting, several people brought up the need to create drinking water improvements that would be sustainable. Uncertain of my role as both a scholar of and participant in the space, I said little during the first half of the meeting. When I finally spoke up, I mentioned how pleased I was to hear the group members emphasizing the importance of sustainability, then said that if we wanted the solutions we discussed to be sustainable, we would need to address how the drinking water gets contaminated by industrial agriculture in the first place. Was that topic on the table for discussion, I asked? The answer was a quick and clear "no" from multiple people. A government representative told me that if we were going to discuss agricultural drinking water contamination, then "agriculture" would need to be at the table too. Later, another government representative said that it was probably financially unrealistic even to build drinking-water filtration systems so that the water from residents' kitchen taps would meet US drinking water standards. Instead, he said, we should probably focus on how to truck in potable drinking water.

As it turns out, the first meeting of that group was also my last, for reasons unrelated to the events that took place. But the discussion I describe here has much in common with new public participation. Professionally managed stakeholder engagement processes such as the one I encountered are usually limited by the convening entity, which is not always open to all possible options; the options that are actually on the table are usually ones that will not harm the profit-making ability of local power holders. That fundamental circumscription limits what facilitators can do (even when they are, as in this case, environmental justice NGO staff).

Despite these drawbacks, public participation is widely seen as a social good that promotes egalitarianism. It gained importance during the events of the 1960s, which saw a large portion of the American public becoming increasingly alienated from government and distrustful of experts. Public participation came to be seen as "a check on the authority and power of experts, [and] a tool for creating community and overcoming social alienation and the meaninglessness of consumer society." But the post-1970s boom in these committees happened within a political, racial, social, and economic context that was undergoing dramatic change (as chapter 3 explores); the proliferation of these committees "occurred alongside the greatest expansion in socioeconomic inequality since the Gilded Age." Walker, McQuarrie, and Lee argue that these participatory processes do not help people "express their essential aspirations and values" but instead discipline them to express aspirations and values that fit within a predetermined array of acceptable topics for discussion. Sheldon Wolin calls this an "inverted totalitarianism," giving elites "democratic authority even as they pursue antidemocratic goals." While the new public participation can be "efforts to arrive at better-informed organizational decisions by relying on the collective wisdom of assembled publics rather than experts," it can also be a form of "lay participation [invited] by elite actors in order to manage or channel the former's voice in support of narrow interests"; public participation mechanisms can function as "collaborative relationships between lay actors and organizational decision makers [designed] to reground the authority of the organization."[31] Ultimately, as suggested by my experience and the experiences of many activists I interviewed, participation and inclusion is encouraged, but only within a very constrained field of what is possible to discuss. As one interviewee told me, activists must not "confuse access with power."

These cautions must be carefully considered by environmental justice activists who consider working on advisory committees. Public participation events can easily fill calendars with meetings, hearings, and phone conferences as activists serve on multitudes of national, state, local, academic, and nonprofit advisory boards. Time spent in such meetings is time not spent on other forms of activism—and activists express widespread skepticism about the efficacy of these initiatives. Perhaps other types of activism would have better results; perhaps public participation would be more fruitful if activists could also help "determine the menu." Many activists feel that their participation is tokenized and their suggestions are disregarded. Experience and observation suggest that environmental justice activists should approach public participation initiatives with healthy skepticism and awareness of what they can and cannot accomplish.

Despite these drawbacks, activists continue to participate in environmental justice advisory committees, for they offer other benefits. These types of participation can promote coalition building, bringing together a number of environmental justice activists who may not typically work closely. Being on advisory committees and other such mechanisms of public participation can also provide insight into how government works and who knows whom, in ways that activists find useful later as they continue to pursue other campaigns. It is also a defensive measure: advisory groups will continue whether environmental justice activists join them or not, and the seats activists leave empty may be filled by someone who may have antithetical goals and interests. Finally, and in part because of these drawbacks, public participation events are now sometimes run by staff from environmental justice organizations themselves, who are hired by government agencies to solicit and manage stakeholder engagement processes related to environmental planning and regulation. This provides more possibility to make more space for the voices of affected communities in such events. However, in these instances environmental justice organizations are still limited by the framework of the task they are hired to complete. Taking on the role of convener and facilitator of such public participation efforts also complicates activists' abilities to switch from collaborative to oppositional relationships with the agencies that are paying them for their facilitation services, as discussed further in the following.

ROUTINIZATION AND INSTITUTIONALIZATION

So far, this chapter has described how the environmental justice movement evolved in California. It began as a set of primarily grassroots, local independent groups using disruptive direct-action tactics; today, it is a formalized movement that has turned to less confrontational tactics, enmeshing itself with the institutions of legislative policy, electoral politics, and nonprofit organizations as it seeks to bring about broader societal changes. But what did the movement's evolution look like day to day? What mundane processes and adjustments—things that I call "processes of routinization"—enabled, or even caused, such a fundamental reshaping? In other words, how did we get from disruptive direct action to bureaucratic compromise with the state and industry, the movement's original enemies?

Routinization via Funding

The first process of routinization that encouraged these movement changes revolves around funding. The environmental justice movement took shape in the 1980s and 1990s, at a time when private funding for the environmental movement was growing rapidly. At this time, traditional unincorporated mass membership associations such as unions, fraternal and sororal organizations, and groups like the Grange or the Odd Fellows had already experienced a steep decline in numbers and power. They were replaced by professionally managed nonprofits funded by private foundations, a configuration that has increasingly become the organizational backbone of progressive activist efforts.[32]

Environmental justice organizations receive a small fraction of the funds that more mainstream environmental groups do, but many environmental justice groups do successfully compete for foundation funds.[33] In order to receive these funds, though, activists must set up appropriate legal structures, including finding a fiscal sponsor or incorporating as a nonprofit organization. Applying for and managing philanthropic or government funding requires good accounting skills, knowledge of the array of funding sources available or the research skills to locate them, and specialized grant-writing skills. Although some funders explicitly target grassroots groups less practiced in these skills, most funders favor organizations with high levels of professionalization and existing bureaucratic infrastructure that can smoothly receive funds, process them, and report on how they are spent.

Many scholars and activists have documented the relationship between the increasing availability of foundation funding, the institutionalization and professionalization of social movements and nonprofits, and the decline of disruptive protest tactics.[34] As activist Henry Clark put it, "It's quite a difficult challenge. The more action-oriented that you are—[the more] community organizing and action-oriented that you are—probably the more difficult it is, probably the less sources of funding that are around because you're involved in some type of controversial type of work."[35] In addition to encouraging professionalization, foundation funding also increases the likelihood that activists will turn to "insider" rather than "outsider" tactics; as Clark points out, the more radical the action, the riskier it is to fund.[36] Funding might be found for noncontroversial activism like educational campaigns or even policy work, but it is much more difficult to get funding to support strikes, direct action, or protest-based organizing. There is thus a kind of selection bias that benefits activist groups already engaged in the moderate, less controversial tactics that funders prefer, and professionalized, insider-type groups are better positioned to apply for and receive such funds. For less moderate groups, funding patterns may indirectly channel their work toward less controversial tactics as they adapt it to existing funding opportunities. Alternately, foundations may directly pressure their grantees to choose less confrontational tactics or to fall in line with their preferred policy solutions.

In a case much discussed among activists, one funder withdrew its funding from a California environmental justice organization because it disapproved of one of the group's priorities—one that its money was not being used to fund. The environmental justice organization sought to keep the legislature from choosing a cap-and-trade mechanism—a market-based system—as a primary method of controlling industrial greenhouse gas emissions. (The cap-and-trade debate is discussed in detail in chapter 5.) The fact that the funder pulled money that it had allocated to an entirely different aspect of the NGO's work shows the amount of leverage funders can exert over NGOs' agendas.[37]

One activist I interviewed commented on some of the pitfalls of foundation-driven activist agendas in his discussion of Senate Bill 375, the Sustainable Communities and Climate Protection Act of 2008. Senate Bill 375 was designed to implement the mandates for greenhouse gas emissions reductions contained in Assembly Bill 32, the California Global Warming Solutions Act of 2006. AB 375 requires the creation of regional sustainable communities plans that can be integrated into broader land use and transportation plans. This activist said that AB 375, while important, somehow became the overriding concern for funders; foundations directed so much funding toward the bill that it drew activists away from working on other important issues. He also complained that funding to lead the development of plans for Los Angeles did not go to local Los Angeles advocacy groups but to San Francisco Bay Area groups, missing an opportunity to support local activism and to incorporate local knowledge into the planning process.

As Henry Clark intimated, most foundation funding generally goes disproportionately to noncontroversial organizations that shy away from disruptive protest and instead favor policy work, collaboration with state and industry, education, and individual behavioral change. The best-funded California environmental justice groups are part of CEJA, which focuses on policy advocacy in the state capitol. In 2012, five out of six of the CEJA organizations had annual revenues of at least $1 million. By contrast, none of the forty-eight member organizations of CEJC (which, you will recall, was created as a kind of counterweight to CEJA) had revenues of $1 million or more in the same year.[38] And while some limited nonfoundation funding for environmental justice work is available, with some city, state, and federal agencies offering small grants, these grants are even *less* likely than foundation grants to fund disruptive activist tactics; at their most radical, they fund policy work, but most go to projects that are not overtly political, such as educational projects or local greening initiatives like community gardens and recycling programs.[39]

Other potential sources of funding are the polluting industries themselves, though environmental justice groups largely shy away from accepting such funds. Indeed, early environmental justice activists criticized the "Big 10" environmental groups for taking funds from polluters (and for having representatives from polluting industries on their boards of directors). Most environmental justice activists are critical of such relationships because they believe accepting money from polluters undercuts activists' ability to hold polluters accountable for their actions. However, some of these funding streams are making inroads into the environmental justice movement as well. At one organizational award ceremony I attended, a poster thanked the event sponsors, including Pacific Gas & Electric, a longtime opponent of some environmental justice activists. The poster also displayed the logo for Latham & Watkins, a law firm that environmental and environmental justice lawyers often face off against in court. (I have a vivid memory of one such lawyer shuddering in distaste when I mentioned the firm's name and then launching into a description of his repeated interactions with them in court.)

Environmental justice activists have also tried other methods of funding their work. As noted earlier in this chapter, one such approach is to take jobs as paid contractors for state agencies that facilitate stakeholder engagement projects on environmental planning and decision-making. These funding streams, however, can present similar challenges to those posed by money from private foundations:

Funders have been kind of changing their focus, and funders always do that. And it has been, I think, overall away from environmental justice, and made us have to characterize [our work] in different ways than as [environmental justice]. More like community development, community assistance. . . . Actually, one of the things that we've been doing to address some of those changes and priorities with foundations is doing more of these pilot projects, where we're kind of consultants on projects. So, we're doing the community engagement piece, or the community facilitation piece, and getting paid for that [by] the county. So basically, in a couple of projects there's been funding given to the county, or we've gotten the county to apply on behalf of communities, or other agencies to apply. . . . So that's been really good, both to help ensure that we can be funded to do this work, and also to make sure that it's done in a way that we feel like is addressing community needs, and having those really drive the project. And so we do a lot—as contractors, we do a lot of internal advocacy within the contracting agencies and parties, that's sort of behind the scenes, about how the project should be run, and how to develop recommendations out of it. It's been a good fit for us so far, but it's a really different kind of funding. It's meant we've really had to figure out, like I said, how do we walk that line, then, when we're advocating with those agencies?

Taking on these kinds of government contracts can put activists in an awkward double position, not unlike those we saw in the earlier discussion of the pitfalls of industry or government collaboration: How do activists manage professional paid relationships that come into conflict with their activist values and commitments? As the activist just quoted puts it, how do they walk that line?

Money is vital to providing movement infrastructure, which buys people time to work on the problems at hand; in an environment of economic scarcity, it is difficult to sustain this kind of work with only volunteers. Funding has also been important to many of the networking and collaboration-building activities that link activists from disparate locations to one another, allowing them to exchange ideas and build a broader movement that transcends local concerns—events like the annual California Communities Against Toxics (CCAT) meetings described in chapter 1, the first and second national environmental justice summits in 1991 and 2002, and even international gatherings such as the World Summit on Sustainable Development in 2002. External funding also enables activists to access and intervene in legal and policy battles and to undertake citizen-science efforts to monitor their exposure to pollutants.

But as vital as it is, external funding also has some drawbacks. As mentioned previously, funders put their fingers on the scale of movement tactics, promoting the continuation and expansion of groups pursuing institutional tactics by funding them more than oppositional, disruptive organizations. Alternately, activists seeking foundation funding tend to adapt to foundations' funding priorities, and they have occasionally been punished when they fail to do so; the migration of activism into nonprofits with paid, professional staff creates a need for external funding that has increasingly pushed the movement away from its disruptive outsider roots and toward institutionalization and insider tactics. External funding has thus changed the landscape of the environmental justice movement, exacerbating tensions within factions of the movement that are either in competition for funds or have different ideas about the best tactics with which to pursue their goals.

Routinization and Incorporation of Protest

The routinization and institutionalization of the environmental justice movement are driven not only by the "carrot" of external funding, as laid out in the preceding section, but also by the "stick" of policing disruptive activist tactics. In the 1960s, the state used a form of protest management that social movement scholars call the "escalated force" model. Under this model, police carried out violent reprisals, using fire hoses, police dogs, beatings, and/or tear gas against nonviolent protesters. Extreme police violence against civil rights protesters, including children, in the 1963 Birmingham protests and against anti-war protesters at the Chicago Democratic Convention of 1968 are iconic examples. More recent examples of police violence against protesters include responses to Indigenous protests in 2016 against the Dakota Access Pipeline and nationwide Black Lives Matter protests in the summer of 2020.[40] Alongside such violent responses to protest, however, the state has also shifted to "negotiated management" tactics; this is the kind of policing with which California environmental justice protests are now typically met. Negotiated management aims to contain the disruptive activity of protest, routinizing the act of protesting to make it as nondisruptive and orderly as possible.[41] As Traci Yoder has put it, the use of negotiated management tactics "shifts the focus from dispersing demonstrations to containing and controlling them through a variety of tactics, including permitting, delimiting free speech 'zones,' and convincing demonstrators to cooperate with police in planning marches and gatherings."[42] Note the language here: the goal of negotiated management is "containing" and "controlling" the potentially disruptive and radical act of protest. In other words, it aims to routinize and institutionalize street activism, and in so doing to defang it. Here, the "stick" of protest policing is largely metaphorical but always backed up by the threat of physical violence.

No one wants to be attacked by dogs, gassed, or beaten, or otherwise risk their life in political protest. However, permitted, orderly public marches run the risk of becoming so well accepted that they lose their "protest" power. As the Washington, D.C. Metro Police commander put it in 2001, "Washington is so sanitized with demonstrations; I don't think people pay them any mind anymore. I mean they're just everyday."[43] As Don Mitchell and Lynn Staeheli write, permitted protest is used "not to silence dissent outright, but rather to regulate it in such a way that dissent can be fully incorporated into, and become part of, the liberal democratic state."[44] Environmental justice activism, in acquiescing to managed, nondisruptive protest, thus risks losing what Frances Fox Piven and Richard Cloward argue is one of the few forms of power available to the poor: the power to disrupt the status quo and thereby force concessions from the ruling elite.[45]

In addition to removing the disruptive power of protest, the bureaucratization of protest has also pushed movement tactics toward established political channels. Just as much funding has routinized advocacy and rewarded institutionalized and professionalized groups, the routinization of protest also shifts the terrain in favor of formalized advocacy groups. These groups can more easily navigate permitting systems and police negotiations, and they have more resources with which to recruit participation in public rallies and marches. And as Piven and Cloward point out, these sorts of groups are very unlikely to use radical and disruptive tactics: "Formally organized groups are not likely to undertake disruptive protests. . . . It is not that disruption and violence are never employed by formally organized groups; it is that, in general, organization constrains against such tactics. Protests can provoke severe repression which formal organizations will not usually risk (secret or underground organizations are better positioned in this respect)."[46]

Indeed, some California environmental justice groups no longer organize protests at all; many have shifted entirely to policy, lobbying, and political work. They are more likely to organize a lobbying day in the state capitol or encourage people to turn out for a public hearing, a press briefing, or a conference than to organize or participate in a street action. The self-identified environmental justice groups that continue to organize marches and protests get permits and hold peaceful, orderly events that follow preplanned routes, remain within police barriers, and end on time with minimal police intervention—a happy outcome for the safety of the protesters, but also a triumph of negotiated management.

What are the effects of the broad shift from disruptive tactics to institutional tactics that I have traced here? The institutionalization of environmental justice advocacy, caused in part by the increasing formalization and professionalization of organizations in response to the paired carrot and stick of funding and routinization of protest, has had mixed outcomes. Some policy victories have been won, but they are significantly watered down—a far cry from activists' original vision. Many of the movement's highest priorities have only been addressed tangentially. For example, efforts to limit the ongoing pollution in low-income communities and communities of color have spawned proliferating advisory committees, measurement tools, opportunities for

FIGURE 13. Police intervening to ensure protesters stay on the sidewalk and do not disrupt traffic, Kettleman City, September 17, 2011. Photo by author.

participation, improvements in reporting problems, some improvements in enforcement actions, and, in some cases, financial investment—trends that I continue to examine in the next chapter. But there have been few direct reductions to the central problem: polluting industries are still sited disproportionately in low-income communities and communities of color. The pollution levels in these places remain a threat to human health, and far higher than in whiter, richer neighborhoods.

Even activists' modest gains would not have happened without their strenuous and ongoing efforts in the policy arena, but institutionalization always raises the question of how far activists should go in their efforts to work with, rather than against, the state. Different activists have different answers to this question, and this division has created and deepened schisms within the movement. What is the best way to promote change? How much compromise is too much compromise? When would a more outsider, radical politics result in more actual gains? These questions echo throughout most activist endeavors, and the answers reflect the political ethos of the age in which the activism takes place. The next chapter further explores the roots of the activist institutionalization described in this chapter, contextualizing the shift traced here by locating it in the changing political landscape of the post-1960s United States and California.

CHAPTER 3

Explaining the Changes in Environmental Justice Activism

Social movements don't just change the world; the world also changes them. Sometimes the changes are the result of calculated decisions made by activists, while at other times activists are swept along by larger social currents of which they may be only partially aware. These decisions, and the broader currents that shape them, are the subject of this chapter.

These broader contexts are often overlooked in popular understandings of protest and social movements, which tend to overemphasize the individual heroic leader and their success against the odds as a result of superior strategy and determination. But social movements aren't only shaped by activists and their individual leaders; the broader world both constrains and propels movements.

Decisions to shift tactics are of course always made within the context of larger social currents, for activists make deliberate tactical shifts in order to respond to changing political contexts. But as we saw in the brief overview of the routinizing effects of funding and protest policing in the previous chapter, tactics also shift because of the accumulation of small decisions that are shaped and reinforced by social and political constraints. Here I present activists' own logic for pursuing increasingly institutionalized approaches to achieving environmental justice. Then I lay out the effects of changing racial politics and neoliberalism on environmental justice activism, for activism is funneled in the direction of what gets traction within those contexts. The historical moment also shapes societal risk perception, which in turn influences what kinds of activism take hold.

As the previous chapter documented, the California environmental justice movement today uses more tactics that engage standard political channels, such as policy advocacy and electoral politics, and fewer "outsider" tactics, such as disruptive street protest and the taking over of public meetings. Critics often see this as evidence that activism is being watered down or co-opted. Proponents see it as evidence of political maturation—a change to be celebrated. In this chapter, I reframe the debate away from these binary "good versus bad" assessments of tactical changes to focus instead on their causes. Explaining *why* the environmental justice movement developed along this particular path, in terms of both activists' strategic choices and the funneling action of the broader political environment, helps us better understand the implications and likely long-term effects of these changes. As this chapter shows, multiple forces both external and internal to the environmental justice movement encouraged the shift toward institutionalization and away from oppositional tactics, ultimately creating a feedback loop that reinforced the movement's trajectory.[1] Without concerted efforts to resist these political and economic currents, movements are slowly remade by the world around them until they are incorporated into existing political structures and therefore no longer a threat to those structures.

ACTIVISTS' REASONS FOR PURSUING INSTITUTIONALIZATION AND INSIDER TACTICS

Many environmental justice activists have actively sought to institutionalize their work by integrating into nonprofits and state structures, and many intentionally adopted nondisruptive institutional tactics. These activists see this approach as broadening the reach of the movement beyond the individual and the local to the systemic. Many activists now see early environmental justice activism, much of which worked primarily to stave off polluting industries through site-by-site battles, as insufficient. As I explore in this chapter, they believe they get more "bang for their buck" by engaging in policy battles in the state capitol, where wins will benefit more people. One activist named the resource-intensive nature of fighting local battles on multiple fronts as one reason environmental justice activists and organizations turned to policy work:

> We started out fighting a lot, putting out fires, a lot of fires. We would go to whatever community was asking for our help, and we'd go put out fires. . . . I think that there's a little bit of a trajectory, where you're first fighting things, and then you're working on policy to try to get to scale. Because, fighting one [thing at a time], like la Montaña—that's an eleven-year fight. That takes a lot of capacity, and we have limited resources.

La Montaña was the subject of a 1990s-era environmental justice campaign in Huntington Park, a largely Latinx, Spanish-speaking neighborhood in Los Angeles. In 1993, Aggregate Recycling Systems was given a site permit to recycle the huge amounts of concrete that were being dug up while building a below-ground railroad to connect the Los Angeles harbor to the downtown. The recycling process first involved piling the crushed concrete at the site, located next to Cottage Street. When the 1994 Northridge earthquake collapsed portions of the Santa Monica freeway, the resulting debris was added to the pile. The concrete pile got so large it became known as la Montaña, or the mountain. It grew to over 600,000 tons of debris that rose over sixty feet tall, towering over the neighboring homes.[2]

The recycling facility and the huge pile of crushed concrete were more than eyesores for the neighbors. Crushing the concrete to recycle it spread hazardous dust throughout the neighborhood, and the parade of trucks going to and from the site kept the concrete dust suspended in the air while adding carcinogenic diesel exhaust to the mix. Activist Linda Marquez suffered the impacts: "[The roar of the concrete crusher] used to go all night. But the worst part is the dust. I call it a phantom dust. You wipe off your furniture, and an hour later it feels gritty again. It's a taste in your mouth that's very flat and terrible. You always want to clear your throat, and after you rinse your mouth, it comes right back. I used to have a garden, but the two trees in front of my house are half dead now."[3]

Residents and their allies eventually got la Montaña cleaned up, but it took years of fighting the recycling company, the government, and the business community. In 2013 the cleanup was finished, and a school named after Linda Marquez was opened on the site—twenty years after the pile was created, fifteen years after the courts ordered the owner of the recycling company to clean up the site in 1998, and nine years after the cleanup finally began in 2004.

This resource-intensive, long-term fight addressed only a single street in a single Los Angeles neighborhood. These kinds of fights are the reason that some activists moved toward institutionalization: they thought it would help them address the root causes of environmental racism and environmental classism rather than taking on the symptoms one by one. One activist described her motivation for shifting to focus on electoral politics, which she saw as likely to build more power for more low-income communities of color than site-by-site battles:

> [The groups we work with] now know that if they want transit or if they want waste, water, or whatever it is that they need, that they want to prioritize—they know the process for that, who to go to. But they're still being disregarded, because they have no political relevance. And that was not something new to us. It was just kind of like, "do we really want to just do this without trying to attack the bigger problem?"

This speaker underscores her belief that without the political power to make large-scale changes, the basic work of helping residents figure out the official channels for extracting services from the government is of limited use. Many policy-oriented activists emphasize that local issues are linked to the broader world in ways that make it difficult to drive progress locally without addressing larger problems, such as the polluter influence on state politics at the capitol.

Other activists also explain the shift toward "insider" political tactics as a calculated decision by activists, though they attribute it to slightly different motivations. One person I interviewed, for example, embraced collaborative, professional, policy-oriented tactics as a way to chart a new course in the environmental justice movement that moves away from what he sees as the failures of past generations. He sees his work as part of a generational shift in environmental justice activists, with new activists choosing new tactics to address the same unsolved problem: communities of color remain disproportionately burdened by pollution despite the many local victories of early environmental justice organizing. He pursues policy work from inside the government because, in his words, "I don't want to be fucking old in 20 years, and say, 'Shit, you know, everything is still the same.'" Another activist also sees it as a generational shift, but he attributes it to the aging of the early environmental justice activists. He compares the tactics of the 1960s and 1970s in which he participated as a young man to those he uses now: "We yelled, we screamed, we threatened. But then, as we mature, we need to realize, how do you fight the enemy from within? You fight him on his own turf now." Still others see policy work as complementing, not supplanting, local action; for these activists, policy work ensures that the hard work of local action isn't wasted when it is overturned by policy changes: "If we don't [do policy], I think we can do a lot of good stuff on the ground, but they can wipe it out with just a piece of paper being signed in Sacramento [the state capital]."

Some activists, however, focus on the risks inherent in this broader move toward institutionalization. The first main risk is that institutionalized and highly professionalized social movements can easily exclude or speak over the intended grassroots beneficiaries of their social movement work if they are not careful. This is a particular challenge mentioned by Penn Loh, who keeps at the front of his mind a movement slogan, first spoken by Dana Alston at the First People of Color Environmental Justice Leadership Summit in 1991: "We Speak for Ourselves." Environmental justice activists used this phrase to emphasize the importance of having people who directly suffer the impacts of pollution speaking for themselves in spaces designed to discuss and resolve these problems, where they were often talked over by government officials, professional environmental groups, and industry representatives. Loh entered the environmental justice movement via Nindakin, an environmental justice group made up of students of color at UC Berkeley in the early 1990s that was affiliated with the Southwest Network for Environmental and Economic Justice. Later, he worked for a Boston-based environmental justice NGO. Reflecting on the challenges of working as a professional to scale up a movement meant to be led from the grassroots, he says: "In that statement, [Alston] challenged us to build a movement led by those most affected—a goal that is easy to say, but hard to do. If we are a movement led by people struggling locally, then how do we build power and use it to achieve broader change regionally, nationally, and internationally?"[4] While most environmental justice organizations aim to empower the residents for whom they work, the organizational structure of nonprofits tends toward the concentration of political power and authority among nonprofit professionals. Legally speaking, the board of directors must have ultimate decision-making authority.[5] This formal, hierarchical structure can blunt the grassroots energy from which activism ultimately draws its power as easily as it can develop and channel it.

The second major risk is collaboration; as social movements institutionalize and seek policy solutions, they enter into collaborations with the state, and sometimes with industry. As chapter 2 showed, these collaborations are difficult and always involve compromise. Some activists see them as incommensurable with "real" environmental justice activism. Others see the possibilities in these increasingly collaborative relationships, at least those with state and federal agencies:

I think over time what happened—the EPA definitely, and other agencies, have tried to do more collaborative processes, and I think it's helped. I mean, the more that they have dialogue with people of color, and communities of color, on these issues, and maybe learn something from them, and there's an honest exchange, things can only improve. Even if it's just that there are friendly people at the agency you can talk to, and give you advice about politically what you might want to try or not try [laughs], and who you should be talking to, and who you should not be listening to. All that stuff, inside information, is extremely valuable, even if it's only that.

Like this speaker, many activists acknowledge that there is little rapid substantive change to be gained from collaborating with state institutions, but they see such collaboration as offering some more moderate rewards in the long term, after they have learned the political ropes. These activists see state collaborations and insider tactics as short-term stepping-stones toward their long-term goals:

I think there's a lot of work to do in the policy front, and the funding front, and the political front, to build the political power to get our people into decision-making roles. I don't know that I trust democracy in this country, but I'm willing to run with the strategy of—right now—a one-to two-to-three-year strategy to influence decision-makers who are currently there, to be on our side. And the five-to-ten-year strategy is to become them—from the local water boards up to the Governor's Office. Elected officials, appointed officials, the whole thing.

Although the changes within the environmental justice movement are not practiced or embraced across the board, the increasing turn to engaging standard channels of politics has been, at least in part, a conscious, strategic decision on the part of activists.

THE CHANGING POLITICAL CONTEXT OF THE CALIFORNIA ENVIRONMENTAL JUSTICE MOVEMENT

However, we cannot attribute the entire trajectory of the environmental justice movement since the 1980s only to activists' own decisions to change tactics. These decisions were made within the broader context of the political and economic climate at the state and national levels, and that context radically constrains the choices that activists make. The world in which today's environmental justice activists operate is not the same world from which the movement was born nearly half a century ago. Of course, the central problems that the movement emerged to address—racism, poverty, and pollution—are still here, and in some cases are even worse today than they were then. But the politics surrounding these deeply embedded features of modern life have changed. Each of the trends I discuss in the remainder of this chapter has contributed to changing the context in which the problems that environmental justice activists seek to fix must be addressed. In this chapter, I address three main contextual threads, each of which is bound up with many others. First, racial politics have changed since the inception of the environmental justice movement in the 1980s. Racism shape-shifts to fit the times, with multiple forms coexisting even as techniques change. Second, the effects of capitalism are currently intensified by neoliberal ideology, which seeks to reduce the role of the state in managing the economy and social life. Third, people's attitudes toward toxic environmental exposures are changing. The perception of the risk from hazardous waste is different now than it was at the height of the 1970s/1980s panic; now, in communities that host hazardous waste landfills, the fact of ongoing risk has become normalized, even as societal knowledge about the dangers of hazardous waste and other toxic substances has grown. This normalization has blunted residents' fear and anger, and with them their willingness to confront state and industry representatives with oppositional tactics. Together, these trends have further pushed the movement toward institutionalized approaches to achieving environmental justice.

Changing Racial Politics

Racism remains deeply entrenched in American life, but America's racial politics have shifted since the 1980s, when activists began explicitly naming and attacking environmental racism. There are three mutually reinforcing vectors of this change in racial politics: demographic change, class mobility and inequality among people of color, and changing practices and understandings of racism. These shifts have both opened up new opportunities for environmental justice activists and introduced new challenges.

Demographic shifts in the electorate have encouraged environmental justice activists to engage in policy advocacy in order to represent the increasingly important "people of color vote." These voters, and among them particularly Latinx, are gaining more political attention, for demographers predict that by 2044, the majority of the US population will be made up of Latinx, Black, and Indigenous people and Asian Pacific Americans. California is at the forefront of this demographic change. In 2000, California became a majority people of color state, and the relative percentage of whites continues to shrink. This change is driven largely by the state's growing Latinx population, which surpassed whites as the single largest racialized group in 2016. The state's electoral politics are changing with the population. In 1980, white votes made up nearly 90 percent of the total votes in California's general presidential election; in 2012, white votes declined to only 56.7 percent of total votes in the general presidential election. In 2016, people of color became the majority of California's eligible voters.[6] Broadly speaking, people of color are more likely to be Democrats (of the 27 percent of Latinx elected officials nationwide who served in a partisan office or were publicly affiliated with a political party in 2007, 91 percent were Democrats), and Democrats are more likely to vote for environmental legislation than Republicans.[7] Thus, the growing population of people of color presents opportunities for environmental justice activists in electoral politics.

Statewide and national polls show that Latinx specifically, like people of color more broadly, are more likely to believe the science of climate change and to favor environmental legislation to slow it than are whites.[8] Because people of color are now the numerical majority, California environmental justice activists use these survey data as leverage, pressuring legislators to support the environmental justice causes that matter to their constituents. As Strela Cervas of the California Environmental Justice Alliance puts it, "To maintain support among California's new and growing majority, decision makers will need to give more weight in their agendas to the environmental concerns of communities of color. . . . The constituencies most impacted by these policies are rapidly growing their political voice and power, demanding to be heard as California takes strides toward environmental health."[9]

As the state's electorate has changed, so has the demographic makeup of California's elected officials. A growing number of people of color are being elected to positions in state government.[10] (This is notable, because the rapid change in the population demographics has outpaced other electoral changes: the percentage of people of color registered to vote in California is not as high as the percentage of people of color in the population at large, and the percentage of politicians and agency staff who are people of color is even further behind the demographic curve.) Some of these officials have backgrounds in environmental justice work.

Some of the earliest California environmental justice campaigns were successful in part because of Latinx political incorporation, and the importance of support from Latinx politicians has grown significantly since. For example, the Madres del Este de Los Angeles, whom we met in chapter 1, benefited from the involvement of Miguel Mendivil and Martha Molina. As Gabriel Gutiérrez writes, both "typified the increasing number of young people from the barrios who were taking leadership roles."[11] Both worked for state Assemblywoman Lucille Roybal-Allard, who shortly afterward was elected to the US House of Representatives in 1992—the first Mexican American woman to serve in the US Congress. By 2002, only one of the thirteen environmental justice bills passed by the state legislature was sponsored by a white legislator; ten were sponsored by Latina, Black, and Asian Pacific American women, and two by Latino men.[12] With its increasing political clout, California's Latino Legislative Caucus has helped pass legislation favored by environmental justice activists, including the state's Global Warming Solutions Act of 2006, which is the subject of chapter 5.[13]

Of course, these demographic changes will not, on their own, give environmental justice activists an automatic win. Sometimes people go into government explicitly to promote environmental justice goals but are limited in what they are able to accomplish. This activist speaks to the constraints they face:

> I think there's been a big change in a lot of our agencies, with people of color now in there. But I keep insisting that unless we dismantle the system and re-mantle it, or redo it, or put it back together, it's always going to be difficult even if everybody was people of color. They want to do the good thing, their heart is in the right place. You have somebody that—"I'm gonna go in there and I'm gonna tear this whole thing apart." They go in there and they try to tear it apart, and pretty soon they're like, "Wow, it doesn't allow me to do this, it doesn't allow me to do that. I can't do this, I can't do that." So we have a problem with our system, the way it's already been built over hundreds of years. So when somebody with all good intentions and everything goes to EPA, goes into the Department of Toxic Substances Control, they start out gung ho, and then they go in and they realize that the system doesn't let them to do what they wanted to do.

In addition to the challenges facing people of color who seek to promote environmental justice from within government, not all Latinx, Black, and Indigenous people and Asian Pacific Americans necessarily want to promote environmental justice in the first place. As Roger Kim, former executive director of the Asian Pacific Environmental Network, says, "Yes, demographic change can work in our favor but you have to do the hard work of investing in the infrastructure to make it so. . . .

California doesn't look like this by chance; there was an incredible amount of work that went in."[14] It is therefore crucial that the movement actively work to recruit support from the increasing numbers of people of color holding office in California.

Sociologist Eduardo Bonilla-Silva's scholarship highlights the importance of these efforts by highlighting a different possible outcome. He expects that the United States will follow the path of many Latin American countries in becoming a "multiracial white supremacy," in which some Latinx, Black, and Indigenous people and Asian Pacific Americans are in power without fundamentally changing the "racial order of things" because they are too invested in the status quo to lead, or even call for, radical changes.[15] Indeed, people of color cannot be *assumed* to be sympathetic to the environmental justice movement's goals, particularly when their political or class loyalties lie elsewhere, or when their paychecks depend on polluting industries. As environmental justice activist Carlos Porras put it in 1994, "There's a lot of political turmoil in southeast LA, which has given us some new Latino faces in city governments here, which before were almost exclusively white. But often we've replaced the white defenders of industry with Latino defenders of industry."[16] Party affiliations also affect environmental attitudes. While Democrats hope to use votes by people of color to bolster their own power, observers are careful to note that "conservatives can count," too, and that, accordingly, conservatives are pursuing tactics of both "suppression and seduction" of voters of color to alternately reduce the impact of their Democratic Party voting patterns or woo them to conservative viewpoints.[17] Republican legislators of color are typically more hostile to environmental issues than their Democratic colleagues; at the national level, the League of Conservation Voters reports, Republican Congressional Hispanic Conference members voted pro-environment in only 10 percent of the 2016 cases tallied. In California, the Latino Republican congressional representatives Devin Nunes and David Valadao from the San Joaquin Valley voted pro-environment in only 5 percent and 3 percent of cases, respectively.[18]

When people of color in government are unsympathetic to environmental justice causes, it complicates activist strategies. This observer describes what happened when a white environmental justice activist and lawyer made a race-based environmental argument to an unsympathetic Black judge:

There have been some small steps I think towards diversifying the character of the decision-makers. But what has also become plainly evident is that diversity for diversity's sake is not enough. And in our own experience in [a] natural gas storage facility case, that argument came flying back in our face in a particularly ironic way. At that point the late, great Luke Cole was our environmental justice expert. And in his initial testimony he said to the tribunal that, traditionally speaking, that environmental justice has not had equal access, these groups have not had equal access to decision-makers. At that particular instance, potentially by design at the Public Utilities Commission, the only African American commissioner and the only African American administrative law judge were assigned to our case. So, in the closing remarks, the commissioner was making his plea to his colleagues that "We have to let Congress do what Congress will do, because it is in the interest of all of us," he said, "The groups complained that their groups can't be heard, because the decision-makers are generally not people of color." He says, "Well, here I am, and I'm telling you, you're wrong, you're going to suffer the consequences of my decision, and that's the way it should be." So, quite clearly, just being a person of color was not enough to win the day.

This story underscores that not all people of color in government will be responsive to environmental justice activists' claims. It also alludes to the possibility that Latinx, Black, and Indigenous people and Asian Pacific Americans may be deliberately used to foil activists' claims of racism, as the speaker mentions that the case was assigned a Black judge and a Black commissioner "potentially by design." This is a familiar dynamic; recall that Chevron's glossy newsletter featured a Q&A with a Black activist that painted the company in a positive light.

A similar suspicion was mentioned by two San Joaquin Valley activists, who wondered if a Latinx council member was deliberately used to try to defuse their claims. (The fact that there was only a single Latinx council member also indicates that some parts of the state lag far behind others in their incorporation of people of color into political roles.) These two activists describe a meeting of the Stanislaus Council of Governments board, which at the time of our interview had sixteen or so white members and was chaired by the single Latinx member. The activists went to the hearing to complain about problems with the board's public outreach process. They were approached before the meeting by the Latino chair, who asked them not to bring up the issue, as it would be on the agenda later. As the Mexican American activist put it, "If you go up there to speak, and it's the white rich farmer guy telling the Mexican guy to be quiet, then there's going to be outrage," but having "the only brown guy coming to talk to us about it" was likely aimed at circumventing such pushback. The exchange was further complicated by the fact that the mere presence of the lone Latinx member of the board, who they suspect is being used against them, is still a sign of progress:

> I know it sounds strange, but living in this area, that's a step towards progress. Because like before, even seeing a Brown or Black person as the Chair of any board of the county or the city; unheard of. So, if you want a silver lining, I guess here's the sign of progress, but yeah, it's still the same.

As these anecdotes show, people of color now occupy a wide range of social, political, and economic positions in California, though not in numbers proportionate to their population. This increase in social and economic mobility has mixed implications for environmental justice causes, for while race-based solidarity can occur across class lines, often it does not.[19] Rich and poor people have quite different experiences of the world. While economic status does not erase the impact of racism on people of color, it profoundly cushions those who can pay for the best private schools, health care, club memberships, and other trappings of upper-class life. Wealth is likely to insulate people from environmental racism, for economically privileged people of color are less likely to live in places that bear heavy pollution burdens than their poorer counterparts, and therefore to experience the need for environmental justice less directly.[20] While little research has examined how race and class combine to affect environmental attitudes, one survey does suggest that environmental support declines across all racial groups as incomes rise: while Latinx and Black people are the most concerned about air pollution in general, concern about air pollution declines among all racial groups for people with incomes over $80,000.[21]

Demographic change is one factor in the changes in the US racial climate since the 1980s, but it is certainly not the only factor that affects environmental justice activism; the shift of some racism from overt to "smiling" has limited the ways that activists can work against environmental racism. This form of less visibly hostile racism, whose proponents deny their own racism, has been called "smiling racism," "color-blind racism," and "racial liberalism." These are, as Bonilla-Silva ironically says, a "kinder and gentler white supremacy."[22] Despite ongoing hate crimes and white supremacist organizing, much racism today is much less overt than it was in the 1960s under Jim Crow. "Smiling" racism became more common after the legal victories of the mid-century civil rights movements, which made illegal the overt forms of racial discrimination of the Jim

Crow era: "Whites only" signs, segregated seating on public transportation, racial covenants that legally barred people of color from living in certain white neighborhoods, sundown towns that legally prevented people of color from being present after dark, and bans on interracial marriage, to name a few. These legal victories over highly visible manifestations of racism remain in place, but the Richard Nixon and Reagan administrations, along with the Warren Burger and William Rehnquist Supreme Courts, severely limited the reach of the civil rights victories of the 1960s, and more recent judicial decisions have continued this trend.[23] Other mechanisms of racism are just as legal as always; unofficial segregation, racialized disparities in wealth, voter suppression, and environmental racism persist, and in some cases have even intensified, over time.

Today, these forms of smiling racism facilitate the persistence of white supremacy at both the institutional and individual levels. When racism is narrowly defined as displays of spectacular violence and overt hate speech, it is easier to frame it as anomalous rather than part of an ongoing system of normal racial violence. This same dynamic plays out in the courts. Narrow legal definitions of racism, which track with popular understandings of racism as individual and overt, have constrained activists' ability to use the courts to address environmental racism. In 2001, *Alexander v. Sandoval* limited the use of civil rights law in environmental justice claims. In this case, the Supreme Court established that the only thing that legally "counted" as racism was a demonstrable *intent* to racially discriminate.[24] Even though this case was not directly about environmental justice activism, it established a precedent that clear evidence of racialized *outcomes* in pollution distribution would not be enough to win civil rights court cases; racist intent must be proved—a nearly impossible task. This ruling did not affect administrative Title VI complaints made to the EPA's Office of Civil Rights, which can consider racialized outcomes of environmental decision-making without proving intent. But efforts using this channel have been highly unsatisfactory. Administrative complaints filed with the EPA Office of Civil Rights have taken years to decades to process, and in its twenty-eight-year history, the office has never made a formal finding that there has been a civil rights violation.[25] (The first preliminary finding in favor of the complainants was not made until 2011 in *Angelita C. v. California Department of Pesticide Regulation*, and the complainants were not at all happy with how their complaint was resolved.)[26]

Similar to how racism has been redefined in ways that benefit the status quo, the state has redefined environmental justice in ways that limit its impact. State and federal agencies, and in some cases industry, have adopted the language of environmental justice. In doing so, they rearticulate it in ways that serve their interests. After President Clinton's 1994 executive order on environmental justice directed all federal agencies to develop environmental justice programs and policies, environmental justice framing was increasingly used in policy settings but was redefined in terms not of *outcomes* but of *processes*. In governmental use, the term often meant simply representation and fair inclusion in environmental decision-making, no matter what decision was eventually made or its actual outcome.[27]

The activists I interviewed experienced the trajectory of racial politics I have documented here; some of them described being subject to fewer instances of overt racism but more instances of "smiling" racism.[28] One federal environmental justice staffer interviewed by Jill Harrison put it this way: "When someone does something that is discriminatory, they are not trying to be obvious about it. . . . Persons became a little more savvy in terms of how they would cover their stripes around the mid-1990s."[29]

The broad, if shallow, reduction of overt forms of racism between the 1980s and the mid-2010s thus reduced the visible racism in encounters between environmental justice advocates and government and industry representatives. This appears to have affected many environmental justice advocates' attitudes toward these entities; the reduction of hostile treatment has made activists more willing to collaborate with government. But at the same time, this cordiality has in some ways taken the wind out of the sails of the movement. Activist anger matters: blatantly racist, sexist, and classist treatment of residents by agency officials and industry representatives served a vital politicizing role in early environmental justice activism of the 1980s. In some cases, the dismissive, harsh treatment activists received at the hands of government regulators and industry representatives angered them more than the environmental hazard itself. The replacement of the worst of this treatment with overtures of inclusion has partially undercut the ability to generate widespread participation in the kinds of disruptive protest that characterized much of the earlier years of environmental justice activism.

Of course, overt racism still happens. However (and notwithstanding the "racial reckoning" of the summer of 2020), occurrences are usually framed as isolated incidents and thus minimized. In 2015, public record act requests revealed a series of email exchanges peppered with racial slurs between two senior scientists at the California Department of Toxic Substances Control (DTSC). The scientists mocked colleagues with Asian names and imitated and mocked what they pretended were Black and Latinx speech patterns as they discussed each other, their colleagues, and their work in communities of color. These types of exchanges might well have been brushed off as meaningless banter by agency leaders during the environmental justice movement's early years, but in 2015, the head of the DTSC quickly disavowed the emails and their content while at the same time framing them as anomalous, downplaying their significance.[30] But how anomalous were they, really? Penny Newman, the white executive director of the environmental justice organization that submitted the public records requests that revealed the racist emails, was "completely disgusted but totally not surprised" by their contents.[31] Senate president pro tem Kevin de León, a member of the Latino Caucus, reported to the *Los Angeles Times* that CalEPA secretary Matthew Rodriguez "has assured me the individuals have already been disciplined and that Cal EPA has made sure this is not widespread behavior at DTSC."[32] (Note this as part of a pattern we have already seen: sympathetic people of color are front and center in this interaction, implicitly undercutting claims of systemic racism.) Racism remains central to American institutions and pervades the experience of environmental justice activists, not only in the siting of polluting industries in communities of color but also in their interactions with state and industry officials.

Impact of the Racialized Political Economy

The changing racial politics described in the previous section are entangled with the changing political economy: the embedding of neoliberal logics within a long history of capitalism. Indeed, the intensification of neoliberal logics has driven many of the political, economic, and social changes in the United States that have remade the context in which environmental justice activists work. David Harvey describes neoliberalism as a theory that "proposes that human well-being can best be advanced by liberating individual entrepreneurial freedoms and skills within an institutional framework characterized by strong private property rights, free markets, and free trade."[33] In such a system, services to the public are provided not by the state but by voluntary associations, churches, and NGOs, which thus take on a new centrality in the public sphere. Neoliberalism emphasizes individual responsibility for life outcomes while minimizing or denying the systematic effects of racism, classism, and privilege in shaping individual life experiences. It moves away from a post-Depression focus on using the power of the state to provide social safety nets and to regulate industry. Instead, neoliberalism encourages a hands-off approach that has reduced the government's ability to intervene in the economy to protect the environment and human health. It has also contributed to rising social inequality. In California, neoliberalism has been contested successfully in discrete political initiatives, such as the successful effort to raise the minimum wage to fifteen dollars an hour by 2022. Nonetheless, it remains a powerful political ideology that influences much of state politics.

Neoliberalism became the dominant political ethos in the 1980s, but it fits within a longer history of racial capitalism in which, as Laura Pulido puts it, "the devaluation of Black (and other nonwhite) bodies . . . creates a landscape of differential value which can be harnessed in diverse ways to facilitate the accumulation of more power and profit than would otherwise be possible."[34] This racialized "landscape of differential value" is created by labor protections and public services that protect whites more than others, insufficient regulation of industry in communities of color, and other forms of racial inequality that increase profits on the backs of Latinx, Black, and Indigenous people and Asian Pacific Americans. Some studies indicate that the 1980s-era rollback of spending on social safety nets and public goods was motivated, in part, by white voters' desire not to have their taxpayer dollars spent on services that, as a result of civil rights era legislation, could become newly available to nonwhites.[35] This effectively denies people of color the many social goods from which whites have long benefited.[36]

Neoliberal racial capitalism sustains and deepens the unequal racial distribution of polluting industries. When former California governor Ronald Reagan began his first term as president in 1981, the EPA was only ten years old. Reagan immediately proposed deep cuts to its budget and staff and tried to roll back federal regulation or devolve responsibility for implementing it to the states, reducing the federal government's power to regulate industry. He also appointed industry defenders to administrative positions designed to oversee environmental regulation of industry, weakening the enforcement of existing regulations.[37] During this time, the EPA had to get approval from the Office of Management and Budget before researching whether a particular chemical should be regulated; before approving the research, the OMB had to perform a cost-benefit economic analysis to determine whether the proposed regulation would be economical. As scholar Michelle Murphy puts it, "The regulatory process could now be stopped before it even began, placing economic considerations before those of science."[38]

The neoliberal project to hobble regulation of industry, and particularly environmental regulation, of course affected society writ large, for everyone depends on clean, safe air, water, and food. But the rollback of regulation posed a particular threat to low-income Latinx, Black, and Indigenous peoples and Asian Pacific Americans, who are more likely to bear the heaviest burden of pollution. The 1980s intensification of neoliberalism thus also intensified racial capitalism and environmental racism: the rollback of environmental protections allowed industries to extract more profit by polluting in communities of color.

Some national environmental organizations acceded to the changing times in the 1980s, exploring business-friendly and market-based approaches to environmentalism. Antitoxics and environmental justice activists, however, came out swinging directly against their corporate opponents, making demands for tighter environmental regulations and more enforcement of them. They made some headway: they helped pass the 1986 Superfund reauthorization; established the Toxic Release Inventory and the Community Right-to-Know Act; shut down some landfills; and prevented many, many incinerators and other new polluting industries from being built, as described in chapter 1. But antitoxics and environmental justice activists were significantly constrained by the prevailing anti-regulatory politics, as a number of scholars have shown. According to geographer Ryan Holifield, the federal government did not use Clinton's executive order on environmental justice to redistribute environmental risk; instead, it used it to "empower" environmental justice communities, build trust for the state, and manage their participation in decision-making—in other words, to embed more deeply the neoliberal forms of environmental management.[39]

This is a typical strategy: to remove dissent by seeming to accede to it. Just as it tries to hide racism behind a smile, the neoliberal state incorporates activists into its processes, using the illusion of participation to tamp down their demands. This is the same strategy as the "negotiated management" policing of protest. The neoliberal state punctures activist anger through seeming compliance and collaboration. It turns protest, disruption, and radical demands into managed activist participation within existing structures, seeking only small measures of incremental progress.

Neoliberal logics also organize the funding described in chapter 2, which largely encourages and rewards institutionalization. As Harrison's analysis of government environmental justice grant-making programs in California and four other states shows, funders often back projects that align with neoliberal logics: those that encourage individual behavioral change, voluntary improvements by industry, and reduced-cost environmental services, such as energy audits, rather than regulatory reform.[40] This national trend does seem to have hit California somewhat more lightly than other states, for Harrison notes that out of the five state-led environmental justice grant programs she studied, the program run by the California EPA was the least influenced by such neoliberal trends.[41] Harrison also notes that CalEPA's environmental justice funding program was more likely than others to fund activists to work on policy and support stakeholder engagement mechanisms, which she describes as less neoliberal than the work funded by other states (although, as chapter 2 showed, stakeholder engagement mechanisms are often constrained in ways that enable neoliberal logics).

The tactics of professionalized NGO activist groups are thus shaped by which activities the granting entities choose to fund. People do what works; efforts that align with neoliberal frameworks (even when they are in service of goals that oppose neoliberalism) are more likely to be the ones that find purchase. This process can be clearly seen in the acrimonious debate over air pollution and carbon markets. The carbon market is one of the clearest examples of neoliberal mechanisms of environmental governance: it is designed to avoid regulation that might stifle profit making. Environmental justice activists consistently oppose these market-based mechanisms, calling instead for direct regulation of pollution sources. The story of the environmental justice movement's fight against cap-and-trade is thus largely a story of its fight *against* neoliberalism—although, as chapter 4 details, it is also a story of neoliberalism's power to determine political outcomes and create division among activists.

Neoliberal capitalism sets the conditions for the compromises and collaborations described in chapter 2, such as the good neighbor agreements between polluting industries and the communities in which they are located. These types of private/public, nonregulatory agreements are also nongeneralizable, addressing the problem of pollution only at the hyper-local level and often only mitigating rather than solving problems. Good neighbor agreements can win some improvements for residents who live in the immediate vicinity of oil refineries and other industrial facilities, but by definition they are limited agreements that do not win benefits for others facing the same problems elsewhere or for other kinds of problems caused by the same facility. (Moving ammonia storage tanks to the other side of a property does not remove the toxic ammonia from the environment, and it does not prevent Chevron from later storing a different toxic chemical near residents' homes.) These voluntary agreements' enforcement mechanisms often rely on the courts for redress and on poorly resourced community groups for oversight; these groups must be ever vigilant for potential breaches, and they must have the resources to go to court when breaches are found.[42] Thus good neighbor agreements are usually a last resort, used only when existing regulation and enforcement are insufficient and the odds of improving it are low. As we see in this example, the neoliberal approach to government influences the problems activists are responding to, the kinds of interventions that are pursued, and the results they get.

Similar largely voluntary initiatives include environmental reporting task forces springing up around California, designed to improve enforcement of existing environmental law.[43] Like good neighbor agreements, environmental reporting task forces are a compromise, chosen as a last resort when existing state enforcement of environmental regulations is lacking. These task forces fill the gap caused by reductions in state funding for on-site investigations of potential violators and subsequent enforcement actions, another manifestation of the anti-regulatory ethos of neoliberal governance. It can be difficult to find information about California's environmental enforcement initiatives, even things as basic as how much state money is spent on enforcement staff and whether that budget is increasing or decreasing—as one senior CalEPA official stated as recently as 2007, "We cannot tell how much enforcement is going on out there."[44] The Natural Resources Defense Council (NRDC) used Freedom of Information Act requests to get as much data about enforcement as it could, and its 2008 report described widely varying inspection rates, enforcement actions, and reporting mechanisms. Although industries were regularly noncompliant with environmental laws—an annual average of 55 percent of workplace safety and health inspections discovered violations—NRDC found a steep decline in "complete inspections" conducted by CalOSHA, from close to four thousand in 1995 to just over one thousand in 2005. The report also found that certain industries seemed to get a pass on enforcement; for the period under study, 94 percent of the hazardous waste violations resulted in "enforcement actions," but less than half of the agricultural pesticide use violations identified received formal enforcement responses. The state water boards reported no enforcement actions at all for between one-third and one-half of the wastewater violations identified.[45]

Neoliberal austerity measures, combined with distaste for regulation, have affected the operations of state enforcement programs. As a report from the environmental justice initiative at the California DTSC put it, "In 2010, proposed state salary reductions and benefit cuts threaten to stretch the thin green line even more as experienced environmental enforcement staffers take early retirement, find better paying jobs or move to other agencies. Already, California lacks sufficient staff to inspect more than a fraction of regulated facilities, let alone unregulated facilities, and resources to pursue more than a small percentage of violations are limited." The same DTSC report noted that in 2009, in response to budget shortfalls, the state had furloughed environmental enforcement staff for a full twenty-six days, "basically provid[ing] polluters with five weeks when state environmental enforcement staff weren't on the job."[46]

When environmental enforcement is weak, low-income communities and communities of color take the brunt of it. As the DTSC report notes, polluting industries and environmental law violations are unevenly distributed:

Environmental enforcement authority in California is decentralized, compartmentalized and fragmented. It's not unusual for state and local environmental agencies to employ different enforcement priorities and strategies. As a result, there are variations in programs, which impact the enforcement of environmental and health laws. A clear result of this fragmentation is that violation rates have been found to be higher in some areas than others, and "hot spots" of unlawful environmental conduct exist in the state. These hot spots are invariably found in EJ communities.[47]

To address this problem, new Identifying Violations Affecting Neighborhoods (IVAN) initiatives were started in 2009. These are designed to make it easier to report environmental problems so that the state can take action, a premise that funnels activist behavior away from radical interventions and toward those that seek to improve upon existing systems. IVAN's goal—to improve government enforcement of environmental regulation—flies in the face of neoliberalism. However, these interventions also bear traces of neoliberal ideologies. Currently, state officials' participation in these initiatives is largely voluntary, and the programs are funded not by the state itself but by a public/private collaboration, with part of the funding coming from private philanthropies. The IVAN initiatives thus partially reflect the neoliberal shifting of responsibility for environmental management away from the state to the community and state-nonstate collaboration, even as its proponents seek to use it to improve a key function of the state: enforcement of environmental regulation.

The IVAN initiatives grew out of the Brawley-based NGO Comité Cívico del Valle's annual leadership summits, which hosted local activists and environmental agency staffers, elected officials, and local opinion leaders. As one participant puts it, "It's evolved from a venting type of conference to a healing, because when we brought government [representatives] there was a lot of frustration on both sides—government, because people don't participate, and people because government is not solving their problems." Over time the summit organizers began to incorporate environmental justice bus tours to view problem sites. The speaker continues:

> In one of those bus tours, we were working with [a staffer from] the Department of Toxic Substances Control, and [he] said, "Hey, you know, I'm taking some classes. Look, I'm using Google Earth. Why don't we start putting some information on there, like a picture that you can write a little bit of something here, and you can take a measurement." I was like, "Oh, that's pretty cool, yeah, let's do that. Let's do the map, and then when we get back, then we'll have a meeting. And after the bus tour, then we discuss this on Google Earth." And so, there was the first version of IVAN, you know, the first model.

The Google Earth tool evolved into a more sophisticated tool on a different platform designed for disaster response, which later changed into something custom built for the participants' purposes. The model has been replicated across the state, and seven regions now use online environmental reporting tools in the IVAN network.[48] Each region has a task force made up of community and government stakeholders and NGOs. The task forces create and support websites at which residents can report their complaints. Then the task forces review them and forward them to the appropriate government bodies. The online tools, which are integrated into existing environmental justice nonprofit work plans and outreach mechanisms, make it easier for people to report problems more quickly and follow what happens to their reports as they wend their way through the convoluted enforcement landscape.

Complaints registered through online IVAN platforms have produced results. For example, an abandoned concentrated animal feedlot operation (CAFO) was leaking waste from untreated manure and rotting animal carcasses into a local waterway. This was cleaned up, and the CAFO was barred from reopening the feedlot in the abandoned site in the floodplain of the New River, where it should never have been located in the first place. The other CAFOs in the area were also audited to bring them into compliance with the law. Other successes include fining companies for illegally disposing of wastewater fluids and the cleanup of homes evacuated because of gas leaks from underground transportation pipes.[49]

The program's successes did not come simply from introducing new reporting technology that gets more "eyes on the ground." Crucially, the program also adds transparency to the process of environmental monitoring and enforcement. It obliges agencies to report back to the affected communities at monthly public meetings, where they give regular updates about actions being taken to resolve the problems. Residents and NGO staff leverage this transparency to better demand action from these newly accessible officials. This process also puts reported problems into the public spotlight, where they are more likely to receive press coverage—which then puts even more political pressure on officials to resolve the problems. The importance of this public transparency is articulated by Ryan Atencio, a DTSC enforcement staffer and the designated "Government Problem Solver" within the IVAN initiative in the Imperial Valley: "Once that list [of reports] goes live, there's nowhere to hide."[50]

Of course, this is not true across the board; cases are sometimes not resolved until activists have pursued extensive follow-up and ratcheted up political pressure. Through these projects, environmental justice activists and nonprofit professionals have learned to better navigate the state's complex, multijurisdictional, and multiscalar environmental enforcement agencies. For example, activist and San Joaquin Valley almond farmer Tom Frantz reported illegal wastewater disposal at a neighboring fracking site first to the CalEPA, and then to the local collaborative environmental justice reporting system (KEEN) within the IVAN network. Both reports included his video documentation of the illegal wastewater disposal taking place. CalEPA sent the complaint to the Central Valley Regional Water Quality Control Board (CVRWQCB), without much effect. Community members continued to press for action from the offending company, Vintage Production, and from the CVRWQCB, but little action was taken. So they brought the complaint to the state-level Environmental Justice Program, which directed the problem further up the chain to the State Water Resources Control Board. The state board intervened and forced the regional body to take action. The regional body settled with Vintage Production, fining it $60,000, but later reviewed the practices of disposing of oil drilling fluids by all the "significant oil and gas operators" in the region and found many additional violations. The settlement agreements for this second wave of violations were used for supplemental environmental projects (SEPs) in disadvantaged communities such as those where the original violation took place. The SEPs were carried out by a local environmental justice organization to train residents in how to press for solutions to drinking water contamination in low-income communities.[51]

Reporting the wastewater dumping through the IVAN system was one piece of a multipronged effort to focus attention on this illegal dumping and, eventually, put a stop to it. However, while the violators in the Vintage Production story were fined (and the fines put to good use), there was no regulation in place that would force violators to clean up their illegal dump site, nor did the state provide funds for cleanup. This is another example of how environmental justice activists contest, bump up against, and participate in neoliberal environmental governance, in which state functions are partly outsourced to individual volunteers and NGO staff, while a lack of sufficient regulation means there is no way to force redress of the problem at hand.

As political scientist Jonathan Fox reminds us, transparency is not the same thing as accountability.[52] Indeed, like participation, transparency can give the illusion of change rather than deliver real substantive change. It takes a great deal of work and a strong and savvy activist network to convert transparency into accountability. The IVAN networks in California rely on a strong NGO infrastructure combined with experienced and well-connected activists—a network that is not available in many parts of the country. The wastewater example was organized around activist Tom Frantz's work. Frantz had years of experience with local environmental justice politics, frequently appeared as a commentator on environmental issues in local and national media outlets, was deeply connected to local environmental justice organizations, had self-taught scientific and regulatory expertise, had experience as a regular litigant with the Association of Irritated Residents (AIR), and had connections to environmental law firms that represent AIR pro bono. He also had a "smoking gun" video of industry caught in the act of breaking the law. While the response process built up around the IVAN tool appears to have ultimately helped address the problem by making it easier for the resident to get his evidence out, it was not the only tactic at Frantz's disposal, and the tool's existence did not itself solve the problem.

Despite the success of the IVAN tools, activists still face stiff challenges, many of which are tied to prevailing neoliberal logics. The IVAN tools can improve the functioning of the state's environmental regulatory apparatus, but only within the constraints of existing environmental regulation, and only insofar as that apparatus is funded to enforce those regulations. Much also depends on how large the fines are for violations. Are they large enough to deter businesses from future violations? If not, polluters may simply see fines as a cost of doing business— one that is offset by their profits.

Environmental justice groups support the IVAN initiatives because they believe the state does not adequately enforce existing environmental laws. If they are successful, these anti-neoliberal programs will *increase*, rather than shrink, the reach and efficacy of the state. But the long-term outcomes of these environmental reporting projects remain to be seen, and it is fair to assume that these programs are able to gain traction because (as we have seen with other seemingly anti-neoliberal tactics and goals) they fit within the broader neoliberal political landscape. Governance techniques of voluntary participation, collaboration, and political processes aimed at transparency are easier to implement than increased regulation or enforcement of existing regulations in an anti-regulatory environment.

As other government programs that have enabled more participation in environmental decision-making have shown, the IVAN programs could be used politically by environmental justice activists' opponents, to argue against the need for further funding or tightening of environmental regulations. After all, don't these existing, innovative IVAN programs already meet the needs of underserved communities? The stopgap measure could thus easily be made to serve as the permanent "solution," though one available only in parts of the state with the nonprofit infrastructure to sustain it. Given the limited resources of environmental justice organizations, activists can get caught between providing these kinds of stopgap services to address pressing immediate needs and working to create broader, more lasting changes to environmental governance. If transparency projects like the IVAN network do not lead to stricter regulations and better public funding for enforcement, they could end up simply reinforcing the status quo. Much will depend on how much activists are able to use the IVAN tools as a springboard for broader political efforts to reform the state.

Ultimately, the key question is not whether there have been some successful outcomes due to the IVAN initiatives, but whether or not the

IVAN projects are causing the state to improve overall environmental enforcement, and in particular, in the places where there are the most potential violators: low-income communities and communities of color. This is a difficult question to answer given the partial and difficult to interpret nature of enforcement data (Clean Air Act violations may be underreported by up to 85 percent), and given the effect of both state and national politics on environmental enforcement (federal environmental enforcement actions declined precipitously during the Trump administration, to the lowest level since the EPA began recording inspections in 1994).[53] A few more recent data points from the Environmental Data & Governance Initiative and the Environmental Integrity project raise as many questions as they answer. Since the beginning of the IVAN programs, the overall budget of CalEPA has increased. However, much of this increase is spent on recycling initiatives; has the budget dedicated to environmental enforcement also increased?[54] During the first three years of the Trump administration, as compared to the first three years of the Obama administration, California saw modest increases in inspections and enforcement actions, but a large decrease in fines.[55] How does this compare to what was happening in California before the Obama administration? California saw a 747 percent increase in Clean Water Act violations during the Trump administration compared to the average number of violations in the prior sixteen years.[56] Do the increases in violations represent environmental actions actually getting worse, or are they the result of increased inspections? Of all the California facilities regulated under the Clean Water Act, 13 percent were in violation for at least nine months of the years 2017–2019.[57] In 2019, there were 1,576 violations for every 1,000 facilities covered under the Clean Water Act, more than one violation per facility.[58] Although the IVAN initiatives and the 2018 establishment of the Bureau of Environmental Justice within California's Department of Justice bode well, clearly much remains to be done.

Environmental justice activists continue to work against health-threatening pollution in immediately threatened local communities, but they increasingly express an interest in being "for something" rather than "against something." This desire pushes activists toward institutionalization and policy work. Adversarial or disruptive organizing tactics such as protests, boycotts, and unionization often work "against something," seeking to end ongoing pollution, prevent a new polluting facility from being built, protect workers from labor exploitation, or draw attention to a crisis or a botched response to one. Working "for something" often draws activists into education, consensus-based problem solving, partnership, political participation, capacity building, and asset-based development—conveniently, the types of techniques that are typically favored by funders over more adversarial tactics.[59] There are both advantages and disadvantages to the ways that activists seek to put this desire to be "for something" into practice in the prevailing neoliberal environment.

In some cases, activists can shift from being "against something" to being "for something" on the same site. When an environmental justice campaign shuts down polluting facilities or prevents new construction of toxic infrastructure, for example, it may then work to add safe outdoor recreational space in the area. For example, the residents who battled the Stringfellow Acid Pit later worked to build a thirteen-acre park, complete with hiking trails and a community garden. As Penny Newman, the executive director of the Center for Community Action and Environmental Justice (CCAEJ), explained, "It was a very different notion of remediation for us." She added, "We wanted to make the community whole."[60]

This mode of being "for something"—investing in and improving a site once cleanup is completed—often goes hand in hand with efforts to benefit from less locally polluting forms of capitalism. For example, Pacoima Beautiful in Los Angeles County successfully pressed for cleanup of the Price-Pfister Faucet Plant Superfund site in its community, then invested significant energy into creating new, safer jobs by transforming the former industrial site into a shopping area that featured a LEED-certified Costco (LEED stands for Leadership in Energy and Environmental Design, a system of environmental certifications from the US Green Building Council). Activists are proud of the LEED certification and the provision of good, stable new jobs at Costco.[61] Similarly, after Youth United for Community Action in East Palo Alto won a landmark campaign to shut down Romic Environmental Technologies' hazardous materials recycling facility, the group transitioned to working with the city to create a business park on the same site.

However, in remediation and redevelopment efforts, the racialized political economy can still make the community vulnerable to capitalist exploitation. In the Bayview-Hunters Point neighborhood of San Francisco, historically a predominantly Black neighborhood with significant public housing stock, activists shut down a PG&E power plant in 2008. Then they participated in the cleanup of the nearby naval shipyard, which had been abandoned in 1974, hazardous waste and all. The local public housing residents had been exposed to pollutants from both sites during operations, then were exposed to toxic dust as the sites were cleaned up. Now that these polluting industries are gone, though, the entire area is being redeveloped, and housing prices are rising. Low-income residents risk being priced out of the area, and public housing residents are threatened with displacement.[62] Such paired clean-up-and-redevelop projects can increase the price of housing, and neoliberal policies tend to cut public housing in areas with a high cost of living. Thus when removal of the environmental threat is not accompanied by restraints on capitalism such as rent control or new public housing, it can end up displacing low-income residents—a process known as "green gentrification," or, as anthropologist Melissa Checker observes in New York City, the "greening and whitening" of the neighborhood.[63]

The desire to work "for something" is also directed into DIY initiatives. Some activists, for example, build community gardens and worker cooperatives—efforts that look to small groups to create the communities and jobs in which they want to live and work rather than to the state for regulation and enforcement. However, this too is not without its drawbacks. Some scholars of the alternative food movement have critiqued community gardens as apolitical interventions that are unlikely to significantly change low-income people's opportunities. They also point out that such interventions neatly map to the neoliberal emphasis on individual responsibility rather than regulatory politics.[64] Environmental justice activists approach these local interventions in ways that both align with and complicate neoliberalism. But activities like these can also provide both community members and activists themselves with short-term rewards: a rich sense of community, tactile pleasure, and a sense of accomplishment to offset the often years-long grind of political campaigns. All these themes are visible in the following passage, in which an activist tells me how her organization's community garden program relates to the group's overall work:

> A lot of the people who've been involved in the gardens were involved in our fracking trainings, and have been going up to Sacramento on different bills, or engaging in different programs. So they've testified at Air District meetings. It's part of our larger organizing; it's not its own thing. There are some participants who are only involved in the garden, but a lot of people are involved in other aspects of the work. . . . It's worked in a couple of different ways. There have been a few people who have become more active, who [initially] only got involved in the garden. And then there are people who had been active, who wanted to do the garden. And so it's happened in both ways. So that's been really neat to see, how people have gotten involved.

And that all came out of our decision to be a little more proactive, and say, "Okay, the community's saying, 'We want community food projects.'" Then it's like, well, we can advocate for cities and counties to try and create these projects, or we can try and entice developers to develop these projects. But why don't we just help the community design and implement the projects? Why don't we just demonstrate that it can be done? And so that's how it got started. So it feels like it's very much part of our organizing. And it's become a good base from which to draw support for other issues and other campaigns.

Some of the DIY-type local interventions such as bike shares, community gardens, and worker cooperatives are created in response to direct requests from the communities that environmental justice nonprofits serve, as in the preceding example. They speak to people's desires to create things that have immediate, tangible impacts on their lives, such as tomatoes you can plant in spring and eat in the summer. This is a far cry from the longer timeline and ambiguous impact of most policy advocacy campaigns.

Projects like this express an ambivalence about the role of the state. They do not look to the state for regulation or funding to address systemic problems; after all, the state has been complicit in creating many of the problems in communities of color in the first place. DIY initiatives build on long histories of cultivating self-reliance in communities of color. For example, Black communities have long fought for fair laws and regulations, but when these were absent they historically have looked inward, building institutions (such as schools and cooperatives) partially or entirely outside the orbit of the state.[65] These programs, like community gardens, align with neoliberalism to the extent that they do not look to the state for solutions, but the motivations are different. This is a response to a state that seems beyond reform, not a desire to get the state "out of the way" so markets can determine the allocation of goods and resources across society.

The Normalization of Risk

The early intense, urgent, disruptive grassroots environmental justice movement tactics grew out of new fears about toxics that came to the forefront of public consciousness in the 1970s. As we saw in chapter 1, fear of hazardous waste among the US populace spiked in the late 1970s and early 1980s after a series of hazardous waste–related disasters, which drove home to the American people (especially those directly affected by these disasters) that existing government regulation was not strong or comprehensive enough to keep them safe.[66] This high public concern with the health impacts of hazardous waste, combined with new awareness that hazardous waste disposal facilities were being sited primarily in low-income communities and communities of color, produced the explosive mix that fueled disruptive activism in the 1980s and 1990s.

Now, over forty years after the passage of the Resource Conservation and Recovery Act, much of the public seems to have simply accepted the fact that they will have some environmental exposure; the risks seem to be normalized. Of the three Class 1 hazardous waste landfills in California, only one continues to be regularly targeted by environmental justice activists. And even there, it has been hard for dedicated activists to turn residents out for events, year after year, decade after decade of living near a hazardous waste landfill. Without a crisis, it is difficult to mobilize people. Similarly, when the crisis is physically invisible or slow moving, activists often struggle to mobilize people. For example, mass pesticide poisonings in California's San Joaquin Valley—urgent crises that severely and visibly affected many people—have spurred political involvement of those impacted.[67] But the routine, mostly imperceptible lower-dose exposures draw much less attention and outrage. One activist from the San Joaquin Valley, Rosenda Mataka, describes it as follows: "Things here in the Valley are so gradual, you know? They're everyday. It's so accepted and part of life, like it's nothing. But if it would hit you all in one day—if all the pesticides you used in this area would just fall on you in one day, then you would think about the impact."[68]

Toxins are so ubiquitous that many people learn to ignore their presence. This dynamic is apparent in an anecdote from anthropologist and cancer patient Lochlann Jain. Jain describes cancer as—like the toxins that cause cancer—so common that it is normalized. In her book, she shares a photo from the parking garage next to the Stanford Medical Center, where she is being treated for cancer. The image shows a sign well known to Californians, which states: "WARNING: This garage contains gasoline and diesel engine exhaust which is known to the state of California to cause cancer and/or reproductive toxicity." California activists waged a lengthy battle to get the signs posted as part of larger right-to-know, antitoxics efforts of the 1980s. Proposition 65, passed in 1986, mandated warnings to alert the public when they are being exposed to known carcinogens. But these signs are now so ubiquitous that they are almost entirely ignored by the public as they go about their daily lives. In Jain's image, the carcinogens warning sign is ominously placed just below a sign pointing the way to Stanford Hospital, where Jain goes for cancer treatment. Jain writes, "The signs are posted everywhere in California, like flags of surrender."[69]

Similarly paradoxical effects were produced by the successes of the 1980s- and 1990s-era environmental justice movement in preventing a wave of new incinerator construction. As described in chapter 2, much early California environmental justice activism grew out of concerns about the location of hazardous waste landfills and incinerators in low-income communities and communities of color. Incinerator proposals politicized a broad spectrum of early activists, who successfully crippled the industry: no new commercial municipal solid waste incinerators have been built in the United States for over twenty-five years.[70] This is one of the major successes of environmental justice organizing in the United States. But paradoxically, the scale of this success removed one of the movement's recruiting tools for addressing many other problems. Because people respond best to immediate, visible crises (rather than slow-moving, invisible threats), and to new impending threats rather than existing threats, the fact that fewer incinerators were being proposed (combined with the offshoring of much polluting manufacturing) reduced the sense of public urgency. The success in reducing new incinerator proposals has reduced one of the driving forces of widespread community politicization around environmental justice concerns.

As this chapter has shown, the tactics of the environmental justice movement described in chapters 1 and 2 grew out of the political and social climates in which they exist. The disruptive tactics of the early movement responded to a new and urgent sense of the dangers of hazardous waste, and residents' fear and anger motivated them to agitate for fundamental change through disruptive forms of protest. But over time, changing racial politics and creeping neoliberalism, both of which exist within the structures of long-standing capitalism, opened up new opportunities for activists to engage in traditional political channels and shifted how other activists thought about creating change. They also reduced residents' sense of crisis and willingness to react aggressively; anger and the sense of urgency were defused for some by corporations' and the state's new façade of collaboration. The state now routinely invites activists to "sit at the table" (though it rarely satiates them), and corporations frame themselves as good neighbors (offering a few limited, difficult-to-enforce concessions).

The movement's shift to insider tactics, incremental and reformist goals, and increasing institutionalization and professionalization has produced some mixed successes and some unforeseen consequences. Activists must constantly negotiate and work within the broader structures of neoliberal capitalism, which work constantly to incorporate and sideline challenges. Engagement in insider tactics of collaboration with the state always runs the risk of co-optation and can divert energy away from pressing problems at the local scale. The channeling of much activism through nonprofit structures also introduces challenges such as the competition for funding and "turf," as well as the concentration of movement power within NGOs and away from residents themselves (though some NGO staff are themselves residents in communities with high levels of pollution). People also often find it easier to "unite against a common enemy" than to unite around an array of policy reforms and institutional relationships. These changes have caused dissension within the movement itself, as many activists feel that the changes are antithetical to the movement's core principles and values.[71] However, nonprofits have provided employment opportunities to some residents in disproportionately polluted places, have fought for state resources, and have assisted innumerable people to take leadership roles in key political struggles. Environmental justice activists have won some policy improvements, have blocked other policies that would have worsened environmental injustice, and have pushed back against polluter influence from local politics all the way up to the state capital and beyond.

Environmental justice activists' seemingly innocuous goals of fair treatment, healthy homes, and safe workplaces actually work against the grain of American politics and global racial capitalism. But activists cannot step outside of this context in working toward these goals, and in this era of institutionalization of activism, they end up working both against and with the grain of American politics. As I see it, environmental justice activists' institutionalization and concomitant efforts in the policy realm are a constructive effort to broaden their impact, and avoiding policy engagement would risk ceding the state entirely to polluters. Yet I also think that disruptive tactics should not be left behind, for they rapidly respond to immediate local threats and offer a much-needed corrective to the tendency to compromise more and more over time—a tactic that will eventually stall forward progress altogether.

In the next two chapters, I offer two case studies that show how these trends have played out on the ground, tracing the successes and failures of both direct action and policy work over time. Chapter 4 offers a case study of the Kettleman City campaign against a local incinerator, a hazardous waste landfill, and other pollution threats. The Kettleman City experience highlights activism that still retains much of its oppositional roots. But it also offers a microcosm of the California environmental justice movement as a whole, showing how activism there has contended with changing racial politics, the normalization of risk, and the other broad trends described in this chapter and the last. Chapter 5 is a detailed case study of the institutionalized processes and tactics of California environmental justice groups' response to the drafting and early implementation of Assembly Bill 32, a precedent-setting climate change policy. It shows these activists walking the fine line of movement institutionalization as they attempt to get the political machine and mainstream environmentalists to incorporate environmental justice principles into their responses to climate change. It also shows the divisions among activists themselves, who are sometimes at odds over how to properly respond to the broad, market-based initiative that forms the core control for industrial greenhouse gas emissions in AB 32; the compromises required for policy change can fracture the movement itself. These case studies thus trace the entanglement of political context and environmental justice values, showing how they work together and against each other to produce complex outcomes—good, bad, and mixed—within the constraints of intensifying neoliberal capitalism, changing racial politics, and shifting risk perception described in this chapter, as well as the impact of philanthropic funding and policing of protest described in chapter 2.

CHAPTER 4

Kettleman City

*Case Study of Community Activism
in Changing Times*

Many Californians who recognize the name "Kettleman City" do so because it is a good place to stop for gas and a snack on the long drive between Los Angeles and the San Francisco Bay Area, passing through the Central Valley's agricultural landscape. But some Californians recognize the name of the tiny town (population 1,439) because it played the David to the Goliath of Waste Management, the country's largest waste company.[1]

Kettleman City, like so many other poor communities of color, was a prime target for a hazardous waste landfill. The town's demographics are comparable to many other places that host hazardous waste facilities: 100 percent of the community is Latinx; 57.5 percent of residents over age twenty-five have less than a ninth-grade education; and the average per capita income is $15,656 per year.[2] Kettleman City hosts one of three Class 1 landfills in California (all three are located in or near predominantly Latinx communities), and the community's opinion was not sought when the landfill was sited. Indeed, residents did not even know about the dump until after it had been permitted and built in 1979. But when a hazardous waste incinerator was proposed on the dump site, the residents made their opposition known, loud and clear. The fight in the late 1980s and early 1990s against the incinerator at the Kettleman City landfill was a paradigmatic early case in the environmental justice movement.[3]

This chapter traces the thirty-plus-year history of environmental justice activism in Kettleman City as a case study within the broader evolution of environmental justice activism. This case study exemplifies the broader trends discussed in chapters 2 and 3 and analyzes how these trends played out on the ground. The Kettleman City story is an early environmental justice success, preventing the construction of a new "locally unwanted land use"—here, an incinerator. These successes added up in town after town; only three of the seventy-five or more new or expanded incinerators proposed since the 1980s were ever built.[4] However, Kettleman City's example also shows how these successes, as important as they are, could not on their own address existing unwanted land uses or the effect of multiple sources of contamination in one location. And these successes left other problems in their wake: the challenge of sustaining broad levels of local activism after the immediate threat ended made it difficult to address the broader structural conditions of capitalism that disproportionately locate pollution in low-income communities and communities of color and that constrain efforts to change the status quo.

The case of Kettleman City shows the unevenness of the environmental justice movement's transition from "protest" to "politics." Many in the environmental justice movement have used the limitations of fighting individual, defensive battles site by site as a reason to scale up into statewide policy advocacy and collaborative work with state agencies. Others have ventured into efforts to build gardens, parks, and other environmental amenities, some of which pursue a DIY model that eschews state involvement. But in Kettleman City, much environmental justice activism remains true to its roots: focused on local sources of polluting health threats and engaged in continued confrontations with industry and state agencies. Of course, Kettleman City activists are also influenced by the broader trends described in chapters 2 and 3: changing racial politics and industrial public relations efforts, pressure to collaborate with state agencies, the opportunities and challenges of increasingly relying on philanthropically funded nonprofit structures to support activism, and the normalization of risk from the nearby hazardous waste landfill. They also face the challenge of pursuing activism within the context of neoliberal policies under capitalism, which mitigate against increasing environmental enforcement budgets and channel environmental activism toward voluntary and market-based (rather than regulatory) measures to contain industry pollution.

In Kettleman City, we can also see the fissures in the movement caused by the disagreement over tactics. The town hosted the first meeting of the newly formed California Environmental Justice Coalition, which was formed as an alternative to the better-funded, exclusive California Environmental Justice Alliance. Finally, in the face of skepticism about the value of participating on government advisory committees and improving the public's ability to participate fairly in environmental decision-making, Kettleman City's difficult history accessing environmental decision-making also shows why activists worked toward these goals in the first place.

THE ANTI-INCINERATOR CAMPAIGN

In the late 1970s, Chemical Waste Management, Inc. (a subsidiary of Waste Management Inc.) built a hazardous waste landfill 3.5 miles away from Kettleman City on land formerly used to store waste mud from nearby oil drilling. As a Class 1 landfill, the facility is authorized to take almost any hazardous substance up to, but excluding, radioactive waste. It is the largest hazardous waste landfill west of the Mississippi. In the 1980s, Chemical Waste began the permitting process to add a hazardous waste incinerator to the existing landfill. The incinerator would burn hazardous waste instead of landfilling it. According to the waste management industry, the push toward incinerators in the 1980s was a response to a national crisis of landfills running out of room for new waste. (However, as David Pellow, Kenneth Gould, and others have written, the "crisis" had other origins, including that the public increasingly did not want to live near them, and industry was blocking or shuttering recycling initiatives.)[5] These incinerators would add dangerous toxins to the air, and the proposed incinerator sites were disproportionately in low-income communities and communities of color, such as Kettleman City.[6]

Many residents of Kettleman City did not even know about the existing hazardous waste landfill just outside of town, where it is not easily visible from the road. Residents did not discover its presence until after it was built—some in 1985, when the dump was fined for operating unauthorized waste ponds, and some not until they learned about the incinerator proposal a few years later.[7] Maricela Mares Alatorre, daughter of activists Mary Lou and Ramon Mares, remembers that her family and neighbors had no idea that the dump existed, or that a hazardous waste incinerator was proposed to be added to it, until Greenpeace organizer Bradley Angel knocked on her door while recruiting residents to attend an upcoming permitting hearing. The hearings, however, were not easy to participate in:

> When we started attending these meetings, we noticed that they were never in town, they were usually in the middle of the day, 45 miles away, where they weren't really accessible to people. And if you could get there, they didn't translate them into Spanish when most of the town speaks Spanish. And we started finding out that there was a pattern to the way these things happen. We started researching the company. We were informed about the Cerrell Report. It was a 1984 document, which was commissioned by the California Waste Management Board where they said how you should choose a town for these kinds of projects. And we found out that they were going around choosing towns that had a large minority population, where people didn't speak English, large immigrant populations, low education, and Catholic.[8] That was actually in the report: Catholic. And we were—we were shocked because we really had no idea. I had no idea that environmental racism existed until we were made aware of that document. And it's like you don't want to have to go to a meeting. You don't want to have to, you know, spend all your time in these boring hearings, and sometimes you don't understand what they're saying. But it makes you mad when we saw the pattern. And we talked to people from other towns, and we started networking, and we saw how they deliberately chose people like us to do these things to. It makes you mad.[9]

Mares Alatorre's story is a common one in communities fighting incinerators and other waste facilities in the 1980s and 1990s. As people across the country learned that toxic industries were being located in politically vulnerable communities, residents faced off with local government officials and industry representatives (who appeared to march in lockstep), resorting to disruptive political tactics when their pleas to government officials fell on deaf ears. In Kettleman City, residents, concerned about the threat to their health, formed a grassroots group to tackle the problem: El Pueblo para el Aire y Agua Limpio (People for Clean Air and Water). Mary Lou and Ramon Mares, and Esperanza and Joe Maya, among others, took leadership roles. Some of El Pueblo's members brought in prior experience with farmworker organizing in the United Farm Workers of America to El Pueblo, while for others El Pueblo was their first experience with organizing.[10]

Like many other groups nationwide, El Pueblo pursued local, direct action and community organizing strategies. However, it was unique in having early access to a lawyer, Luke Cole at California Rural Legal Assistance (CRLA), who used the case as a test for the use of civil rights law to address pollution in communities of color.[11] The organization also had the support of organizers from the large environmental group

Greenpeace, which (unlike many other large national and international environmental organizations) embraced direct-action tactics and at the time, at least on the West Coast, invested in local antitoxics and environmental justice organizing. In addition to their work with Greenpeace and CRLA, activists also attracted support from the Southwest Network for Environmental and Economic Justice, Las Madres del Este de Los Angeles, Citizen Action, Rev. Jesse Jackson, a UC Berkeley student group (Nindakin: People of Color for Environmental Justice), and a wide array of others.[12]

One of the most iconic moments in the campaign occurred at a 1988 public hearing about the toxic waste incinerator proposal. By the time this hearing took place, residents had lost faith in both state and industry officials and came prepared to confront them:

> So, before this meeting, I'm at my home, and we said, "Well, whenever we don't like something, we're going to have to let them know." All their same lies. So, I made hundreds of copies of this piece of paper with the word "NO" real bold on it. It's just that, "NO." I said, when we don't like something, we're going to scream "No!" So, we all had those with us.

The circumstances of the hearing underscored how Kettleman City residents were being excluded from the normal process of government decision-making. Like other hearings, this one was not in Kettleman City but in the county seat in Hanford, thirty miles away. Although it was held in the winter, the hearing was not scheduled for one of the comfortable, well-heated spaces available in town such as the high school auditorium. Rather, the hearing was held in the County Fairground building, a building about the size of a football field that was, as one resident told me, "an exhibit barn for arts and crafts, or your animals or whatever. One of those big galvanized buildings made out of sheet metal or something. It's cold. Cement floor." The planning commission sat elevated at the front of the room, with portable heaters at their feet and hot coffee on their table. Open space, microphones, and then about fifty rows of seats lay before them, followed by bleachers. Behind the bleachers, there was empty concrete that stretched until the end of the building.[13]

Luke Cole and Sheila Foster describe provisions made for Spanish-speaking residents as follows:

> Kettleman City residents showed up at the meeting in force. About 200 people came by bus and carpool from Kettleman City, and, as one of their leaders made clear, "We're here, we want to testify on this project, and we

brought our own translator." The chair of the Kings County Planning Commission looked down on the crowd and said, "That request has been denied. The translation is taking place in the back of the room and it won't happen up here." Residents looked at where the Planning Commissioner was pointing: they looked from the Planning Commission up on their dais, they looked at the open space and the microphones, they looked at all the rows of chairs, and they looked at the bleachers. And then they looked way back behind the bleachers, nearly at the rear of the room, where there was one forlorn man sitting surrounded by a little circle of about twenty-five empty chairs. The Planning Commission chair said again, "Why don't you go back there? There are monitors back there. We are all in the same room."[14]

Kettleman City residents had come prepared to press their cause, and this arrangement did not suit them at all. One activist describes what happened at the meeting as follows:

It was supposed to be open all day for people that wanted to go and say whether they're for [the incinerator], against it, or have questions for the supervisors. And we had a certain time we were supposed to be there. We were bused over there. Some people took their cars, and some people went on their own, but when we got there, they didn't let us speak 'til about 9:00 or 10:00 that evening. They let other people speak first that should have spoke during the day. They were getting us to be tired so we would just go home, you know, and leave them alone. Then they didn't have the translators they were supposed to have had. They had some translators. We asked for the translators and then they said, "Well, the translators are going to be in the back of the building. Go to the back." They told us to go in the back! Go to the back of the room for the translators. And we all went, "No!" You know, "You bring the translators to us when we're up there speaking!" So we go, "No!" And then we said, "*Adelante!*" and we all went forward with our "No! No!" "We're not going to go to the back of the room!" . . . And they were shocked that we did that. Why would they send us to the back of the room? That's discrimination there in itself. So, they didn't have translators, and it was just waiting for somebody to do something wrong, to jump on us, to fight with us. You couldn't even go to the bathroom, 'cause they were waiting for you in there to do something, the Chem Waste employees. It was just really, really bad.

Negative encounters like these, in which state decision-makers and industry representatives blatantly disrespected residents, drew more people into the fight, as this early incinerator opponent describes:

When the people that needed the translation started understanding what they were trying to do to them and how they were being disrespected, that made them more active. So that's how we got more people to get into the fight for the incinerator.

Another iconic moment of disruption took place later in the campaign, the day before another hearing, when activists blockaded the entryway to the landfill with an old school bus and chained themselves to its axle. An activist who had been part of a successful campaign to oppose the construction of another incinerator in nearby Alpaugh helped out in Kettleman City. Greenpeace stored the bus on her property until it was needed and used her home as a planning area for the demonstration. She describes the opportunity to have supporters from out of town staying with her as a strange but wonderful experience. A Kettleman City resident who also hosted out-of-town supporters had a similar experience:

> One time I housed a lot of people from Greenpeace at my house. They were at my house for almost two weeks, and they camped in my backyard. They came to canvas. I didn't even know what that word meant. . . . But I remember seeing them coming in with money in the evening. I didn't even know what was going on. We were so green to all this. So I was asked if I could house them and I said, "Yeah." Well, they all came over to help us and I don't even know who they were. And I remember that I used to cook for them. They would not eat meat, so I would cook a big pot of pinto beans every day, and they would eat the whole damn pot—[laughter]—of beans and salsa. I always had that, and I don't know who furnished the pasta, but they always had big bags of pasta and I would cook the pasta. And they stayed at my house for that long. The posters were made in my backyard. The canvas banners were done there. I housed a lot of people throughout the years in my home—strangers, you know? Strangers because I never seen them before, but they came to help. I didn't even know what the organization Greenpeace was, or who they were, who Bradley [Angel] was, you know? But I learned throughout the years.

During this period, environmental justice activism felt like it was becoming a national mass movement, with Kettleman City as one of many hot spots. In addition to the student activists and others brought by Greenpeace, residents from other affected communities such as San Francisco's Bayview-Hunters Point, East Los Angeles, and Alpaugh visited Kettleman City to lend their support. One Kettleman City activist remembers those days fondly:

> I think all of it was a high point. I was really amazed that people outside Kettleman City actually cared for us, what happened to us. We started networking and all these people came to our aid. Who were they? Why did they care? We couldn't understand that. Like Bradley [Angel] and his organizations, and Luke Cole with the lawyers. Why did they care? We're just a poor Hispanic migrant little town, you know? But they knew more of what Chem Waste was doing. We were not the only site in the United States.

We found out later that there were other dumpsites, and that they have the same pattern [of locating dumps in politically disadvantaged communities] throughout.

Kettleman City activists returned the favor, giving their support to people elsewhere and strengthening the emerging network of grassroots environmental justice activists. They went to the First National People of Color Environmental Leadership Summit in Washington, D.C., in 1991, which helped bring together people facing similar problems across the country. They traveled to Los Angeles and other California locations, as well as New York, Alabama, and the town of Playas de Rosarito, ten miles south of the US-Mexico border. These visits were not just to provide moral support, but to share tactics and information about their common corporate opponents. The meetings laid bare the lies that Chemical Waste was telling on each side. For example, the residents of Playas de Rosarito had been told that the people of Kettleman City were supportive of the incinerator proposal—a lie that Kettleman City residents quickly debunked when they met. The Mexican residents had wanted to come see the landfill in Kettleman City as they considered their options but were told no by Chemical Waste; at the same time, Chemical Waste was telling Kettleman City residents that they could come see the landfill anytime, because the company had nothing to hide. The Kettleman City activists therefore planned a visit to the dump without mentioning to Chemical Waste that they would be accompanied by several busloads of Mexican residents from Playas de Rosarito and local press. The Mexican visitors returned home and successfully blocked the building of the incinerator proposed for their town.

As Kettleman City residents met activists from elsewhere, many developed broader political critiques about waste infrastructure writ large, broadening their opposition beyond the early "not in my backyard" beliefs. Mary Lou Mares shared the following:

We started going to statewide conferences and meeting other people who were fighting other terrible stuff. There was Stormy Williams, she was fighting in the Mojave Desert. Everybody says, "Why can't you put this incinerator in the desert or somewhere where people don't . . . ?" And she would get up and say, "Wait a minute, I live in the desert!" [Laughter] At first, you are so ignorant that it's easy to say, "Put it in the desert," but you start meeting people and you start understanding that there is no place to put an incinerator because the air belongs to everybody and it has currents and it goes around and comes around. You just cannot put anything into the air.[15]

Despite the efforts by Kettleman City residents and allies, the Kings County Planning Commission nevertheless voted to approve the incinerator construction. Kettleman City is an unincorporated community, which means the people have no local governance structure of their own but rather are governed from a distance by a county board of supervisors, located forty miles away in the whiter and more affluent county seat of Hanford (where the public hearings took place). At that time, Kettleman City had little representation on the Planning Commission, which was mostly made up of people who did not live near the dump. The county stood to increase its revenues through taxing the landfill operators (although, as Kettleman City residents complained, precious few of those resources were reinvested in Kettleman City itself—an example of how racial capitalism functions at the county level).

El Pueblo appealed the decision to the Kings County Board of Supervisors, who upheld the incinerator approval. El Pueblo and its legal supporters at CRLA filed a class-action lawsuit against Kings County in 1991. In 1992, a superior court judge overturned the Kings County approval of the incinerator, ruling that it was based on an inadequate environmental impact report and that the public permitting process had failed to meaningfully involve the local population, since residents in the predominantly Spanish-speaking town had received the relevant documents only in English. Chemical Waste Management filed an appeal, but then withdrew the incinerator application in 1993. One activist describes the immense relief she and her friend felt after winning the protracted campaign:

> [My friend] and I just cried and cried the day we got the announcement. The reporter came first to my house, saying, "Tell us what you're doing, what's your next this and that, your next strategy," and then along came the general manager of Chem Waste and he comes up to us and he says, "It's over. The lawsuit, it's over. We're withdrawing the plan to put in the incinerator." I said, "What?!" He said that they are not doing the incinerator. "Oh, I gotta go see [my friend]!" And I go to [my friend's house] and we just hugged and cried and cried. It was [many] years of struggle, you know, it was great. It was so good.

Kettleman City's fight against the incinerator was often framed as an epic David versus Goliath battle between the largest waste management company in the country and a tiny, low-income Latinx community in a largely forgotten part of California. The activists' victory became a symbol of the movement's vitality and potential.[16] It also inspired environmental justice activists across the country. The Kettleman City residents' visits to and from other communities confronting similar problems helped activists see the bigger picture, that this was not a local but a systemic problem. This campaign thus helped nurture the broader environmental justice movement, both in California and the nation.

AFTER THE ANTI-INCINERATOR CAMPAIGN

Kettleman City's story does not end with the defeat of the incinerator. After all, residents still lived next door to a hazardous waste landfill, and new problems kept surfacing. As the broader environmental justice movement changed, so too did the organizing in Kettleman City. As Kettleman City activists have learned more about multiple sources of exposure, their early focus on toxic waste has grown to include a broader focus on pollution in general. Residents are exposed to an array of different pollutants every day, but regulatory regimes largely regulate threats one by one rather than accounting for the total burden they place on human health.[17] Advocates for policy change therefore press for regulation of pollutants according to their cumulative impacts, which highlights the fact that even when individual threats are within legal limits (which is not always the case in Kettleman City), their cumulative impact can still threaten human health.

Although Kettleman City activists have expanded their focus beyond hazardous waste, the hazardous waste landfill remains a core concern, and their tactics are still frequently oppositional rather than collaborative. And unlike other contemporary environmental justice activism, El Pueblo has not expanded its issue area into work creating environmental amenities such as parks and community gardens, nor has climate change become a core component of its work. Its members do not spend a lot of time lobbying in the state capitol. In this way El Pueblo retains much of the character of the early efforts of the environmental justice movement.

There has been plenty to keep activists busy. Kettleman City activists continue to fight off new threats while at the same time grappling with the mixed implications of concessions they extract from their opponents. As one activist says, "I ended up coming back to live in Kettleman City after college. And I found out that even though we had defeated the incinerator, there was still lots of activity up there [at the landfill] that they were trying to bring in." In the 1990s, there was a fight over an unwanted toxic rail car, which had been moved from place to place throughout the county and eventually ended up in the landfill. In 1997,

El Pueblo sued Chemical Waste. They alleged flaws in the company's environmental impact report, which was submitted as part of the permitting process for a new development in the landfill. On the advice of its lawyer, El Pueblo settled the case for $75,000 of seed money. With the seed money, the group created a foundation (a particular kind of legal, institutional tax entity) that allowed it to successfully apply for further funding, with which it built a community center:

> So, we were fighting this and Luke [Cole] says, "Well, I don't think we are going to win this case." And, the people from Buttonwillow [which has one of the two other Class 1 hazardous waste landfills in California], lost their case. And they were all scared 'cause they were going to have to pay lawyers and all that. I didn't want to leave the people in Kettleman City with a debt that they would have to pay for the lawyers' fees and all that. So we sat down and we talked about it [with Chem Waste], and they said, "What do you want?" And I said, "Well, I want you to be a better neighbor to us." They came up with the money to start the community building and the money to maintain it. The more toxics they accept, the more money the community building gets. We have the Head Start program in there. We have other county people that come in, like once a month, immunization or stuff like that, coming out of the building. Then, we have the community building. It's small, but it's good enough for the people to have meetings or parties or whatever. But, it's still maintained with Chem Waste money. . . . [My friend] was one of those people that didn't think it was right that we built that community building with that money. . . . . At that point, I was almost the last one, and people look to me to make decisions. And it's hard when they put that kind of burden on your shoulders, and you try to make the best decision for everybody. I know this building, it's maintained with blood money, but I hope some good comes out of it. I hope so.

Activists are glad for the community center, but they are wary of Chemical Waste's financial support of it. They worry that that funding might be used for leverage, to silence further criticism of the company. They are also unhappy that Chemical Waste Management is using it to improve its image in the community:

> Part of the monies to build this community center came from community block development grants. I talked to one of the county supervisors, because she wanted to know if we really wanted part of those monies to help us build the community center. And I said, "Well, we do." 'Cause we were still protesting against Chem Waste at that time, even though we had already won that settlement, which was just seed money to build the community center. It wasn't enough to build the community center. And she said, "Well, I don't understand. Why are you guys still complaining? Do you want this or do you not want this? Do you want this building?" I said, "Yes, we want the building. But we don't want it to buy our silence."

Last year the general manager of Chem Waste approached us and he had the gall to ask us whether we would be willing to let them name this the Chem Waste Kettleman City Community Center if we would accept more settlement funds. So we've constantly, constantly had to keep on our toes. A few years back Congresswoman Maxine Waters and a couple of other Congressmen formed a committee where they went out and talked to communities that had large landfills among them to ask them what benefits they've gotten from living next to these facilities. And of course Chem Waste was there with a big, long list of stuff that they donate to the community and whatnot. And one of the things that they listed as having donated to the community was the community center. And I said, "Wait a minute." I said, "You didn't donate it. That was because we sued you." And the Congressmen were there. They said, "Is that true?" I said, "Yes, it's true. We sued them. This didn't come out of their pocket. This was from lawsuit funds." So it's like if we just turn our backs or let our guard down a little bit, something new will happen.

Environmental justice activists often file lawsuits like the one described here, intended to block polluting projects. When these suits fail, activists extract what funds and concessions from polluters they can. In Kettleman City, Chemical Waste has continually tried to expand the landfill, and other companies seek to add other types of polluting projects nearby. For example, in 2005, the Westlake Farms Composting Facility was approved for construction, which would import human sewage from Los Angeles, compost it, and then spread it on Kings County farmland, next to Kettleman City. The Kettleman City activists filed a lawsuit against the human waste disposal project. They eventually settled the case, extracting some concessions to limit new air pollution and provide modest local benefits: the Los Angeles County sanitation districts agreed to give $30,000 a year to the West Hills Community College District (which includes colleges in Coalinga and Lemoore, each about twenty-five miles away from Kettleman City). The Los Angeles sanitation districts also agreed to use natural gas rather than diesel powered trucks to transport the sludge, which would add fewer health-threatening pollutants to the local air.[18] The human sewage composting project became operational in 2016.

During this entire decade, the landfill continued to grow in size, with regular expansions permitted by the California DTSC. This has caused other skirmishes between residents and Chemical Waste. In 2006, it appeared that the hazardous waste landfill in Kettleman City was illegally accepting radioactive waste, or at least pursuing efforts to do so legally in the future. After state senator Barbara Boxer expressed her opposition and activists threatened a lawsuit, landfill managers quickly issued a statement promising to cease their efforts.[19] In 2008 a bioreactor was permitted to enable the landfill to use liquid to speed up the decomposition of nonhazardous waste.

Some of these battles have used disruptive tactics in addition to the legal challenges described earlier. While activism in response to these new threats was subdued compared to the larger mobilizations of the initial anti-incinerator fight, it retained a disruptive flair. Maricela Mares Alatorre describes actions taken by her son Miguel at a public hearing regarding the Kettleman City hazardous waste dump. She partially disavows his tactics, but describes them sympathetically:

> My son is involved in a group that was formed last year called KPOP. It's Kids Protecting Our Planet. He's gone to a lot of hearings since he was very, very little. My son's been involved in a lot of protests, he's passed out a lot of flyers. He's very outspoken. . . . They were at a protest in March, the KPOP kids, where they almost got arrested. It was kind of scary. You never want to see your kid arrested like that. The EPA was having a hearing about whether Kettleman City is an environmental justice community or not. The kids wrote a list of 50 things that they'd rather be doing than coming to the hearing. They'd rather be watching TV, they'd rather be skating, they'd rather be playing basketball, they'd rather be playing soccer. On and on and on. They said, "And you still think that I'm not affected by having this in my community? Come on." And then these little radicals went out and got garbage bags, and they came in, and they propped them up in front of the EPA people, and they said, "You dump your garbage here all the time, why don't you take some of our garbage home? Don't you like it? It's safe. It's not even toxic." And then, they went and they opened the bags, and they dumped them on the table in front of the EPA people. And of course, they had policemen in the audience. They always do, I don't know why. They're always scared like we're going to, you know, act up or do something horrendous. And he and the other KPOP kids, they dumped the garbage on the table, which I wasn't expecting. I wasn't necessarily, you know, proud of that. But they were passionate, and they felt it, and it was important to them. And I remember one of the Chem Waste people getting up in my face and saying, "You don't even know how to raise a kid. Look at how your kid acts." He said, "My kid wouldn't do that." I said, "At least your kid doesn't have to be here defending his life. Mine does." They were so angry. They wanted the kids thrown out, they wanted them arrested, they were so angry at these kids who were just there defending themselves. Really, I mean, the garbage was nasty, but it's nothing compared to what they do every single day up there [at the landfill].[20]

Although these actions are less disruptive than those used in the post-incinerator activist campaigns, the children's actions show that some residents are still willing to break the norms of "civility" in the face of

FIGURE 14. Maricela Mares Alatorre and thirteen-year-old son Miguel Alatorre at a protest in front of the Chemical Waste Management hazardous waste landfill, Kettleman City, November 16, 2007. Photo by author.

ongoing threats. While Chemical Waste staff tried to shame Alatorre for her son's behavior, she defended his actions, reframing the problem as caused by the company's actions, not her son's disruptive behavior.

The Birth Defect Cluster

Close to twenty years after the incinerator struggle, the town found itself once again in the spotlight. Over the years there had been scattered health complaints that Kettleman City residents suspected might be linked to the hazardous waste landfill. Mary Lou Mares recalls one such incident in a 2007 interview:

> There was a friend of ours—her child was born with that open-head syndrome, I don't know what you call it. A lot of people blamed Chem Waste, but how can you prove it? They keep saying the incinerator was going to dump only minute amounts of particles per day, which at the end of the year was gonna look like a mountain, you know. And then, the supervisors would say, "Well, you don't know technology. You don't know about new stuff." But we know you are trying to experiment on us with the new stuff, and I don't want to know more about it. Find out on yourself if you want it so bad.[21]

In 2009, Chemical Waste again sought permits to expand the Kettleman City landfill, this time planning to double its size. Activists conducting a community-led health survey discovered that five children had been born with cleft palate and other birth defects within a fifteen-month period between 2007 and 2008; three of these infants died within their first year of life. Later, nine more babies with similar birth defects were discovered. In a town of just under fifteen hundred residents, these numbers were alarmingly high. Even the activists conducting the study, who were well-versed in the pollution to which they were daily exposed, were surprised by their findings.

As a result of the birth defects, some residents signed up with personal injury lawyers, and others worked with a lawyer who wanted to get the entire town relocated. The mothers of the children with birth defects and of those who had died gave countless interviews to the press. El Pueblo and its allies began a new phase of work. They tried to block Chemical Waste's permit to increase the size of the landfill while pressuring health authorities to acknowledge and then investigate the birth defects, some of which had not made it into the government's official health records. Local health authorities resisted, and activists moved on to the politicians in the state capitol. Eventually, then governor Schwarzenegger intervened, ordering the State Department of Public Health and the California Environmental Protection Agency to investigate the birth defects.

In early responses to the activists, government officials claimed that the number of birth defects was not especially high for a town of that size. Activists also complained that an early fact sheet distributed by the state listed poor individual behaviors as a cause of birth defects (such as drinking, smoking, doing drugs, or eating poorly during pregnancy), and gave short shrift to exposure to toxins as a potential cause—a seeming attempt to shift the blame away from environmental pollutants onto individual behaviors.[22] Both actions produced public outcry among the mothers and activists in Kettleman City. A later report concluded that the mothers had taken appropriate precautions to protect their fetuses while pregnant.[23] However, the investigators ultimately found no causative link between the birth defects and the hazardous waste landfill or other environmental contaminants.

Activists were unhappy with the design of the study. No tissue samples were taken to test which environmental contaminants might be present within residents' bodies, although activists had repeatedly requested such biomonitoring. They charged that environmental samples were

FIGURE 15. Rey León (with megaphone), Linda McKay (with sign, in front), and other activists marching with Kettleman City residents to protest the birth defect cluster and planned expansion of the Chemical Waste Management hazardous waste landfill, Kettleman City, July 18, 2009. Photo by author.

taken well after the period of exposure that could have triggered the birth defects, during a period when the landfill was nearing capacity and therefore accepting less waste; the site had been much more active when the mothers were potentially exposed. The analysis did not address how the multiple toxins to which Kettleman City residents are exposed could interact to cause poor health outcomes: air pollution, drinking water contamination, pesticide exposure, and the possibility of contamination from the hazardous waste landfill.[24] And the investigation relied on Chemical Waste Management's self-reported pollution data despite its history of violations.[25] This is not uncommon; environmental enforcement relies heavily on data generated by industries themselves about their own practices.[26]

Even if tissue samples had been taken, cumulative impacts of multiple toxic exposures considered, and environmental monitoring data gathered closer to the time of the mothers' potential exposure and by the state itself, it would have been difficult to establish a causative link between the birth defects and potential environmental exposure from the hazardous waste landfill or other sources. The town's small size reduces the validity of the kind of conventional statistical analysis relied on by regulators, and the birth defect cluster was therefore seen as potentially just a statistical anomaly.[27] It is difficult even in laboratory environments to prove causation. In politically vulnerable places like Kettleman City—targets of environmental racism and environmental classism—residents are often exposed to a combination of air pollution, water contamination, and pesticide drift, in addition to the possibility of exposure to hazardous waste. In these cases it is nearly impossible to draw definite causal (rather than correlative) links between particular environmental pollutants and associated health outcomes. There is no clear "pre-" and "post-" exposure status to make comparison easy, and there are many confounding factors from many sources. Kettleman City and other rural agricultural towns like it also have large populations of farmworkers, many of whom move regularly to find new work. They are thus exposed to different pollutants in different locations throughout their lives. Thus, the very thing that makes many Kettleman City residents more susceptible to health problems in the aggregate—their multiple exposures to environmental pollutants over the life course—is also the thing used to deny specific environmental connections to their individual health problems.[28]

State agencies often use the lack of scientific proof of a causal link to a singular source as a reason not to take action, unless residents can apply sufficient political pressure. As sociologist Lauren Richter puts it, "the type of monitoring, data production, and analysis deemed actionable by the state are neither conducive to nor aligned with decades of methodological advancement in the science of cumulative chemical contamination in ecosystems and human bodies."[29] Because of the difficulties in scientifically linking environmental exposures to individual health outcomes, activists call for regulations that follow the precautionary principle. Such regulations would shift from requiring the victim to prove harm to instead requiring industry to prove the safety of the pollutants and processes in question. Adopting this approach would radically reorganize environmental regulation and the economy and has gained little support in government.

After the Kettleman City health study found no direct causal link between the landfill and the birth defect cluster, Chemical Waste declared itself vindicated and moved forward with its plans to double the size of the landfill. The company also moved forward with efforts to extend the permit of the site's relatively new bioreactor. During this time, activists pushed the EPA to pay closer attention to the landfill's management. Around the same time, President Obama appointed Jared Blumenthal to head the EPA's Region 9 offices, which oversee the Pacific Southwest. Blumenthal began an internal investigation into his agency's dealings with the landfill, and in April 2010 the EPA charged Chemical Waste with violating PCB disposal rules. Activists discovered that the EPA had found traces of PCBs in soil near the facility as early as 2007 but had done nothing about it. The EPA also found that Chemical Waste had disposed of prohibited waste for five years, between 2005 and 2010, and that its lab analyses had been flawed due to problems with the calibration of its measurement tools. Chem Waste was fined $400,000 and required to upgrade its laboratory to the tune of $600,000. Several months later, the California DTSC fined Chemical Waste Management $46,000 for failing to report spills of toxic materials as required by law—the latest in a string of such violations documented by the DTSC since 1983.[30] Yet the EPA continued to assert that none of these problems posed a health threat to local residents. In 2012, the California Department of Public Health reported that the birth defect rates in Kettleman City appeared to be returning to the baseline rates seen before the birth defects identified by activists in 2008–2009, and in 2014 the County Board of Supervisors approved the permit to expand the landfill, allowing the landfill to expand to accommodate an extra 5.2 million metric tons of waste.[31] No legal settlement was ever made to the parents of the children born with birth defects.

Beyond the Birth Defect Cluster

Throughout the long fight over the birth defects and the proposed expansion of the landfill, activists also continued to respond to other potential pollution threats. Around this time, they learned that a new 600-megawatt power plant slated for construction in the neighboring town of Avenal was being exempted from the most up-to-date versions of federal clean air regulation, instead being grandfathered in under older, looser rules. Activists were still concerned about the Westlake Farms Composting Facility's human waste recycling project, which had yet to be finalized at the time of the birth defect cluster.[32] Residents also lived with the persistent air pollution of the Central Valley, one of the most polluted air basins in the nation—in EPA parlance, an "extreme non-attainment zone" because its air pollution had exceeded federal and state air pollution standards for years.[33] Indeed, once a year regional news outlets all dutifully report on the "F" grades given to the air quality in many San Joaquin Valley counties by the American Lung

FIGURE 16. San Joaquin Valley air pollution, as seen over State Route 99, October 14, 2011. Photo by author, previously published in Perkins, Voices from the Valley.

Association. In addition to this regional air pollution problem, Kettleman City residents are exposed to localized pollution as a result of living directly adjacent to Interstate 5, a core north-south transportation corridor heavily traveled by diesel trucks, which emit carcinogenic exhaust. Finally, government studies conducted after the investigation of the birth defect cluster found traces of pesticides on the floors inside Kettleman City homes, though at levels declared not to be health threats. Such studies also raised the public's awareness of the (already documented but not widely known) contamination of the town's drinking water, which contained benzene and arsenic beyond the legal limits.[34] While arsenic is naturally found in the local soils, the benzene contamination of the groundwater is a result of earlier nearby oil drilling, dating back to the 1920s. Indeed, two of the street names of the small town refer back to this past: General Petroleum Avenue and Standard Oil Avenue.

Activists tackled these sources of pollution with support from foundation and government grants, as well as services donated by environmental law firms. El Pueblo and its allies challenged in court the fossil fuel plant to be built in neighboring Avenal, for which the EPA had waived the current clean air regulations. Their fellow complainants included Greenaction for Health and Environmental Justice, the Sierra

FIGURE 17. Kettleman City street signs, July 18, 2009. General Petroleum Avenue and Standard Oil Avenue are two of the main roads running through the residential part of Kettleman City. Photo by author.

Club, and the Center for Biological Diversity, and they were legally represented by Earthjustice and the Center on Race, Poverty and the Environment. The lawsuit was ultimately successful, with the 9th Circuit Court of Appeals declaring the EPA's exemptions illegal. By 2015, the power plant was defeated.[35]

Legal actions were not always so successful, especially when they made direct charges of racism rather than targeting procedural problems. In 2011, activists in Kettleman City and their legal representatives filed a complaint with the EPA's Office of Civil Rights over the fact that their original 1994 complaint alleging racial discrimination in the siting of California's three Class 1 hazardous waste landfills in Latinx communities had not been responded to in a timely manner. Indeed, by the time the 2011 complaint was filed, sixteen years had passed from the time the original complaint was filed, without any response from the state, a fate common to many civil rights complaints lodged with the EPA. In 2012, the EPA provided an official response by dismissing the case.

To improve air quality, local activists sought to reduce pollution from truck exhaust in large and small ways. They applied for and received a small grant from the EPA to post signs asking truckers, who often left their engines idling for long periods of time while in town, to instead turn them off. Doing so would reduce the localized air pollution generated by the idling engines. (Note the alignment of government funding with a voluntary, neoliberal response to pollution.)[36] Activists also joined a statewide initiative to reform the regulation of freight and goods movement.

Activists also worked to get residents access to clean drinking water. In Kettleman City, as in many small San Joaquin Valley towns, residents drink the groundwater that sits directly underneath the valley's vast landscape of chemical-intensive agriculture. This groundwater is often polluted by fertilizers, pesticides, and other contaminants that have seeped into the water table over the decades.[37] But groundwater is not the only water nearby; the California Aqueduct flows right by Kettleman City. The water in the aqueduct originates from the snowpack in California's Sierra Nevada mountain range, where it flows downhill and is channeled into myriad aqueducts and canals. This mountain water makes its way south through the San Joaquin Valley, where it is used for irrigating farmland, then is pumped up and over the Tehachapi mountains into Los Angeles, where it is used as drinking water. This long journey provides a vivid example of the phrase used in California water politics, that "water runs uphill toward money."

It is unusual for a town such as Kettleman City to get permission to use this surface water from the Sierra Nevada, for in California, water rights have a long, complex history and are still hotly contested. But with help from "insider" environmental justice advocates working within the government, Kettleman City did get permission to use water from the aqueduct. However, the town could not afford to build a new water purification system to treat the water and hook it up to the existing water infrastructure. Chemical Waste Management volunteered to help pay off the debt on the existing water system in order to make it financially feasible for the town to build the new system. However, the company later put conditions on the offer, using the donation as leverage over the town: it made the money contingent upon the approval of its permit to double the size of the landfill, which was stalled by the ongoing investigation into the birth defect cluster. The landfill's managers claimed that without the expansion, they would not be able to afford the donation—even though their parent company, Waste Management,

FIGURE 18. The aqueduct carries clean mountain water through the San Joaquin Valley to Los Angeles. San Joaquin Valley farmers are allowed to use the water for irrigation, but local drinking water typically comes from often-polluted wells. Photo by author, previously published in Perkins, Voices from the Valley.

had company-wide annual profits of $1.9 billion.[38] To date, the drinking water problem has not been resolved. The benzene from the well water is now being removed from the water and vented directly into the air in Kettleman City, while the arsenic in the tap water, including at the school, remains above legally allowable limits.[39] The State Water Board provides a $10,000 a month grant to allot residents thirty gallons of bottled water per month.[40] Plans to build a new water treatment facility to enable access to the Aqueduct water began in 2009. Chemical Waste received its permit to expand the landfill and paid off the community service district's debt so that they could apply for a grant to build the new water treatment facility. It was completed in 2019, but as of 2020 was still not operational.[41]

Activists from Kettleman City remained largely focused locally, on Kettleman City itself, regularly directly targeting local polluters with protests and lawsuits. However, other NGOs pursued more insider tactics, seeking to influence statewide policy advocacy on behalf of Kettleman City and the other two towns that host the state's three Class 1 hazardous waste landfills. The California Environmental Justice Alliance (CEJA) worked to pass Assembly Bills 1330 and 1329. Neither

El Pueblo nor its primary nonprofit partner, Greenaction for Health and Environmental Justice, is a member of CEJA, but Kettleman City activists' longtime collaborators and frequent legal representatives at the Center on Race, Poverty and the Environment were part of the network. AB 1330, which did not pass, was introduced by Assembly Speaker John Pérez to, among other things, identify "environmental justice communities" and prioritize funneling state resources to them. AB 1329, also introduced by Pérez, was passed in 2014 and requires the DTSC "to prioritize an enforcement action" to reduce the disproportionate environmental impact in the "most impacted environmental justice communities," as identified by CalEPA. One CEJA activist describes AB 1329's history as follows:

> *Interviewee:* There was Kettleman City, there was Buttonwillow [which hosts another Class 1 hazardous waste landfill in the San Joaquin Valley]. They were both going through hazardous-waste expansion permits. There were also proposals to ship radioactive waste to the hazardous-waste facilities. At the same time, there were a lot of illegal-dumping issues that were coming up, and there were a lot of bio-solids issues.

> *Interviewer:* The sewage sludge stuff [for example, the Westlake Farms human waste composting facility next to Kettleman City].

> *Interviewee:* Exactly. There was stuff going on in Hinkley, and stuff going on in the [San Joaquin] Valley. Our new lawyer's project was to tackle all of these different things. This was a real civil rights issue. All of the Class 1 hazardous waste in California, all of those processing facilities are in low-income communities of color. So it started off as, the DTSC, the Department of Toxic Substances Control, needs to create a plan for how to reduce these impacts on communities. One of the frustrations we often have is that the legislation says, "Create a plan," but then there's no requirement to actually do anything with the plan. So the original bill was: you create a plan, and then DTSC needs to create regulations to implement what comes out of the plan.

> *Interviewer:* And the plan would be to mitigate?

> *Interviewee:* To mitigate and to reduce those disproportionate impacts. They've created plans before on, like, how do we reduce waste, and how do we divert more into recycling, and stuff like that. But they haven't talked, specifically, about, how do we reduce the disproportionate impact?

> *Interviewer:* Okay. And even those other plans—they would make plans, and then they wouldn't implement them?

> *Interviewee:* They don't necessarily, they kind of sit on a shelf. And so this bill was, we create a plan, and we create regulations based on that plan, that then get implemented, that actually will reduce the impact.

> *Interviewer:* And having the legislature force the issue.

Interviewee: Forcing it, and also creating a mechanism where there'd be some oversight, so if [DTSC] didn't do that, then we could go back to the legislature and be, like, "Hey, look, the bill said this. You're not doing that," as opposed to just leaving it up to [the agencies] to decide what to do. That didn't get very far with DTSC and the various committees, because it was a little, like, "What's all this about?" In that original conception, there was this enforcement piece, to make sure that enforcement happens in the communities that are housing these things. And so that was a piece of it. The great irony was that the language around developing the plan, and around the regulation coming out of it, sort of got taken out of 1329. We were left with the enforcement piece. And then in July, DTSC announced that it was proposing to grant the expansion permit for Chem Waste in Kettleman City. They said, "Hey, we're going to [let the Kettleman City landfill double in size], but we're also going to create a plan to reduce hazardous waste disposal in the state by 50 percent by 2025." So we had language in 1329 about a plan that they didn't like, but they came back and they took the idea of a plan, and they were, like, "We're going to give this permit out now, but we're going to create a plan."

As this activist points out, the bill was significantly watered down from the original vision: it replaced a legislatively mandated plan to reduce waste with a plan that depended on the state agency in question to voluntarily create one—which, as we have seen with voluntary actions in general, is a weak tool. In addition, the new voluntary plan was announced alongside the decision to approve the landfill's proposal. Nonetheless, activists did win language that prioritizes the enforcement of environmental laws in communities identified by the California EPA as "the most impacted environmental justice communities."[42]

To identify and map these "most impacted" communities, activists also participated in government workshops to help develop the California Communities Environmental Health Screening Tool, or CalEnviroScreen. In a roundabout way, this tool was a result of Assembly Bill 32, the California Global Warming Solutions Act of 2006, as well as years of work promoting the concept of cumulative health impacts.[43] As chapter 5 details, AB 32 legislated a cap-and-trade program as the cornerstone of California's efforts to reduce greenhouse gas emissions from industrial sources. Funds generated from the sale of emissions permits went into the Greenhouse Gas Reduction Fund to be spent on projects to further reduce greenhouse gas emissions. In response to AB 32, Senate Bill 535, passed in 2012, mandated that one-quarter of the proceeds in the Greenhouse Gas Reduction Fund benefit "disadvantaged communities," and that 10 percent of the Greenhouse Gas Reduction Fund be spent directly in those communities. The bill tasked CalEPA with creating a system to identify those communities. The result was CalEnviroScreen, which the Office of Environmental Health Hazard Assessment designed, building on many years of activist engagement with the EPA around the subject of cumulative health impacts.

CalEnviroScreen was used to create the 2014 list of disadvantaged communities (which included Kettleman City) that would receive the money from AB 535. CalEnviroScreen will likely be used for other legislative purposes, such as fulfilling the mandate of AB 1329 to prioritize environmental enforcement in "environmental justice communities." Given the landfill's long history of legal violations, extra attention to the enforcement of environmental laws will be useful in Kettleman City, but it will not solve the problem of cumulative impact from multiple legally allowable pollution sources, which cluster disproportionately around low-income communities and communities of color.

Many environmental justice activists hope that CalEnviroScreen can be used for more aggressive purposes in the future. Here, a Kettleman City activist describes her hopes for the tool:

> I think that the whole cumulative impact movement—that's the big deal right now, cumulative. And that's fantastic. But they're using it to leverage funding to vulnerable communities, like CalEnviroScreen. . . . They're using it to leverage those funds that are available for environmentally impacted communities. We need to go a step beyond that, and make sure that they use that for the planning process, that if you say, for example, Kettleman City, that's designated as the top ten percent of California communities that are environmentally vulnerable. When you see that, you say, "Oh, I'm not going to permit this new project that's going to pollute there, because they're a vulnerable community. It says over here, on their screening tool."
>
> I think that that's the logical next step, that we use that for the permit process, not just for leveraging funds. Because leveraging funds is just throwing money at the problem after. It needs to be a preventative thing, too, and they need to use it when they're even thinking about signing these facilities.

While activists hope the tool will be used to limit new industrial development in already overpolluted communities, commercial interests are working to make sure that does not happen.

THE IMPACT OF THE CHANGING POLITICAL CONTEXT ON KETTLEMAN CITY ACTIVISM

As described in chapters 2 and 3, the California environmental justice movement—and Kettleman City activism—has evolved along with the changing political context. Industry and government have changed their tactics; changing racial politics means that there are fewer displays of overt racism. Chemical Waste has instituted new public relations efforts targeting the local community and hired a Latino as the community relations staffer for the landfill. Indeed, Chemical Waste's parent company, Waste Management, now professes its commitment to environmental justice.[44] Waste Management is a member of the Business Network for Environmental Justice, formed in 1995 by the National Association of Manufacturers. In 2012 the vice president for federal public affairs, Sue Briggum, was even featured in the video series made by the EPA Office of Environmental Justice to commemorate its twentieth anniversary.

These changed tactics have complicated activists' ability to recruit continued opposition to the dump, for some residents feel they have less to be angry about now that officials are less likely to ignore or insult them. Activists have also won more opportunities to participate in environmental decision-making processes. As compared to the anti-incinerator battle, public hearings are now more likely to be translated, and documentation is more likely to be offered in multiple languages. This reduces people's anger and sense of being disrespected—emotions that helped contribute to their early willingness to use disruptive tactics. Many residents have also become exhausted by the protracted fight and are now somewhat resigned to the dump's seemingly eternal presence, or they have been replaced by newcomers unfamiliar with the town's history with the landfill.

Participation, Public Relations, and Changing Forms of Racism

As longtime Kettleman City activists describe, the newly cordial relations between Chemical Waste and residents make it more difficult for them to create real and lasting change. The seemingly cooperative relationship with the landfill administrator, for example, does not reduce the risks posed by the landfill itself:

Interviewee 1: Bob Henry's the general manager [at the landfill]. He's a very nice man. I mean, it's his job, and I understand. He's never told us—at least not like Sylvia Vickers—remember their old manager? Who would call us ignorant people, and stupid people? He's pretty smooth. But his business is detrimental to our health, so unfortunately—

Interviewee 2: Yeah. He—he is a nice person.

Interviewee 1: He's a nice man.

Interviewee 2: We've got nothing bad to say about him. He never treats us bad or, you know, stuff like that. It's just like she said, it's his business. And it's our business, you know, to be against it, so—always that low conflict. But he is a nice person to talk to and stuff. He doesn't make you feel bad. Like that day [on the tour of the landfill], he didn't make me feel bad or say, "Oh, you're with them." He's like, "Oh, go take a tour. Go have something to eat." You know, he was really nice. But, yeah, and they—

Interviewee 1: But the bottom line is they still store chemicals there.

Interviewee 2: Yeah.

Interviewee 1: They still have, you know, 98 diesel trucks per day running through our town. They're still going to have gases escaping. Just last year they got slapped on the wrist by EPA because they didn't have their water, their liquid monitors on in the—the municipal and toxic waste that was layered. So there was leakage there for ten years that was never monitored. They've gotten fined for improper storage of PCBs. You know, no matter how nice they are, no matter how many tours you go on, that doesn't make that go away. And like we said he's a nice man, but you know, he's in a business that we don't agree with.

Despite Chemical Waste's kinder face, activists find that some of these broad changes are only skin deep. For example, one activist recounts taking a tour of the municipal landfill in neighboring Avenal, where Kettleman City youth attend high school:

You know why they give money to schools. It's like the municipal dump in Avenal. I took a tour of that a couple of months ago, and the manager said the worst thing when he came out. We're concerned about [that landfill] 'cause it's a local community, our kids go to high school there, we don't have a high school. They go to Avenal High School. He came out, and the first thing he did was extend his hand and say, "Do you know how much money I've given to Avenal High School?" Before he said anything else. [Laughter] And then we took the tour, and they had these long pipes in the landfill that monitor liquid leakage and gas emissions. And we said, "Well, how much is going to be leaking out? I mean you have all these monitors." "Oh, EPA requires them, but we don't expect anything to leak. Nothing's going to leak." I said, "Why would EPA require leakage monitors if they didn't expect it to leak?" I said, "Everything leaks when it's breaking down." I said, "I'm not a scientist, but I know when stuff is decomposing, it turns to liquid." "No, not here." And then we saw these big, huge holes and all this machinery moving all this dirt around. And we said, "You know, there's a very high incidence of Valley Fever here in Avenal and Kettleman City."[45] I said, "And I can't imagine that you moving these tons of earth is going to help it." I said, "What are you going to do to prevent that? I mean, is there a plan?" And he says, "Oh well, you have to resign yourself to the fact that living in the Valley, you're going to get Valley Fever. So you might as well get it over with." The

attitude is like, you're going to get sick anyway, why fight it? Just unbeliev-
able the arrogance in people that work in these businesses. They can explain
anything away. They can justify anything.

Although this activist is unmoved by the increasingly friendly landfill
staff, the same cannot be said of all residents. Beyond the emotional
wear and tear of sustained social change efforts, many are less motivated to continue the landfill fight without the impetus of anger at disre-
spect and overt racism. As described in chapter 3, the changing political
backdrop of the state and nation, particularly the shift from overt racism to "smiling" racism, has complicated activism. In the following an
activist describes her observations on changing racial politics from the
vantage point of a lifetime of participation in the movement:

> I think in the past, it was easier to fight, because the racism was more blatant.
> It's different now. . . . I remember during the incinerator fight when I was
> a teenager, the big talk was the meeting where they told everyone, "If you
> speak Spanish, go to the back of the room." And now they have interpreters
> there, and they ask you, "Do you need a headset to interpret?" and all that.
> You know, they're smarter about it. They'll hire people that speak Spanish,
> that look like us, culturally, that act like us, culturally, but that are really
> company people. . . . I've seen company spokespeople come and go, come
> and go, in the past 25 years. But the most recent one is Latino. He speaks
> Spanish. They brought him to live in the town, and so people relate to him.
> He goes to church with everybody. His wife started teaching Catechism. He
> goes around shaking everyone's hand after church. People relate to that. The
> companies weren't that smart before, but now they are.

As this activist points out, when residents are angry at blatant racism, it
is "easier to fight" for environmental justice causes. The pleasant, neigh-
borly Latino company representative—an example of the company's
increasing civility—has undercut this activist's ability to mobilize her
neighbors against the landfill. In the late 1980s and early 1990s, Kettleman City was almost entirely united in its fight against the hazardous
waste incinerator, but Chemical Waste's new friendliness and its Latino
PR man have gained it supporters in town, as this activist describes:

> At the September 18th meeting, the company spokesperson walked in with
> all these people with these shirts that said, "I'm a Kettleman City resident,
> and I support Waste Management." And it was disheartening. Our first reac-
> tion was, "Oh, let's pack up and go home. The people want this." But then
> I started looking at those people, and those people have been here less than
> five years. They don't own homes; they're all renters. A lot of them don't have
> documents. They're undocumented. So, he's talking to them, and sounds real
> nice, and he's giving them a tee shirt, and they showed up. But do they, in

their heart—does anyone in their heart, could they say, "I want more toxic waste where I live," with a straight face? I dare them to say that.

As this activist points out, many of Chemical Waste's new supporters have no experience of the town's long history with the company or with its previous violations and disdainful attitude toward residents. These supporters, she implies, are uninformed about the history of the landfill and politically vulnerable because of their undocumented status. This shift in population over time is another struggle for activists, as long-term supporters leave and new people move in. After defeating the incinerator in the early 1990s, some activists moved away because of fears about the health impacts of the landfill. Others have passed away. Many left for work; farmworkers make up much of the population of this town, and the agricultural labor market's employment practices make it hard to stay in one place for long. One resident said he was blackballed from local employment in response to his activism. But some stalwart activists still remain. The activists in town who now make up the core of the movement are part of a family in which three generations have been working to improve environmental conditions.

Activists are also now better able to access government environmental officials. Again, a Kettleman City resident and activist reflects:

I think we have an unprecedented access to people at agencies that are making decisions. I mean, when my parents were involved in the struggle, I don't recall them being able to call up someone at DTSC and get a meeting now. So, we have an access that wasn't there before, and that's because we work in coalitions, and we get them to come out and listen to problems. . . . So that's a good thing, that we have that kind of access. How much of a difference does it make? I don't know. But, we can get them!

This activist is very well positioned to assess what the town has gotten out of its increased access to state decision-makers and environmental agencies, so the fact that she does not articulate tangible outcomes is significant.

Of course, activists had some wins with the state in the 2000s and 2010s. For example, during the Obama era, activists convinced the federal EPA's Region 9 office to pay more attention to environmental enforcement. They got state politicians to pressure local politicians into doing a formal health study of the birth defect cluster. Starting in 2013, they got the State Water Board to provide $10,000/month to buy residents thirty gallons of bottled water each month. The state has also helped to finance the new drinking water system, and it helped the town get permission to access the California Aqueduct water. However, none of these things were easily won, and not all have had the intended effect. In assessing the outcomes of the improved access to state officials, the preceding speaker may be thinking less of these small gains than she is of the many remaining problems: the air pollution, the pesticide drift, the contaminated drinking water coming out of taps and school fountains, the children with birth defects, and the ever-increasing amount of hazardous waste being stored nearby.

Collaborative and Oppositional Politics

The trends described here—the improvements in participation and access to legislators and state agency representatives—are part of the slow, uneven shift away from oppositional to collaborative tactics in California environmental justice activism. As described in chapters 2 and 3, this broad shift manifests in several ways: an array of stakeholder engagement initiatives organized by state agencies, activists' work to create environmental reporting networks that interface with existing state infrastructure, and the increasing numbers of environmental justice activists and people of color serving in state government. However, not all environmental justice activists across the state participate equally in these forms of collaboration, and such forms of collaboration do not always produce results.

Kettleman City activists remain skeptical of these shifts, and some continue to use more oppositional, confrontational tactics. One activist expresses her position this way, after first acknowledging that enacting some of her ideas for what should happen in government would draw her into more institutional channels:

> I guess that would mean that we have to work on legislation, and lobby, and all that stuff. The thing with that is that you have to be nice, and you have to be polite, and all that stuff. And sometimes I don't want to be nice or polite! [Laughs] I think that's the organizer part that I like, because people say, "Oh, you're angry," and all that. Well, you know what? I feel like I'm fighting for my life, and my community's life.

As this activist describes, some personalities are better suited for collaboration and some for confrontation. She describes another activist, Matt, with whom she works closely, as built for confrontation:

> Matt drives me nuts sometimes, because Matt's a crusader. Matt should have been born in another era, because he has a crusade, and he's going to—to the

death. And a lot of people don't understand that, but I admire that, because there is no compromising with Matt—none! None. It's a source of frustration, and it's a source of pride, too, because if we had more people like that, this would be a very different movement. [Pause] It would probably be a more poor movement! [Laughs]

The speaker here identifies the combative activist style as a double-edged sword. She thinks having more of this type of person would make for a stronger movement, but also knows it would be problematic in the current era of institutionalization, foundation funding dependent on collaboration, and insider tactics. At the same time, this activist is wary of people of color being tokenized within government:

It's dangerous to [support] someone just because of their race, to say, "Oh, he's Latino, and I'm glad he's there because they needed a brown person." Because we don't want a brown person that's just there because they want to check it off their list: "Oh, we have a brown person; we have an African American person. We have an Asian person." We don't want them to be someone that they just check off their list. But at the same time, I know what it's like to come from an immigrant family, farmworker family, with a poor background, and you get educated, and you want a job that makes up for all your struggles to get that education. I mean, I know where [the activists that go into government] are coming from. But I still want to hold them accountable that they're not just that brown face on the checklist. So it's a struggle.

Although the broader California environmental justice movement has been increasingly scaling up to address statewide policy issues, Kettleman City activists are part of another stream within that movement that remains focused largely on local and, to some extent, regional concerns. This is in part because El Pueblo remains a grassroots community group, and members can only do so much.

The Role of Nonprofit Organizations

El Pueblo's external support from nonprofits is vital to its ability to keep going. While Greenpeace played key organizing roles in the early campaign, it closed down its US grassroots toxics campaign in 1997. The Greenpeace organizer most involved with Kettleman City, Bradley Angel, then formed Greenaction for Health and Environmental Justice, which continues to support environmental justice organizing in Kettleman City and elsewhere. The legal support provided to the early movement by CRLA continues through lead CRLA lawyer Luke Cole's organization, the Center on Race, Poverty and the Environment. Cole passed away in 2009, but his organization survives him. Earthjustice also provides occasional legal support to Kettleman City activists.

Despite these close relationships, there can be trouble when on-the-ground resident activists—longtime disruptors—become paid staff within professional NGOs. One Kettleman City resident took on a part-time position at Greenaction in 2011. However, her new role as a paid staff member was weaponized by Chemical Waste Management staff:

> One of the new things that they try to attack—the company spokesman has gone out and told people, "[She] works for Greenaction. She's a paid advocate. She's a paid advocate. She makes all this money to go out and oppose. She wouldn't be opposing if she didn't make all that money." ... I said, "I think that my record of 25 years in the environmental justice movement should speak for the fact that I believe in what I'm doing, whether I'm paid or not." I said, "And I'm sorry that I have to have a job to feed my family, but my message wouldn't change, whether I was being paid or not."
>
> Sometimes I think that—it makes me mad that they say that, and I think, "Well, you know what? I'm going to quit, and I'm going to get another job, and I'm going to do this on the side. What are they going to say then?" But then, why should I quit? Why shouldn't I making a living doing something that I was going to do anyway? But that's a new thing that they've got me and [the other resident who works for Greenaction], that we're paid advocates. ... And it turned really ugly, because they were going for personal attacks. When I went up to speak, all of those people were shouting, "How much money do you make? How much money do you make? Tell us how much you make!"

Activists' work with and for nonprofits has provided immeasurable support for the environmental justice cause in California. However, these kinds of formal institutional connections can also be used to call into question residents' status as "authentic" voices of the community. The tactic of painting local activism as the work of "outside agitators" or paid operatives has a long history in many activist movements: the civil rights movement, labor union organizing, the Black Lives Matter protests in the summer of 2020—all were said to be the work of outside agitators, whether Communists or antifascist groups called "antifa." In the San Joaquin Valley, entrenched economic interests have denigrated grassroots local activism as really originating from "outsiders" in San Francisco, who are labeled with the conservative epithets "environmentalists" and "Communists."

There are other disadvantages, too. When activists work in paid positions at nonprofits, the organizations must spend time fundraising to pay activists' salaries. Not only does this fundraising take up time that could otherwise be spent on activism, but organizations often tailor the projects they take on to available funding. One Kettleman City activist describes this in her discussion on how contemporary environmental justice activism has changed from its earliest years:

> I think it has to be more strategic now, and I'm not sure if that's a good thing, or a bad thing. I mean, I think it's good to have a mission, and a focus, but strategically, you have to work towards wherever your funding stream is, and so I think that limits people. That limits them on which fights they're going to pick up, and that's unfortunate, because it's a different feeling than when you would say, "This is wrong. We're going to go and fight that." Now it's like, "This is wrong, but I don't know if we have any funding to work towards that." So that kind of gives people what I call "cubicle mentality," where you're working towards whatever your grant is. And that's—it's a little constricting.

As this speaker points out, movement institutionalization shapes movement strategy toward what can be funded; as I pointed out in chapter 2, funders are less likely to fund disruptive activism. This activist further points out that the friendlier face of industry has made invisible the effects of decades of disruptive action. Many residents do not see that current benefits provided by local industries are concessions that were forced out of them by prior rounds of oppositional activism:

> It makes me mad that Waste Management can get away with that stuff. If somebody doesn't say something, they will. And what makes me even angrier is when I think of all those good things that they promised the town, that they're going to fix our water; they're going to get sidewalks for us. They're going to give money to the schools, and all that. People don't realize that if we hadn't made such a fuss, they wouldn't even be getting that stuff. They're trying to compensate for all the opposition that we put up. They're trying to compensate by giving people stuff, and people don't realize that, that they would have pushed it through without giving them a dime.

Movement Schisms Caused by Diverging Tactics

The scaling up of California environmental justice activism into state-level policy advocacy has been uneven. Kettleman City activists have tended to remain local and continue disruptive and legal tactics, but work by other environmental justice groups on statewide policy advocacy impacts them. Not all groups that have scaled up into state politics have been able to effectively involve all of the people across the state who will be impacted by the policy changes they advocate. It is

FIGURE 19. Inaugural meeting of the California Environmental Justice Coalition, Kettleman City, November 8, 2014. Photo by author, previously published in Perkins, "Slideshow: Environmental Justice Coalition Founding Conference."

increasingly difficult for these groups to embody the "We Speak for Ourselves" slogan of the early environmental justice movement, which prioritized the voices and strategic decision-making capacity of grassroots activists. Policy work is complex, is highly technical, and often hinges on exclusive behind-closed-doors negotiations and last-minute decisions about compromise, making it impossible to engage in lengthy community consultations at each step. Because statewide policy efforts have many more stakeholders, it's far more difficult to arrive at a consensus than when work is on the small scale of the individual town. This tension between the desire to scale up and the problem of adequate representation and involvement of grassroots activists and residents is only intensified by the ideological differences over tactics, personality conflicts, competition for funds and "turf," and other areas of difference. All of these differences have strained the movement's cohesion and created schisms, despite these groups' common goals.

One example of how these conflicts play out in movement alliances and organization structures is the creation of CEJA and CEJC, described in chapter 2. When CEJA formed, it excluded Kettleman City's activist group El Pueblo para el Aire y Agua Limipo and their allies at Greenaction. As a result, in the fall of 2014, Kettleman City hosted the first meeting of the newly formed California Environmental Justice Coalition (CEJC), an open organization that aims to bring together voices from across the environmental justice movement to weigh in on political concerns in the state capitol. (The meetings were held in the Kettleman City community center, showing how residents make use of the funds provided for the building by Chemical Waste to organize for environmental justice.) However, because CEJC lacks the funding stream and staffing of CEJA (CEJA has sixteen staff members at the time of this writing, while CEJC has none), CEJC has been a less visible presence in state politics.

Environmental Injustices Go Unaddressed by Elite Environmentalism

While tensions internal to the environmental justice movement inevitably crop up, environmental justice organizations are still unified by their focus on low-income communities and communities of color. For the most part, they also eschew the market-based forms of environmentalism that much of the broader environmental movement has embraced since the neoliberal turn of the 1980s. These distinctions are vivid in the example of the charging station for electric cars in Kettleman City. In 2018, Tesla opened one of its two first supercharger stations in the country at the Kettleman City exit from Interstate 5. At $35,000–$124,000 per car, Tesla's cheapest electric cars cost more than twice the $15,656 average annual income of Kettleman City residents. The supercharger station starkly juxtaposes the high-status, environmentally conscious consumer products available to the wealthy with the hazardous conditions in which the poorest live, highlighting the divergent environmental realities of Californians. This reality is likely invisible to the Tesla owners who stop in Kettleman City, who generally do not venture beyond the small part of town made up of the off-ramp businesses that cluster around the freeway exit. The Tesla drivers likely leave their homes in safer, healthier neighborhoods and pass through the San Joaquin Valley agricultural landscape without much noticing it, except perhaps to hold their noses and complain about the smell of manure as they pass by the concentrated animal feeding operation of cows at Harris Ranch. If they notice the California Aqueduct that runs parallel to and periodically crisscrosses under the freeway, most won't understand the long history of water politics that shapes who can and cannot access this clean mountain water, which makes its long journey from the Sierra Nevada to Central Valley agriculture and thirsty Los Angeles consumers while bypassing the many small, poor San Joaquin Valley towns in desperate need of clean drinking water. They will pull off briefly in Kettleman City to recharge the car and perhaps rest in the Tesla customer lounge, complete with craft drinks and a place to play with their children and pets. They may even amble over to the faux "Western town" storefronts built nearby in 2014 to attract their business, never realizing that a more accurate history of the West is only a few blocks farther away, where oil and agriculture have left their mark on the land and the people across generations. After their short break, the Tesla drivers will get back on the road, headed toward their final destination somewhere else, the perpetually environmentally threatened Kettleman City receding in their rearview mirrors. As a result, the example of the Tesla supercharger station in Kettleman City is also a reminder that market-based environmental products such as Tesla's do little to directly address the pollution borne by the state's poorest, who must continually defend themselves against the environmental threats of racial capitalism.[46]

KETTLEMAN CITY AS A MICROCOSM OF (UNEVEN) CHANGES IN THE ENVIRONMENTAL JUSTICE MOVEMENT

Kettleman City's thirty-plus years of environmental justice activism highlight a number of dilemmas for contemporary environmental justice activism. First, its history of residents' exclusion from participating in legally required public processes of environmental decision-making shows how important improving these decision-making processes has been. However, its recent history shows that improved processes of decision-making and increased public participation do not necessarily result in more favorable outcomes for activists, and there is a cost to cooperation with either state agencies or industries. When interactions with state agencies turn from negative to pleasant, residents are less motivated to oppose them. The example of Kettleman City also shows how institutionalizing activism into nonprofits can play an important role in sustaining community activism over time but can also provide an opportunity for opposing industries to target paid activists as inauthentic voices controlled by outside political forces. Kettleman City also shows that activists can extract some concessions from industry, such as financial mitigation, local amenities, and investments (community center funding, school donations, money to help build drinking water infrastructure). While environmental justice activists work hard for these concessions, they would prefer the direct reduction of health risks through greater pollution control instead. As was also described in chapter 3, however, even such concessions can undercut community opposition to the industry in question, which makes it harder to exert political pressure to more meaningfully resolve continuing pollution and risk.

The anti-incinerator struggle was a victory that continues to give. There is no hazardous waste incinerator on the site of the landfill. Therefore, the dioxins and other pollutants that would have resulted from it are not being added to the air hour after hour, month after month, year after year. The defeat of the power plant in nearby Avenal represents a similar victory. Both show that if not for activists' strenuous efforts over decades, Kettleman City residents would be living with even more pollution than they do now. But despite these victories, residents still live with a hazardous waste landfill, industrial agriculture, and a sewage sludge operation nearby. The air they breathe, the water in their kitchen taps, and much of the land around them contains substances hazardous to the environment and to human health, and so their struggle continues. Where Kettleman City activists remain largely locally focused, the next chapter turns to activists pursuing policy change in the state capitol to address another problem that also disproportionately affects marginalized communities: climate change.

California Climate Change Bill AB 32

Case Study of Policy Advocacy

Chapter 4 showed how early activist tactics and strategies played out in Kettleman City, and how activism there changed over the years as the broader political context facilitated movement institutionalization into nonprofits and the state. Here, I describe a series of fights led by the more recent style of California environmental justice activism: the battle to shape the state's landmark climate change bill, the California Global Warming Solutions Act of 2006 (AB 32). This case study traces the workings of scaled-up, state-level, professionalized policy advocacy and describes both the risks and benefits of this approach. It highlights tensions between oppositional and collaborative approaches to working with the state, focusing on how the larger racialized, neoliberal frameworks of capitalism have constrained environmental justice activism. As I show here, much of the early fight over AB 32 was a kind of last-ditch action against a neoliberal market-based environmental "solution": the cap-and-trade approach that was eventually implemented. While environmental justice advocates were able to use their allies in the legislature to influence the content of what became the Global Warming Solutions Act, the implementation was up to the California Air Resources Board (ARB), and advocates were unable to stop cap-and-trade.[1]

This chapter begins with the lead-up to the law's passing in 2006 and traces the events of the next eight years, describing both the negotiations over the bill's content and the specifics of early implementation efforts (which included a lawsuit brought by environmental justice activists against the state ARB). The focus on this period of the passing and implementation of AB 32 provides a close-up analysis of several key moments of the bill's early life that have had lasting impacts on climate change policy, raising questions that continue to plague later policy advocacy efforts, summarized at the end of the chapter.

This chapter shows how limited the power of governmental environmental justice advisory committees is, as well as the divergence of opinion between environmental justice activists who try to get what they can from existing systems and those who press for better systems. This particular fight strained the California environmental justice movement, with some activists resigning themselves to California's cap-and-trade programs for the revenues it would provide to environmentally vulnerable communities and others continuing to oppose it wholesale, seeing it as violating the founding principles of the movement. The events described here dramatize the changing political context to which environmental justice activism has had to adjust.

While a comprehensive study of AB 32 is beyond the scope of this chapter, some of the bill's technical details are examined in depth. These details show how minute differences of wording can make the difference between policies that environmental justice activists see as beneficial to their interests and those that may do further harm to the communities they serve. They also show the level of technical mastery required to do state-level environmental policy advocacy—mastery that favors professionalized activism supported by paid staff in nonprofit organizational structures, the situation that is most likely to provide the time and training required by policy work. Tracing the evolution of these details' inclusion and exclusion in the bill, as it was negotiated, shows another form of expertise required of activists: the ability to track a maze of multiple policy, electoral, and legal initiatives over time. This also favors paid advocates who can devote themselves full-time to the effort.

CLIMATE CHANGE AND THE ENVIRONMENTAL JUSTICE MOVEMENT

Although much of the early environmental justice movement focused on local campaigns against particular polluters, as in Kettleman City, local issues are related to larger issues, at both the national and the global levels. To keep these broader impacts, such as climate change, from disproportionately blowing back on already environmentally marginalized communities, environmental justice activists have often

FIGURE 20. Oil refineries abutting residential areas of Wilmington, November 16, 2013. Photo by author, previously published in Perkins, "Research Trip to Los Angeles."

scaled up to work on these larger issues. One clear example of how the drivers of global climate change have also long generated local risk in low income communities and communities of color is the oil explosion in Wilmington, a predominantly Latinx neighborhood in LA.

Wilmington directly abuts the Port of Los Angeles and also sits adjacent to multiple other industrial sites and polluting activities. Some of the modest ranch houses that line Wilmington's residential streets have oil refineries as next-door neighbors, looming above their roofs a stone's throw away. Residents from this neighborhood have long lived with high air pollution levels and the threat of industrial accidents that face all fence-line communities. In the 1960s, one long-term resident recalls, the Fletcher Oil Refinery across the street from his house exploded. His father, pregnant mother, five siblings, and grandmother and grandfather next door all felt it:

> It was near dinner time, around 5 o'clock. Mom just yelled, "Kids, come and eat!" So I'm on the way, treading down the hallway, six years old, killing time, and my little sister, we're all growing up there. And then "boom," explosion. It was so loud—I mean you could hear it, obviously. But it shook the whole ground so much, it knocked me down. So, here I was running down the hallway, fell down, because the whole house just rattled so much,

FIGURE 21. Aftermath of the Fletcher Oil Refinery explosions and fire, Carson, March 28, 1969. Photographer unknown, Herald Examiner Collection, Los Angeles Public Library.

you know, we fell down. And then we could see one of the storage tanks burning.... You know that things are on fire, the potential that's spreading and getting worse—you don't wait to see. So, mom and dad say, "Okay kids, we're all going to jump in the car, we're going to take off and we're going to go down to nanny or grandma's house and Aunt Lupe's house," and they're like, eight blocks away. So, we're all out running into the station wagon, and then boom, a second one blows up. And then you could feel the heat wave too. It is so hot.

A third explosion quickly followed. Accidents and chaos quickly made driving impossible. The family escaped on foot, jumping over the back fence and running, all suffering from first- to third-degree burns. When the debris settled, investigators found that a thirty-thousand-gallon tank of oil had exploded, causing the lid to fly about seven hundred feet and land on nearby Main Street, and four other tanks went up in flames as a result. Ultimately, 154 people were injured and 2 died.[2]

Disasters like this are not the only threat of living so close to heavy industrial operations. The air is dense with pollution in places like

FIGURE 22. Port of Los Angeles, November 15, 2013. Photo by author, previously published in Perkins, "Research Trip to Los Angeles."

Wilmington: ships come into the port; cranes, trucks, and railway cars remove cargo from the ships to be transported around the country; and oil refineries next door and urban fracking fields elsewhere in Los Angeles fuel this industrial economy.[3] All of these pump pollutants into the air people breathe, threatening humans with asthma, acute bronchitis, and premature death.[4] These are the local threats that activists in Wilmington fight. But the fight has scaled up, for the same fossil-fuel transports and industries that pollute the air also emit the greenhouse gases that contribute to climate change. Environmental justice activists battling such industries have therefore long been battling climate change, although most only began to explicitly frame their work that way in the 2000s.

In the global climate change arena, environmental justice activists alternately work with and against the broader environmental movement. Environmentalists who work on climate change tend to focus on the impact of greenhouse gas emissions on global climate change, while California environmental justice advocates pair the impact of greenhouse gas emissions on global climate change with the local impact of the associated air pollutants in places like Wilmington. But as Angela Park has argued, the broader environmental movement would also benefit from adopting an environmental justice framework. When environmentalists frame greenhouse gas emissions only as a global problem and a global pollutant, they lose an opportunity to widen their political base by linking climate change to people's daily and local concerns: transportation, public health, jobs, and pollution from industrial facilities. These are the areas of life that environmental justice advocates are already tackling. It is desperately important to broaden the base of support for climate legislation, because a large proportion of the US population does not believe that man-made climate change is real. Given the coming changes in demographics described in chapter 3 (by 2042, the majority of the US population is projected to be made up of people of color), Park argues that it is increasingly important to connect with Latinx, Black, and Indigenous people and Asian Pacific Americans to create and sustain effective climate change responses. Environmental justice advocates are ideal ambassadors for this work of connecting climate change impacts with local, felt issues in order to draw in the communities of color with whom they are already working.[5]

The urgency of climate change brings these conflicting approaches into contact with one another, exacerbating existing disagreements between environmental groups and environmental justice groups. It also highlights the difference between the two groups of activists that originally caused the movements to part ways: much of the US climate change movement remains dominated by upper- and middle-class white people, who are often willing to gloss over the exclusion of people of color and the working class. As Park eloquently puts it:

> To many in the environmental justice movement, bringing up issues of race, class and power is like the burden of Sisyphus, the protagonist of the Greek myth who was forced to roll a boulder up a steep hill, only to have it roll down so he could roll it up again. There is immense frustration in raising the same issues and naming the same dynamics, over and over. At the same time, they are often maligned for being overly sensitive or stuck on this "race issue" in a dynamic similar to what other subordinated groups experience when they flag discrimination or disparate impact, intentional or not.[6]

Mainstream environmental groups are often wary of partnering with environmental justice groups, if they consider them at all. Environmental justice advocates have their own reservations about such partnerships. One environmental justice advocate involved in the AB 32 struggle puts it bluntly: "Usually in this type of arrangement when mainstream environmental and environmental justice groups collaborate on a single issue, we get 'screwed.'"[7]

While the California experience of creating climate change policy serves as a microcosm of the ongoing tensions between environmental justice activists and the broader environmental movement, it perhaps more crucially highlights the benefits and limitations of policy advocacy as a tactic within the environmental justice movement itself. The rest of this chapter focuses on the involvement of environmental justice activists in six key early stages of the California Global Warming Solutions Act from 2006 to roughly 2014, before turning to a brief update on what has happened since. First, it examines the years before the 2006 passage of the bill, tracing environmental justice activists' opposition to the inclusion of cap-and-trade as the bill was drafted and amended, articulating how activists succeeded in inserting environmental justice safeguards into the bill. It then turns to the period after the bill's passage, from 2007 to 2008, as environmental justice activists advised ARB on the first contentious Scoping Plan that would guide the bill's implementation. It lays out environmental justice activists' lawsuit against ARB over the first Scoping Plan, which was litigated between 2009 and 2012. It then describes the activists' and ARB's creation of the five-year update to the Scoping Plan, which took place between 2013 and 2014. It traces the period from 2009 to 2012, when activists sought to leverage their limited successes with the plan for implementation of AB 32 to benefit "environmental justice communities" by directing revenues from the cap-and-trade plans into these locations. A final section briefly summarizes how the conflicts of these early years have persisted in the politics that continue to surround AB 32's ongoing existence.

THE FIRST BATTLE: NEGOTIATING AND PASSING THE BILL

California passed pioneering clean air regulations in the 1980s that established the nation's first fuel and other energy efficiency standards. These regulations paved the way for later regulation of greenhouse gases, but for years, policy efforts targeting climate change failed.[8] Eventually, in 2006, the state passed Assembly Bill 32 (AB 32), the Global Warming Solutions Act.

AB 32 required that by 2020 greenhouse gas emissions be reduced to the levels from 1990, and by 2050 to 80 percent below the 1990 levels. The bill, only thirteen pages long, charged ARB with developing a plan to accomplish these goals but gave ARB wide latitude in how to do so. (In comparison, the national Waxman-Markey climate bill of 2009 was over fourteen hundred pages, leaving much less up to the discretion of the implementing agencies.)[9] AB 32 would allow ARB to regulate greenhouse gas emissions either through direct regulation (sometimes called "command and control" regulation) or through market-based mechanisms. In the former, the state could mandate pollution reduction levels for entire industries and/or specific facilities; in the latter, market incentives, rather than direct regulation, would encourage polluters to reduce their emissions. These market-based mechanisms aim to reduce emissions at the state level without setting limits on particular polluters or in particular areas. Over time, the ARB developed a complex plan to implement AB 32 that included both command-and-control and market-based mechanisms. However, the centerpiece of the plan to reduce greenhouse gas emissions from industrial sources was a market-based cap-and-trade system.

Under a cap-and-trade plan, the state does not reduce emissions at any particular point of origin, whether it be particular facilities, industries, or regions. Instead, it sets a state level for overall allowable carbon emissions—the "cap"—and creates a market in which the rights to emit greenhouse gases are bought and sold. This gives individual emitters the option to either reduce their own emissions or purchase unused emission credits from other emitters. Often "offsets" are built into the system. For example, an individual industrial facility may continue to emit greenhouse gases by paying for an environmental benefit elsewhere. For example, the facility might pay to keep a forest from being cut down so that it continues to do what forests do: absorb carbon dioxide from the air. Some of these might be international offsets, as with the REDD (Reducing Emissions from Deforestation and forest Degradation) programs. These programs use money from industrialized countries to preserve forests in developing countries. In 2010, California began working toward creating agreements that would allow California polluters to pay for forest offsets outside of California instead of reducing pollution inside California, much to the consternation of California environmental justice activists and some Indigenous groups in countries that would be the recipients of such offsets. California environmental justice activists want carbon emissions and associated cuts in health-threatening air pollution to take place in California's most polluted communities, while some Indigenous groups in Latin America fear their land tenure will be threatened by REDD programming that may kick them off their lands to "save" it.[10]

Environmental justice groups have a number of concerns about cap-and-trade, which potentially intensifies existing patterns of environmental inequality. Greenhouse gas–emitting facilities are disproportionately located in low-income communities and communities of color, and while greenhouse gas emissions alone are not thought to pose a direct health threat to surrounding communities, they are usually accompanied by emissions of other air pollutants that do.[11] If cap-and-trade causes carbon emissions to increase in some locations (despite causing a net reduction at the state level), local air pollution could also increase in those same places. For example, industries in low-income communities and communities of color expand their production over time might decide it is cheaper to purchase carbon credits than to reduce their carbon emissions. This would reduce emissions in other areas (the areas where industries are selling their unused credits) while increasing pollution in the target areas. These types of localized increases and state-level decreases in air pollution would intensify existing inequalities. Similarly, if offsets go national or global, the benefits of retaining forests would accrue to other states or countries rather than improving the air quality for environmentally burdened communities in California. As people of color are disproportionately among those exposed to the highest pollution levels, such offset programs would fit neatly into existing structures of racial capitalism.

Despite these problems, which were obvious to environmental justice activists, two large mainstream environmental groups supported AB 32: Environmental Defense Fund (EDF) and the Natural Resources Defense Council (NRDC). These two groups practically cosponsored AB 32 with the legislators who formally introduced it. EDF made a point of including environmental justice advocates in the creation of the bill and hired a Latino staffer specifically to promote the bill to legislators of color and environmental justice organizations. It did so, at least in part, as a defensive measure, worried that the California environmental justice community would enlist the Latino Caucus and other legislators of color to block AB 32 if it did not address their concerns.[12] This evidences environmental justice activists' increasing clout in state politics, due in large part to their connections to the increasingly large number of voters of color and the legislators they elect. The environmental justice advocates participated to ensure that the reduction of greenhouse gases at the state level would be accompanied by public health improvements at the local level.

Early versions of AB 32 included a directive for ARB to use a cap-and-trade system, but as noted earlier, the final bill simply gave ARB the option to use a cap-and-trade system. The cap-and-trade requirement was dropped in large part because of environmental justice activists' participation in the legislative process. Some of these activists have long been anti-corporate. Indeed, early activists expressed opposition to corporations in one of the seventeen "Principles of Environmental Justice" formalized at the 1991 First National People of Color Environmental Leadership Summit, which stated that "Environmental Justice opposes the destructive operations of multi-national corporations." Some saw environmental justice activism as emerging in the 1980s to offer an explicit alternative to the dominant market-based discourses of the time.

Environmental justice activists (like some environmentalist groups) had concerns about the cap-and-trade system above and beyond its potential to exacerbate environmental inequality through air pollution "hot spots" as previously described. First, they were skeptical that cap-and-trade programs would reduce greenhouse gas emissions overall: the state might set the carbon cap too high, or it might allow offsets that do not truly reduce carbon emissions.[13] Offsets fail when they are allocated to conservation projects already planned, which would occur regardless of the offset. Offsets also fail when they do not change the overall balance of emission versus absorption: an offset might avoid forest destruction in one location but destroy a different forest somewhere else as a result. In policy language, these failures are referred to as problems of "additionality" and "leakage." Furthermore, important details of the design of cap-and-trade programs are vulnerable to corporate lobbying. They also worried that market-based solutions tended to shut out input from community members. While low-income people do not have the financial capital to participate in *market* systems for buying and selling greenhouse gas credits that influence how emissions are distributed in space, they can participate in *political* systems that funnel decisions about industry emissions and locations through processes of public comment, processes that were mandated by the environmental regulations passed in the 1970s.

Instead of market-based solutions, environmental justice advocates favored direct regulation of greenhouse gas emissions. But even among the market-based alternatives, cap-and-trade seemed like the worst option. Environmental justice activists preferred a carbon fee program, known as cap-and-fee, under which the state applies carbon fees to increase the price of fossil fuels and encourage the use of renewable energy sources. Activists argued that the carbon fee would reduce greenhouse gas emissions (and therefore the accompanying air pollutants) more evenly across all regions. Carbon fees are also more transparent and much simpler to administer than cap-and-trade, which is so complex as to require an entire new bureaucracy to administer it.[14] A carbon fee would be put in place through existing government structures. Environmental justice advocates generally prefer transparent systems so that they can more easily track and organize around the issues that affect their constituents. Under a cap-and-trade system, affected parties do not know where emissions are traded to until after the fact, and even then, the information can be difficult to come by because the names of the companies that participate in auctions, as well as the bids they place, are not made public.[15] The carbon fee's simplicity and transparency make it less vulnerable to problems of corruption and "leakage."

Environmental justice advocates did not get all that they had hoped for in AB 32. Like most bills, AB 32 was passed through a multifaceted political process involving not only environmental and environmental justice activists, but also party politics, pressure from polluting industries, the chamber of commerce, and perceived voter preferences. But environmental justice advocates did lobby for and extract some key concessions, which became particularly important in their battle against the first Scoping Plan that ARB developed to carry out the Global Warming Solutions Act. As the activists would claim in court, the first Scoping Plan did not fulfill the environmental justice requirements they had worked so hard to include in the bill's language.

First, the bill's language *allowed* the implementation plan to use market-based regulation of greenhouse gas emissions (broadly understood to mean cap-and-trade), but it did not *require* it. This language represented a compromise between two groups: the Republican Party, Governor Arnold Schwarzenegger, and EDF favored a cap-and-trade mechanism, while Democratic representatives and the environmental justice community were against it.[16] One interviewee describes this process as follows:

> I was involved in that process, and in one particular phone call where we were negotiating with the Schwarzenegger administration. It was over what would be in and what would be out and how it would be worded, and they wanted us to sign off on the difference between "may" and "shall" on cap-and-trade. And there was just no way that environmental justice advocates were going to say that this program "shall" include cap-and-trade, and that's what the governor's office wanted. We told them, "Look, we're not going to do it. We're just not going to support it. We will bite our tongue with "may," but if you put in "shall," we're going to oppose, and we're going to oppose as forcefully as we possibly can, and we will do everything we can to stop this bill from going through.

The bill's final language did indeed say "may" instead of "shall." This compromise should have effectively postponed decision-making about cap-and-trade to the implementation phase of the bill. However, within a year after the bill was passed—before ARB had even created the Scoping Plan, a process that should have involved assessing cap-and-trade against other options—Governor Schwarzenegger began negotiating regional and international cap-and-trade programs.[17]

Second, environmental justice groups successfully lobbied to include the directive that the chosen greenhouse gas reduction strategies must take into consideration "the potential for direct, indirect, and cumulative emission impacts" in communities that already had high levels of air pollution.[18] AB 32 requires that there be no increases in criteria air pollutants as defined by the EPA, which include ozone, particulate matter, lead, carbon monoxide, sulfur oxides, and nitrogen oxides. The inclusion of this language was significant, for it promised not only that *specific air pollutants* would not increase under the plan, but also that the *cumulative toxins* to which low-income communities and communities of color are exposed would not increase. As we have seen, cumulative impacts are a key environmental justice concept that takes into account all the pollutants to which people are exposed in particular places. Environmental justice advocates frequently push for regulatory bodies to make decisions based not just on legally acceptable increases in individual pollutants, but on the ways that individual pollutants add to the toxic burden of already highly polluted communities. However, an overwhelming majority of public policy does not incorporate an analysis of cumulative impacts in decision-making.[19]

Three other provisions in the bill directly addressed additional environmental justice concerns. First, AB 32 mandated that an environmental justice advisory committee be formed to advise ARB on the development of the implementation plan. According to the bill, this advisory committee would be made up of "representatives from communities in the State with the most significant exposure to air pollution, including, but not limited to, communities with minority populations or low-income populations, or both"—in other words, residents of "environmental justice communities."[20] Second, the bill required public workshops to be held in these communities so that residents could comment on implementation plans for achieving the mandated reductions. Finally, the bill included a "Community Empowerment Amendment" that ensured that "activities undertaken . . . do not disproportionately impact low-income communities" and that "the state board shall ensure that greenhouse gas emission reduction rules, regulations, programs, mechanisms, and incentives under its jurisdiction, where applicable and to the extent feasible, direct public and private investment toward the most disadvantaged communities in California."[21] While the inclusion of these provisions and this language evidences environmental justice activists' (and their constituents') increasing clout in the legislature, this moment turned out to be a high-water mark for activists' influence on the Global Warming Solutions Act.

THE FIGHT CONTINUES: IMPLEMENTATION

The Environmental Justice Advisory Committee (EJAC) mandated by AB 32 was intended to give activists a formal role in advising ARB on its Scoping Plan, developed to guide implementation of the bill. The EJAC was convened through an informal process, with Jane Williams of the California Communities Against Toxics (CCAT) playing an important role and a number of leading environmental justice advocates participating.

Committee members were appointed by ARB in January 2007 and conducted meetings through 2009. During these two years, they met with ARB staff to learn about the agency's work on the bill and to make recommendations for how the bill should be implemented across a number of highly technical areas. They made official recommendations for revisions to ARB's reports on early action measures, the regulation for the mandatory reporting of greenhouse gas emissions, a draft and the final Scoping Plan, the low-carbon fuel standard, and the proposed screening method for identifying low-income communities with heavy air pollution. The Scoping Plan, in particular, was the focus of much of their work. The EJAC proposed a three-pronged approach to reduce emissions that combined direct regulation, financial support to help industries reduce their emissions, and a carbon fee to incentivize compliance.[22] The committee explicitly advised against the market-based mechanism of cap-and-trade. As scholars have repeatedly pointed out, structural racism is deeply rooted in the broad, long-lasting framework of capitalism, making capitalist interventions unlikely to address the root of the problem.[23] As the EJAC put it, "It is market-based decisions, within a framework of structural racism in planning and zoning decisions, that [have] created the disparate impact of pollution that exists today; relying on that same mechanism as the 'solution' will only deepen the disparate impact."[24]

Committee members faced a difficult battle to block cap-and-trade. Even though the language of AB 32 ultimately called for the bill to "maximize co-benefits," such as reducing air pollution by reducing greenhouse gases, some politicians and government officials argued that using climate change legislation to address air pollution was inappropriate. This point of view was clearly articulated by Dan Scopec, then the undersecretary for the California EPA. (Scopec is an example of the "revolving door" between industry and the EPA; when he left the EPA, he became the vice president of regulatory and legislative affairs for San Diego Gas & Electric and Southern California Gas Co.) Scopec put it this way:

> [A] lot of people use the issue of global warming to tackle the problems that they've been working on for the last 10, 15, 20, 30 years, and I think that these problems are not necessarily related to global warming. I think that's a folly that we all have to be careful about. . . . The challenge is so great that it should be the sole focus of this effort. Using the umbrella of global warming to satisfy other agendas is really going to distract from the solution and create inefficiency. So as we go forward, I hope that we can all focus in this effort on the problem of reducing greenhouse gases and not try to solve everyone else's unsolvable problems in other areas.[25]

This quotation highlights the institutional resistance to incorporating environmental justice concerns into climate change legislation. Here, Scopec dismisses environmental justice activists' concerns as "unsolvable problems." Unlike climate change, he implies, environmental racism and environmental classism are inevitable, not even worth addressing.

The EJAC did support many of the tools included in the draft and final Scoping Plan, including energy conservation measures and increases in the production of renewable energy. However, the committee's suggestions were not binding on the ARB. (See chapter 2 for a more extensive critique of the problems with such advisory groups.) According to the environmental justice advocates, ARB did not incorporate most of their suggestions into the Scoping Plan, nor even meaningfully respond to many of them.[26] One activist writes, "While the ARB followed the letter of the law in creating the committee, it did not live up to the spirit of the law," and committee members "consistently felt as if the ARB had already made up its mind on key aspects of implementation of AB 32 before EJAC had the opportunity to provide input."[27] All the activists' time and effort felt wasted, diverted from other work, for despite committee members' staunch opposition to cap-and-trade, it was proposed as the key mechanism for meeting emissions reduction targets.

ONE MORE TRY: THE LAWSUIT

In 2009 a number of environmental justice advocates and organizations, including individuals who had been members of the EJAC, sued ARB over the Scoping Plan.[28] The plaintiffs charged that the outcomes of implementing the Scoping Plan as written would violate a number of the provisions and mandates in the original bill. They also charged that the process of creating and adopting the plan had violated procedures required by the California Environmental Quality Act. The cap-and-trade proposal was at the heart of many of these claims.

Shortly after environmental justice activists filed their suit, EDF asked the court for permission to intervene in the case on the side of ARB.[29] EDF is a staunch supporter of market-based environmentalism in general, and cap-and-trade in particular. The group made a name for itself by adopting a collaborative approach with business that it calls "third wave environmentalism." (Fittingly, longtime executive director Fred Krupp first described this approach in the logging industry's trade journal, *Pulp and Paper*.)[30] Judge Goldsmith, who heard the case, did not allow EDF to join the lawsuit alongside ARB as an affected party, but he did later allow it to participate as an amicus curiae, or "friend of the court," allowing it to offer information relevant to the case. Relations between EDF and the environmental justice advocates, which had never been strong, quickly turned downright chilly.[31] (See the appendix for an overview of environmental and environmental justice opinions about cap-and-trade at the time of the lawsuit.)

Reform-oriented organizations each choose their own methods for achieving their goals. Some partner with more powerful entities to achieve some of their goals while compromising others; some work to pull together enough popular support to force more powerful entities to change course. EDF has chosen the first path. In its own words, "EDF . . . is more than willing to stand up to polluters—but it will also sit down with them if there's a chance to make progress on key goals. . . . They deal with the world as it is, not as they wish it to be."[32] This approach has inspired vehement criticism from others in the environmental movement. In an article titled "Environmental Defense Fund: Stop Your Sell-Out to the Gas Industry," Wenonah Hauter, the executive director of Food and Water Watch, criticizes EDF's effort to promote a middle path between the interests of anti-fracking activists and anti-regulation businesses:

[EDF comes] swooping into states where there is a strong grassroots movement against fracking and shilling for the oil and gas industry. They will claim to represent environmentalists while they promote regulation that is so weak even the gas industry can live with it. Of course, everyone in the environmental movement knows that this is EDF's modus operandi. In fact, for years, public interest advocates have rolled their eyes and complained to one another in private about how EDF undercuts their work time and time again. But everyone is afraid to speak out because they might upset funders, who are turned off by disagreements among environmentalists. Maybe it's time to redefine exactly what protecting the environment means. People are ready to fight for what they really want. They don't want to settle for some weak compromise that was negotiated without a strong fight.[33]

Here, Hauter points out the gulf between the tactics and locus of power in organizations like EDF (which, as she frames it, seems co-opted by industry) and those of local grassroots organizations. Like EDF, environmental justice advocates recognize the need to attract more political support for climate change legislation. However, unlike EDF, environmental justice activists see political support coming not from industry but from residents in low-income communities and communities of color. Their constituency is victim of disproportionate pollution, not polluters.[34] Hauter's criticism also highlights the influence of funders on environmental activism, which she argues has limited grassroots groups' abilities to protest the actions of another environmental organization, EDF. Funders have made their preferences clear in California's climate change battles, too. One foundation withdrew funding from a California environmental justice organization over its participation in the lawsuit against ARB that attempted to stop cap-and-trade, even though its funds were not going toward the lawsuit.

EDF is not the only mainstream environmental organization to espouse the pragmatic, "collaborative" attempt to work with industry rather than against it. Many large, mainstream environmental organizations in the United States (with the partial exception of the Sierra Club) have supported a cap-and-trade mechanism.[35] During the lawsuit, environmental justice advocates found themselves at odds with not only EDF but also NRDC, the Union of Concerned Scientists, and the Nature Conservancy.[36] However, the press coverage's simplification of the conflict into "environmentalists" versus "environmental justice activists" was misleading. In fact, many environmental organizations opposed cap-and-trade: the Sierra Club, Greenpeace, Friends of the Earth, Rainforest Action Network, and the Center for Biological Diversity have all publicly called for the reconsideration of cap-and-trade and international offsets.[37] This case shows that despite the very real tensions between the environmental movement and the environmental justice movement, the borders between the two movements are increasingly fuzzy.

In 2011, Judge Goldsmith ruled in favor of the ARB, rejecting environmental justice activists' claims that the Scoping Plan violated the intent of the original Global Warming Solutions Act.[38] He ruled that the legislature intended ARB to draw on its own expertise to interpret AB 32 and applied the standard of judicial deference to agency rulemaking: in order to overrule ARB's interpretation, the court would have had to find its decision-making process not merely flawed but "arbitrary, capricious or without reasonable or rational basis." The judge repeatedly stressed this deference in his responses to the individual allegations detailed by the environmental justice groups. For example, he wrote: "Given the latitude of ARB's quasi-legislative powers, it is within its discretion, *right or wrong*, in interpreting AB 32, to choose cap-and-trade as the primary methodology [emphasis added]." The decision was upheld on appeal on the grounds of judicial deference, with the judge writing, "It is not for the court to reweigh the conflicting views and opinions that were expressed on these complex issues, *which in the end are largely matters of judgment in all events* [emphasis added]."[39]

The courts' deference to agency expertise is not unusual in California legal practice, but it is a particular problem for environmental justice activists, who have a long history of criticizing scientific and regulatory experts for not sufficiently attending to the problems of low-income communities and communities of color. Environmental justice advocates are sensitive to the fact that those with political and economic power behind them can manipulate research and regulation. They are also sensitive to the ways in which research and policy, when created by people not intimately familiar with local contexts, can ignore important questions or get things wrong.[40] The environmental justice slogan "We Speak for Ourselves" encapsulates the grassroots movement's efforts to push back against experts who would speak for them on a variety of issues; it asserts that the lived experiences of people from polluted neighborhoods are also a form of expertise, one that must be incorporated into scientific and regulatory processes.

Judge Goldsmith did rule in favor of the plaintiffs on one argument, finding that ARB did not follow the procedures required by the California Environmental Quality Act in its creation of the Scoping Plan. His ruling was a procedural victory, as many of the environmental justice movement's legal victories are; these victories are easier to achieve than those that more directly intervene in the outcome of the problem at hand. In this case, Judge Goldsmith wrote:

> The Scoping Plan fails to provide meaningful information or discussion about the carbon fee (or carbon tax) alternative in the scant two paragraphs devoted to this important alternative. The brief fifteen-line reference to the carbon fee alternative consists almost entirely of bare conclusions justifying the cap-and-trade decision. . . . ARB seeks to create a *fait accompli* by premature establishment of a cap-and-trade program before alternatives can be exposed to public comment and properly evaluated by ARB itself.[41]

This ruling placed a temporary halt on the ARB implementation of *all* aspects of AB 32 (not just cap-and-trade). This caused consternation among much of the rest of the environmental community, who felt that the lawsuit had blocked progress on climate change action. (Indeed, shortly after this ruling, I helped host one of the environmental justice lawyers active in this case to speak at a weekly environmental studies seminar at UC Santa Cruz, where he received a decidedly chilly reception.) However, with the support of environmental justice activists who brought the suit, the court eventually allowed ARB to move toward implementing everything in the Scoping Plan except the cap-and-trade mechanism.

At this point, the political climate changed yet again; in 2010, Democrat Jerry Brown was elected as the next governor of California, replacing the Republican Schwarzenegger. Environmental justice activists hoped that Brown's election might redirect climate politics away from market-based responses—or at least away from cap-and-trade. After his 2011 installment as governor, forty-one groups from California and beyond signed a letter to him asking that he "rescue the California Global Warming Solutions Act of 2006 (AB 32) from the uncritical trust in markets that characterized [former governor] Arnold Schwarzenegger's approach to addressing climate change."[42] However, Governor Brown made no such intervention. In the meantime, when ARB appealed Judge Goldsmith's decision to halt the implementation of AB 32, the Court of Appeals quickly ruled that the cap-and-trade program could move forward with the rest of the Scoping Plan *while* the ARB added the necessary analysis about *alternatives* to cap-and-trade to the Scoping Plan. This decision shows just how shallow procedural victories can be in the context of capitalism. Indeed, the ARB added the required analysis to the Scoping Plan without changing its final decision; the procedural "victory" consisted of having the documents meant to guide decision-making retroactively doctored without ever actually seriously informing the consideration of alternatives to the final decision.

Many activists who had participated diligently on the ARB advisory board left the process embittered. As one put it:

> We were not very successful, basically because it was—we didn't recognize that it was primarily a political engagement that the governor had in mind. He wanted a market-driven program. He was going to get a market-driven program. He replaced people in ARB to get the folks that were going to support that. And we focused more—we were kind of naively focused on— "We're just going to bring up good recommendations, technical recommendations. We can show that this is doable." And we should have understood, I think, from the beginning that this was a political project, that if we could have the best ideas in the world without the political means to back it up, we weren't going to get anywhere. But we didn't recognize that 'til it was too late. So, basically, except for a few recommendations that got included, we got our ass handed to us. So, the final Scoping Plan did not include a significant number of the recommendations that we particularly wanted.

This activist learned that advisory committees often funnel activists into procedural and technical fights that sidestep meaningful change. He also learned that access to and participation in state spaces is not the same as having real power to influence their outcomes.

At first, the legislative and advisory committee work around AB 32 served to unite environmental justice activists. But after a series of losses and differences of opinion about how to proceed, the movement began to fragment, and many activists drifted away from the AB 32 fight and toward other projects, as this activist describes:

> People were demoralized. It was the end of the recession [that began in 2008], everybody is scrambling to make sure that they just kept their doors open. There were efforts to kind of regroup the folks around AB 32. We made several efforts to kind of get people together and we couldn't do it. You couldn't blame them. I'm not critical of them at all. I'm just saying that's where the movement was at. . . . We weren't coming together. [One group] was doing this thing, and [other people] were doing their thing. Folks that are doing work around water, folks that were doing work around ag, everybody doing good stuff, but no communication, there's no cooperation. We'd go to Sacramento and see each other, "Oh, what are you doing up there?" We didn't know, which was not a good thing. That's just where things were. And [as of 2015,] the movement hasn't quite regrouped since then from my perspective, the California EJ movement. They're still pretty fragmented. So, the California movement, it's looked to a lot as a movement that achieved a lot. And taken together we're pretty strong. But I think people don't realize just still how disjointed we are, and that's a problem.

As a final, rearguard action, environmental justice activists filed a civil rights complaint with the US EPA in 2012 about the AB 32 implementation, but the complaint was quickly dismissed. The EPA found that the complaint was not yet "ripe" for review, as it addressed the possibility of future racialized air pollution outcomes resulting from cap-and-trade—an outcome that had not yet happened. The groups that filed the complaint were critical of the EPA's application of this legal standard, angry that they had to wait until after "the ax falls" before remedying the problem instead of taking preventative action.[43] Advocates challenged the dismissal of the complaint, but the challenge was unsuccessful.

CONTINUING SKIRMISHES: AB 32 BECOMES LAW

The EJAC was never formally ended by the ARB, nor did its members have fixed terms of service. Nonetheless, the committee had stopped meeting shortly before committee members decided to sue the ARB in 2009. However, the language of AB 32 requires that the EJAC advise the ARB on updates to its Scoping Plan, which happens every five years. Accordingly, ARB sent out a request for environmental justice representatives to join the EJAC and advise the agency on the development of the 2013 Scoping Plan Update. The new committee met during 2013 and 2014.

Only two of the original members signed up to be on the committee for a second time. The first advisory committee had been made up of longtime environmental justice leaders who pursued a hard line against the ARB, buoyed by their recent legislative successes in getting environmental justice interests into the language of AB 32.[44] One observer describes it this way:

> [Environmental justice lawyer] Luke [Cole] used to say that getting community members at the table would change outcomes. He would say, "If you're not at the table, you're on the menu." But what I've seen in actual practice, with the [US EPA's National Environmental Justice Advisory Council] or the AB 32 Environmental Justice Advisory Committee, is that the community gets a seat at the table, or they're represented there. They got a seat at the table, but they were still on the menu. The menu didn't change, despite them being there. And the frustration and anger that those members had about what it was like to be on the AB 32 Advisory Committee. . . . It was a great case study on why being at the table not only doesn't help you, but it sucks your time and energy. And you end up with nothing. . . . It would be my view that these advisory committees really are just a waste of time.

Despite this disillusionment, two people from the original committee participated, and one organization that had participated in the first round sent another representative. Of the twelve participants in the second committee, 75 percent of the organizations and 83 percent of the people participating in the committee were new. The second committee therefore included a broader array of organizational representatives, some from groups that older activists did not see as environmental justice organizations. One participant in both committees described the difference in motivation, discussing the first group's decision to pursue the lawsuit:

> We were pretty united. Nothing like that could happen with the current committee. We would never be united enough to sue ARB. Most of them wouldn't want to. It was different this time around. It was a much less radical group in total. A lot of the people were there because they're concerned about housing, and planting trees. . . . This time I was one of the most radical people on the committee, because the old guys were all gone, and the new group they got was pretty much mainstream environmentalism. It was not an environmental justice committee any longer. Because it wasn't made up of people who work on the ground with communities any longer, like it was the first time. So, you're not environmental justice if you're not working with—hand in hand, side by side with people who fit the environmental justice community. You know, they're not representing people. They're representing ideas.

The new population of committee representatives and the presence of a professional facilitator, hired to guide the process, led to a markedly different experience, one that seems to encapsulate the environmental justice movement's shift toward institutionalization and collaboration. Where the relationship between the first committee and the ARB was frequently marked by tension and disagreement, the second environmental justice advisory committee had a more amicable experience. ARB staff and environmental justice committee members even went out to dinner at the end of the second round of committee meetings. As one activist who participated in both rounds of the committee observed, "That would never have happened during the first round." An evaluation of the committee's experience during the second round also articulates this new smiling surface, noting, "Both ARB staff and EJAC members were respectful and went out of the way to not repeat the experiences of the previous EJAC; everyone worked together and not everyone had to agree, which was fine."[45]

However, the second committee's recommendations were perhaps less incisive and visionary than the first's. One observer describes the recommendations proposed by the first advisory committee in bold terms:

> Those recommendations were outstanding. They would have made this the most farsighted, innovative effort to reduce greenhouse gas emissions with equity at the center in the whole country, it would have been amazing. And [ARB would] be farther along in achieving some of their goals, if they had taken some of our recommendations.

In contrast, the second committee's recommendations were far more moderate, incremental, and pragmatic, according to the same participant:

> *Interviewee:* We made recommendations, and they ended up being pretty generic. They ended up being so generic in some cases that ARB totally agrees with them. [Laughs] Which probably shouldn't happen, if you're a true environmental justice committee. But just to get them to move a little bit in that direction sometimes is worthwhile. And that was the reason I thought I would be on the committee again, just to try and get a few small changes.
>
> *Interviewer:* So have you found in round two that any of your group's recommendations have been adopted?
>
> *Interviewee:* Not the good recommendations.

Notions of civility are powerful enough that there is a pressure to see civility as a positive outcome in and of itself, regardless of the outcome for the political questions at hand. While the official evaluation (and some EJAC participants) viewed the second committee's less contentious relationship with the ARB as a good thing in itself, it is hard to say that the more amicable process led to better outcomes for environmental justice communities. Perhaps the second round was more amicable because the biggest bone of contention, cap-and-trade, had already been taken off the table, or perhaps it was because the participants were a different set of people, from organizations with different aims and different methods than the original committee. But this raises the question: How effective is it to work with industry or the state on friendly terms? As shown in chapter 4, Kettleman City activists found that newly friendly relations with Waste Management seemed to attenuate the anger that made residents want to protest, and the veneer of civility made disruptive tactics seem gauche or over-the-top, as when the town's young people dumped garbage on the speakers' table at a public forum. Activists and scholars would both do well to remember that norms of civility can be applied to political ends that do not favor justice.

The EJAC is only one of many similar advisory bodies operating throughout California. Environmental justice activists join these committees in hopes that if agencies can be made to understand environmental justice activists' concerns, regulatory outcomes will be better. But as the bitter failing of the first EJAC committee shows, this is not always true, whether the committee relations are fiery and confrontational or friendly and serene. One observer says,

> The organizers with whom I've worked, and many of them elsewhere, say, "Advisory committees are a bunch of bunk. Don't go to anybody's meeting unless it's your agenda. And if it's not your agenda, make it your agenda." So, there's a particular agitational component to that, which doesn't necessarily lead to one getting invited back.

But if the "agitational" types of participants don't get invited back, or choose not to participate, who does? Their absence creates a vacuum into which less confrontational participants step. Another activist reflects further on the process:

> *Interviewee:* We could have been more forceful if we'd had more people on there who wanted to be that way. As it was, we had a real cordial meeting with the staff all the time. On the last day, I said, "Unfortunately, I really feel your whole plan is fatally flawed." And they didn't want to hear that, but I had to tell them that. I mean, that's what I was thinking. I wasn't being belligerent about it.
>
> *Interviewer:* The first environmental justice committee was more forceful, and it wasn't particularly any more effective . . . ?
>
> *Interviewee:* No, we may have actually been more effective this time, by making small gains. But we're not saving the planet, either. You know, we're not doing what's needed. That's the bottom line.

Here, the interviewee points out the problems with both approaches to activism: the "agitational," disruptive activist may not be invited to the table at all, but the collaborative, institutional, incremental reformist gains only small concessions. For the above activist, while policy work can make small gains, these small gains are nowhere near enough. Other committee members do see these small gains as slowly adding up to long-term benefits:

> The first step is getting [environmental justice] in there as policy, is getting it recognized as something that needs to be considered. And as frustrating as it is, ARB is actually now taking up some of the issues that we were concerned about in 2008. So, they're looking at agriculture, they're looking at more industry regulation, they're looking at the effect of co-pollutants. Who knows

what they're going to do with this stuff, or if we're going to like any of it. But they're at least beginning to take the things that we had talked about, and they're actually starting to look at them. So, there's always this delay. There is the time when we've talked about it, and the time when there's action. Our struggle is trying to get that delay to be less and less and less, until actually people are looking at this before they do their policy choices, that they're actually considering these kinds of impacts earlier, rather than after the fact.

Many environmental justice activists continue to persist with committee work in order to effect this slow and incremental change, but many others are far more skeptical. The latter activists do not object to advisory committees just because they do not have a strong enough or immediate enough effect on policy. Advisory committees can also have actively damaging effects. For example, committee participation is sometimes used to defuse and delegitimize activist critiques. When the EJAC sued ARB in 2006, the agency chair, Mary Nichols, commented on a blog post written by a legal observer about the lawsuit: "Our process for developing the Scoping Plan was unprecedented in its openness and transparency, including many opportunities for substantive comment and interaction. . . . Ironically, some of the plaintiffs sit on ARB's Environmental Justice Advisory Committee (created by AB32) and enjoyed unparalleled access to ARB staff and board members throughout plan preparation."[46] Here, Nichols attempts to use committee members' participation to justify and validate the decision-making process and to serve as an alibi for the ARB's eventual decision. Because they participated in the process, the ARB chair implies, their critique of its outcome is illegitimate—even though ARB did not follow their highest-priority recommendation, to not use cap-and-trade. According to another activist who was part of the AB 32 lawsuit, this rhetoric is often used to deflect activists' concerns about outcomes:

> That's now a very common tactic to say, "They were at the table, we included all stakeholders. We went out and got public comment, we had translators there we gave Spanish speakers twice as much time to talk. Gosh, the outcome didn't change at all." Gee, I wonder why. When the new AB 32 scoping plan revision started again and they restarted the EJAC, I was like, "We are not going to do this because ARB does what it wants and it is just jumping through hoops."[47]

These government advisory committees have no direct power to influence legislation or its implementation through creating binding agreements. One participant in both EJAC committees underscores this point, noting that the second iteration of the committee was disbanded by the agency it was advising:

> So this time, they said, "Okay, you're done. We're disbanding the committee. In five years, we'll have another update." And I said, "Wait a minute! You're promising over the next few years to work on these different issues. I think we should meet at least once or twice a year to be updated on how things are going, and to give you more advice." They didn't say anything.

Advisory committee recommendations are just that: recommendations. The institution being advised has no obligation to adopt them. If these committees have any power at all, it does not derive from the committee assignment itself. In the case of AB 32, activists' original power came from their connection to Latinx legislators representing swing votes for the passage of AB 32. But after the legislation was passed and the bill went into the implementation phase, the legislators no longer held power over it. In this phase, the agencies took over as the key actors, and environmental justice activists' connections to legislators of color carried far less weight. Of course, the EJAC derived some small moral authority as the representative of low-income communities and people of color. But this was only a trickle of power—not enough to overturn the market-based cap-and-trade scheme supported by the full power of capitalism.[48]

Even before cap-and-trade was officially a done deal, some environmental activists were making plans to use the revenues it would create to help communities overburdened with pollution. Between 2009 and 2012, they worked on a bill to create a special fund from the profits of carbon trading to be spent on projects in communities that bear a disproportionate exposure to pollution in California. The first EJAC committee explicitly rejected this approach, feeling that people living in heavily polluted areas needed pollution reduction more than money from polluters. As Angela Johnson Meszaros, who cochaired the first AB 32 EJAC, said, she'd "rather have clean air than a gold-plated inhaler."[49] But other environmental activists forged ahead on their own, undercutting the ongoing attempts to keep cap-and-trade out of the AB 32 implementation. One activist describes the efforts by Coalition for Clean Air to get such a fund established:

> My biggest problem with it, and I had a huge problem with it, was the process by which Coalition for Clean Air decided to move forward with this proposal, because it was being done in the context of an ongoing battle of whether or not there would be a cap-and-trade program. . . . And Coalition

for Clean Air decided to start working on this policy of making sure that cap-and-trade revenue would be spent in EJ communities without coordinating well with those environmental justice organizations.

And what happened is, it gives [agency] people something to point to and say, "Oh, well, we'll take care of you with this. . . ." The policy is a good policy, but it shouldn't have been proposed at a time where the whole idea of cap-and-trade was still a little bit iffy. The organization should've worked more closely with the environmental justice allies that were involved in it, so it was better coordinated. . . . Now there's going to be hundreds of millions of dollars spent in environmental justice communities as a result of the success of the policy. But it's a little tainted in terms of . . . it was a very difficult process, and relationships were really strained over it. And I'm hoping that this all works out successfully in the end. The chances of cap-and-trade going away at this stage are pretty slim. But the concerns of environmental justice still exist.

With support from several environmental and environmental justice groups, including Coalition for Clean Air and the California Environmental Justice Alliance (CEJA), the use of cap-and-trade revenues in environmental justice communities was eventually enshrined in SB 535, passed in 2010. SB 535 requires CalEPA to identify disadvantaged communities and invest a portion of the revenues created by the cap-and-trade system in those communities: 25 percent on projects that benefit disadvantaged communities, directly or indirectly, and 10 percent on projects physically located within disadvantaged communities.

There was no consensus about this bill from the environmental justice community: at different points some traditional environmental justice organizations supported it, some opposed it, and many remained ambivalent.[50] A supporter of SB 535 described why CEJA chose to support the bill:

The reason we engaged in that bill was because we felt like AB 32 is an important law in California, and the EJ groups that were part of CEJA worked really hard to make recommendations so that the state wouldn't mess it up in implementation, and to make sure that environmental justice communities were prioritized in the implementation of AB 32. We were in it to make sure that AB 32 got implemented correctly, and that some of those funds would get into EJ communities, and also so that the funds would stay revenue-neutral, meaning that it wouldn't be cap-and-trade money. And at some point, because of the policy process, the funds did purely become cap-and-trade funds. At that point CEJA decided to pull out of being a sponsor. We just felt too uncomfortable. There were a couple of lawsuits that [Communities for a Better Environment] and [Center on Race, Poverty and the Environment] had filed around cap-and-trade. So, we felt like it was going against what we were standing for. And then at some point, last year, I think, we decided to re-engage again, after a lot of conversation around: these funds are moving, and whether we like it or not, they're either going to get into EJ communities, or they're not. And if they do get into EJ communities, they can actually pay for all these things that we want. Like if we wanted Solar for All, and we wanted solar projects in low-income communities, people are constantly asking, "Where are you going to get the revenue, and the funds?" This could be a huge place to get that. So, after a lot of conversation, we came to an agreement that CEJA should support the bill. . . . So that's a bill where we felt like we were in, and then we were out, and then we were in again.

As this activist intimates, some environmental justice activists were already working to secure access to cap-and-trade profits while other activists were still trying to stop cap-and-trade—a clear source of strife. Another environmental justice activist argues that the cap-and-trade revenues are only a temporary stopgap for environmental issues, and that disbursal of the funds will further pit environmental justice groups against each other:

Interviewee: I don't think they're ever going to get much money, and I know they're going to be fighting for it, hard, even with each other, in the end. Because they're going to have to apply for that money, and they're going to have to write grants for it, and it's going to be everybody trying to get the same small crumbs from cap-and-trade. And personally, I just won't go there. Money's not the issue to solve environmental justice—it's putting a Band-Aid on environmental justice problems. It's like they say, "Yeah, we got $100,000 now for south and west Fresno that we can use to help subsidize you buying electric cars, or hybrids, or something. Or insulating your homes." It won't be enough money to do much. It'll make a few jobs, and it'll be like a Band-Aid, yet the big companies will still keep polluting the air in those areas. Nothing will change, in terms of pollution. The few hybrid or electric cars they get, you would never notice it in terms of air pollution. Yet everybody would think that they're taking care of those communities. I mean, we need a massive effort to take care of those communities! You need every car in those communities to be an electric car with a range of 150 miles. And then they need solar panels on every rooftop, and of course, every home needs insulation, and low water appliances, and fixtures, and all of that.

Interviewer: And you've still got the pollution from industry.

Interviewee: Yeah. You've still got to get rid of that, you know. So, I don't know. I just don't like Band-Aid approaches, where the polluters think they reluctantly did something because it's the right thing to do, maybe. Because in the end, I don't see that much change. What I do see is more and more stuff actually is coming up to the [San Joaquin] Valley to be dumped up here.

Many groups felt they were in a double bind. Of course they wanted money for the communities they represented, which needed such investment. But even after the battle over cap-and-trade had largely been lost, they still worried over the source of these funds. As a Kettleman City activist said of the proceeds of a settlement with the neighboring landfill that fund the town's community center, the funds felt "tainted" to some.

As illustrated by the story of AB 32, concessions given within racial capitalism do not change its underlying features. Concessions like the ability to participate in political decision-making via hearings and advisory committees rarely change the most important decisions made, though they do use up a lot of activists' time and give power brokers a potential weapon against criticism. Concessions like the cap-and-trade revenue fund do not necessarily reduce pollution; in the words of Meszaros, they may only offer the means to metaphorically gold-plate your inhaler—and, at the same time, place activists in competition with each other for the money. While environmental justice activists are widely opposed to cap-and-trade and offsets, for both ideological and practical reasons, the ultimate victory of the market-based cap-and-trade agreement did not unify activists against it; instead, it incentivized division, at least for a time. Eventually, some groups came around on SB 535, and the bill was ultimately passed.[51] While the internal conflicts described here can be seen in some ways as just a bump in the road of coalition politics, they are also indicative of the complex political climate in which environmental justice activists must work. Activists rarely get all of what they want in the political realm, and they must constantly negotiate existing systems in order to extract even small concessions.

THE FOREVER WAR

While AB 32 has been passed and cap-and-trade implemented, this is not a closed chapter in California environmental justice history. The conflicts that animated its early years persist as environmental justice activists continue to try to shape California climate change policy. After the debacle of the first EJAC's work with the ARB, activists worked with political allies to change the composition of the board itself. In 2015, the state legislature passed AB 1288, requiring the ARB to create two additional seats, to be filled by people who work "directly with communities in the state that are most significantly burdened by, and vulnerable to, high levels of pollution, including, but not limited to, communities with diverse racial and ethnic populations and communities with low-income populations."[52] In 2017, ARB created a new staff position to serve as an environmental justice liaison, the assistant executive officer for environmental justice; in 2021, the position was expanded and converted into a more senior position, with the title deputy executive officer for environmental justice.[53]

As for the proceeds from the Greenhous Gas Reduction Fund, new legislation was passed in 2016 that increased the amount of funds to be spent on projects physically located in and benefiting disadvantaged communities, raising it from 10 percent of the fund's revenues to 25 percent.[54] But it is hard to tell how much, or even whether, the funds are actively reducing health-threatening pollution levels in such communities. Some spending has clear connections to climate change and to environmental health, but other expenditures are farther away from the original goal of using the funds to reduce carbon emissions or environmental justice activists' broader goals of improving the health of their communities. One of these questionable expenditures is Governor Brown's 2013 grab of $500 million from the fund, which he called a "loan" to the state's general fund (and which was later repaid).

As one interviewee predicted earlier in this chapter, some expenditures have pitted causes against each other. Groups must make "asks" of the Greenhouse Gas Reduction Fund, and they face stiff competition. In 2017, Julie Cart reported that of the less than $1 billion available from the fund, the "lawmakers' wish lists total $3.5 billion, the governor wants $1.5 billion, and the supplicants came in seeking more than $2 billion." She also quotes Max Podemski, planning director for the environmental justice group Pacoima Beautiful, who "was preparing an ask for the first time and wasn't ready for the rush when the public was welcomed to the floor. 'I was sitting there, and all of a sudden there was a stampede' to the microphone."[55]

Official uses of the fund money are also frequently divisive. After a failed effort to pass a water tax, the legislature decided in 2019 to use greenhouse gas reduction funds to help improve drinking water quality for the million Californians who don't have access to clean, potable drinking water in their homes. This use of funds has angered some mainstream environmentalists, because it does not focus directly on greenhouse gas reduction, echoing earlier critiques of using AB 32 to address not just climate change but also air pollution in low-income communities and communities of color. In contrast, many environmental justice advocates have celebrated this decision. As the Asian Pacific Environmental Network's Marie Choi put it, "For us, solutions aren't about carbon counting, it's about making our neighborhoods and people healthy and whole again."[56]

The fight for climate justice in California continues. The original Global Warming Solutions Act, the 2006 AB 32, required greenhouse gas emissions to be reduced to 1990 levels by 2020 and to 80 percent below 1990 levels by 2050. In 2016, the legislature passed a new bill, SB 32, which gave ARB a new interim emissions goal: to reduce emissions levels to 40 percent of 1990 levels by 2030. The 2020 goals were met early, but it is unclear how much of this success was due to AB 32 policies (themselves numerous) or other factors. It remains unclear whether the program will be able to meet the goals for 2030 and 2050.[57]

Prior legislation had also set cap-and-trade to expire in 2020, so in 2017 new legislation was passed extending cap-and-trade beyond 2020. Again, this put environmental justice activists at odds with mainstream environmentalists and oil and gas industries. EDF again played a leading role promoting the bill, and environmental justice organizations again opposed it.[58] Environmental justice activists seized the opportunity, once again pressuring legislators to get rid of cap-and-trade and focus on climate change legislation that would better serve the needs of low-income communities and communities of color. However, despite the opposition of fifty environmental and environmental justice groups, in 2017 the legislature extended cap-and-trade from 2020 to 2030.[59] Environmental justice activists were highly critical of new concessions given to the oil industry, especially those that curtailed state agencies' abilities to directly regulate the greenhouse gas emissions of polluting industries. This constrained local air districts' ability to set carbon dioxide limits on some air pollution emitters that were already covered by cap-and-trade, undercutting environmental justice activists' efforts to set a lower emissions limit for oil refineries in the San Francisco Bay Area. It also prevented ARB from adding any new greenhouse gas regulations to oil and gas facilities; activists had been pushing for this addition as part of the implementation of 2016's AB 197, which required direct emission reductions.[60]

While environmental justice advocates lost ground with the passage of AB 398, the bill extending the life of cap-and-trade, it was passed with a companion bill, AB 617, aimed at improving air quality in heavily polluted locations. AB 617 mandated that local air monitoring plans and/or emission reduction plans be generated with community input. In the first round of AB 617 implementation, ten pilot communities were selected from the regions of the state with the worst air pollution.[61] While it is too early to determine the outcomes, an early assessment suggests that the effort increased public engagement with air quality planning—although, as we have seen already several times, public engagement does not necessarily lead to material reductions in pollution.[62] For measurable reductions, environmental justice activists and others concerned about air pollution must have actual influence on (not just participation in) the creation of the actual plans. Those plans must be enforced by local air pollution control districts and the state ARB, and the public engagement process must retain its funding and influence over time.[63] Many things could prevent these conditions from being met. Accordingly, some activists criticized AB 398, arguing that it was simply a Band-Aid designed to get the extension of cap-and-trade through the legislature, not a meaningful bill itself. CEJA codirectors Strela Cervas and Amy Vanderwarker wrote that AB 617

> currently lacks the teeth and specificity needed to ensure that it will lead to improved health and air quality in our communities. With the range of concessions in AB 398, [AB 617] was simply not enough to justify the full package. . . . This is sadly too often the case in environmental policy: for a win, compromises are made that negatively impact low-income communities and communities of color.[64]

Despite activists' unhappiness with AB 398 and its companion, AB 617, Governor Brown capitalized on California's reputation as a climate leader to host the Global Climate Action Summit in San Francisco in 2018, which drew attendees from around the world. To draw attention to the problems with the bill (and with market-based climate policy in general), environmental justice activists helped organize a pre-summit march that was linked to other protests taking place around the country. In the San Francisco march, an estimated thirty thousand participants protested Brown's embrace of market-based strategies and pressed the governor to end oil and gas production in California.[65]

Governor Brown did not renounce his support for cap-and-trade at the summit, nor did he commit to stopping the production of oil and gas in the state. However, he did sign a bill, passed by the legislature, that required 100 percent use of zero-carbon electricity by 2045 (SB 100)—a goal made less impressive by the fact that "carbon-free" doesn't necessarily mean "renewable."[66] According to the bill, by 2045, up to 40 percent of the state's electricity usage can be provided by hydropower, nuclear, or natural gas combined with carbon capture and storage. At the same time, Governor Brown also signed an executive order to make the California economy carbon neutral by 2045. Here again, carbon "neutrality" relies on a complex series of equivalencies and trades; it does not mean zero carbon dioxide emissions in California itself.[67]

California continues to be one of the largest oil and gas producers in the country, and the Western States Petroleum Association wields enormous power (and money) in the state capitol to defend its interests, as seen in the 2017 extension of cap-and-trade.[68] Between 2011 and 2018, Governor Brown approved more than twenty-one thousand new permits for oil and gas drilling, with the majority of the projects located in communities of color with higher-than-average poverty rates, a sign of the continuing strength of racial capitalism.[69] Thus, the state had one set of policies designed to slow climate change and another set that hastened it.[70]

The state's controversial effort to approve international carbon offsets continues as well. The program that began in 2010 as REDD was later renamed the Tropical Forest Standard. The question of participating in domestic offsets had split the California Yurok tribe, which eventually agreed to use the carbon stored in its forests to sell offsets to California polluters. The question of the new Tropical Forest Standard similarly divided Indigenous groups in other countries, as well as the California environmental community. Larger mainstream environmental groups (including, predictably, EDF) supported the global offsets, while environmental justice activists and many Indigenous groups from Latin America opposed it. Despite the lack of consensus, in 2019 ARB voted to approve the Tropical Forest Standard.[71]

The different priorities of environmental justice activists, environmentalists, and California environmental regulatory bodies continue to reverberate through California politics, and, increasingly, national politics. After Joe Biden was elected to the presidency in 2020, longtime California Air Resources Board chair Mary Nichols emerged as the top contender for the position of national EPA administrator. California environmental justice activists submitted a letter to the Biden-Harris transition team opposing her appointment. They critiqued her embrace of cap-and-trade, her support of carbon offsets, her disregard of many of the key proposals made to ARB by the EJAC, and the ongoing racism within the agency under her watch.[72] Nichols was replaced with another candidate, likely as a result of the California environmental justice movement's opposition to her candidacy.

As the story of Nichols's candidacy shows, the environmental justice movement continues to push the environmental movement writ

FIGURE 23. Delegation of Indigenous leaders touring California to oppose the REDD program of international forest carbon offsets, Berkeley, October 16, 2021. Berenice Sanchez Lozada from Mexico at right, US-based Tom Goldtooth of Indigenous Environmental Network at left. Photo by author.

large to do more and do better. As CEJA executive director Gladys Limón put it, "[Nichols has] had just indelible achievements. That can't be questioned. . . . (But) it's unacceptable to continue down that path in a way that disregards communities that have borne the brunt of our fossil fuel-based economy and who have the worst air pollution." Nichols's removal from candidacy rankled parts of the broader environmental movement, but few environmentalists made their dissatisfaction public—a sign of the environmental justice movement's growing power.[73]

The dissatisfaction with cap-and-trade continues, and its equity outcomes are not yet fully understood. Some research into the question highlights concerns similar to those environmental justice activists raised years before. In 2016 and 2018, Lara Cushing and colleagues released papers showing that many industrial facilities actually increased their emissions after cap-and-trade was put into place—just as activists had warned they would. Cushing and colleagues compared the first three years of the operation of cap-and-trade to the two years before the program was implemented and found that 52 percent of the regulated industrial facilities increased greenhouse gas emissions and their associated co-pollutants, even as total statewide emissions remained below the cap set by ARB. The researchers also found that facilities that increased their emissions were more likely to be located in neighborhoods with higher proportions of people of color, lower incomes, and few English-speaking households, just as activists had predicted. However, the researchers did not definitively attribute these outcomes to cap-and-trade, and argued that the outcomes they wrote about may change over time, either as the overall cap decreases or through new policy initiatives designed to reduce out-of-state offsets and improve equity outcomes.[74] In contrast, Danae Hernandez-Cortes and Kyle Meng find some positive equity outcomes in the post cap-and-trade period, asserting that between 2013 and 2017, cap-and-trade began to narrow the gap between disadvantaged groups' pollutant exposure and that of other populations.[75] Both sets of research have had their methodologies critiqued.[76] Additionally, some scholars have argued that the reduction in California's greenhouse gas emissions after cap-and-trade's implementation were largely due to factors other than cap-and-trade itself, such as importing out-of-state energy that is less carbon intensive, rather than actually cutting greenhouse gas emissions generated within California itself.[77] If so, the benefits of reducing the co-pollutants that accompany greenhouse gas emissions are accruing to places outside of California rather than to California's environmentally disadvantaged communities. Environmental justice activists' efforts to steer climate change policy toward interventions that would meaningfully limit greenhouse gas emissions while simultaneously improving the health of the people who currently bear the brunt of the pollution from industrial facilities continue unabated.

As this chapter has shown, some of California's actions show promise for reducing both greenhouse gas emissions and health-threatening air pollutants, and activists working in the policy and legislative arena continue to have some successes. In addition to those already described, they have successfully ensured that electricity generated by incinerating trash does not count as "renewable energy" in California, and they have reduced some of the harmful impacts of solar energy generated on large-scale solar farms, particularly those on Indigenous lands in the California deserts.[78] However, the history of climate change politics in California thus far suggests that environmental justice advocates must continue to pay close attention to policy for it to have any chance of prioritizing the needs of low-income communities and communities of color. As the debates over cap-and-trade and offsets show, legislators must pay attention to not only *if* benefits or negative impacts accrue, but *where* they accrue.

Environmentalists and politicians across the country continue to debate how to best tackle climate change via policy interventions, and California's experience is worth learning from. California has long been a trendsetter for US environmental policy and leads the nation in efforts to reduce greenhouse gas emissions. Since its launch in 2012, California has operated the second largest cap-and-trade market in the world, after Europe. The state's carbon market scheme has expanded beyond its borders; California is part of the Western Climate Initiative, which shared the carbon trading markets of California and the Canadian provinces Quebec and Ontario until Ontario pulled out in 2018. If its Tropical Forest Standard moves forward, California's carbon market will be integrated into international offsets as well. California's role as a model for other states and the federal government amplifies the importance of what happens there, as debates about a national "Green New Deal" that continually reference California have shown. But California's experience with climate change policy should be seen as not just a model, but also a warning, for the deep environmental and equity problems that remain.

The dizzying array of climate policy initiatives, and the technical details of many of them, show the importance of having environmental justice activists who can devote time to understanding, following, and intervening in these policies. This task is far easier when it is undertaken as a paid, full-time job; it is difficult to achieve this comprehensive understanding during the little time left over after work and family obligations. Thus, the environmental justice movement's involvement in statewide climate policy both results from and drives the movement's trends toward professionalization and institutionalization. The case of AB 32 shows both the limitations and the importance of policy advocacy, as legislators need environmental justice activists to counterbalance pressures from industry, which largely represents the interests of racial capitalism. Without environmental justice activists, the state's environmental outcomes would be far worse.

Addressing climate change poses an enormous challenge. It is difficult to make people understand that climate change is both real and extremely serious. It is difficult to make legislators and voters do something about it. It is especially difficult to do what is most needed for both people and the planet—to directly reduce greenhouse gas emissions and associated air pollution at their source in the places that emit the highest levels of both—as the battles over cap-and-trade and offsets shows. The level of change required from corporations, governments, and communities to respond effectively to climate change is staggering. The powerful will continue to offload as many costs as possible away from themselves, leaving the less powerful to bear much of the burden. At this moment, California—and the world—needs environmental justice activists to keep the needs of the less powerful at the forefront of climate change response. It is the right thing to do, and it is also the strategic thing to do, for without confronting the entrenched powers necessary to reducing greenhouse gas emissions and pollution at their points of origin, in the places where the world's most disadvantaged live, we cannot hope to slow climate change. Professional environmental justice activists employed by NGOs do their best, but they need mass movements, both to give their efforts more weight and to keep them accountable to the lived realities of low-income communities and communities of color.

Conclusion

Dilemmas of Contemporary
Environmental Justice Activism

I spoke to environmental justice activists across the state while researching this book, and I heard multiple interpretations of whether or not
California's environmental justice activism is succeeding. Some activists gave me enthusiastic descriptions of all the movement has accomplished, while others were demoralized, telling me that the more things
change, the more they stay the same. Both are understandable responses
to the facts at hand. Many things have changed since the early years
of environmental justice activism. Much of the movement has shifted
from a largely grassroots, disruptive movement to a professionalized
movement institutionalized inside nonprofits and the state. The movement's goals are now enshrined in policy, at least in theory: government
statutes direct both the federal and state government to consider the
environmental justice implications of all decisions made by all branches
of government. In 2014, the EPA celebrated the twentieth anniversary
of President Clinton's executive order on environmental justice. Environmental injustice is tackled in college classes throughout the nation
and an ever-increasing number of nonprofits.

California environmental justice activists have even more reasons to
celebrate. The California Environmental Protection Agency now has a
full-time assistant secretary for environmental justice and tribal affairs,
and similar positions exist in a number of its boards and agencies.
Former environmental justice activists occupy positions in the California Public Utilities Commission, the Department of Toxic Substances

Control, the State Water Board, the Air Resources Board, the governor's office, and more. Environmental justice activists occupy both elected and appointed positions in city governments and on local and regional regulatory boards. Activists and community residents regularly attend government hearings that are now equipped to allow both English speakers and monolingual Spanish speakers to participate. Some media outlets and journalists consistently cover environmental justice activists' work. Activists have flexed their muscles on policy advocacy initiatives in the state capitol, playing important roles in halting the construction of incinerators and power plants, walking back the agricultural industry's exemption from the Clean Air Act, creating pesticide buffer zones, banning the brain-damaging pesticide chlorpyrifos, gradually cleaning up the ports of Los Angeles and Long Beach, passing the nation's first law recognizing clean drinking water as a human right, and reducing air pollution levels across the state, among many other efforts.

Other seeming successes have had decidedly mixed results. Some companies (even those opposed by environmental justice advocates) now regularly use environmental justice language. Environmental justice activists are invited to participate on steering committees and advisory boards. Hostility between activists and government has, by and large, decreased, and in some places activists collaborate with government and corporations; many environmental justice activists have framed awards and public recognition from a variety of state agencies on their office walls.

And yet these many years later, much also remains the same. Study after study, including a twenty-year update to the iconic 1987 report *Toxic Wastes and Race*, documents the disproportionate burden of pollution that low-income communities and communities of color continue to bear.[1] Residents of these communities are surrounded by heavy air pollution, noise, and unpleasant smells. They live near ports and refineries, with diesel fumes permeating the air and dangerous chemicals stored nearby; they live near mega-dairies that leach nitrates from cow manure into their drinking water, create bad odors, and draw flies; they live next to agricultural fields from which pesticides drift into their homes; they live near toxic waste landfills and illegally dumped wastewater from fracking; and they live near factories that leak toxins and pollute the air. Accidents at industrial facilities next door send neighbors alternately running through the streets or sheltering in place in their homes. Residents turn on the taps in their kitchen sinks and watch brown or sediment-filled water come out—or, perhaps worse, seemingly clean water that looks and tastes fine but is contaminated with arsenic, nitrates, or pesticides. They live near sites where urban fracking vibrates the earth, cracking the windows and foundations of their homes, and where parents check air pollution alerts to see if it is safe for their children to play outdoors. While some problems have been improved, many have not. California pesticide use levels have not meaningfully decreased; indeed, 2018 use levels were the third highest since 1990, when standardized reporting began.[2] And now we know more about the dangers these conditions pose: scholars increasingly report the damage wreaked on community health, linking pollution exposure to more hospital visits; higher rates of cancer, asthma, and other illness; and earlier death.[3] The little research that tracks racialized groups' comparative exposure to pollutants over time shows mixed results, but most find little significant change.[4]

Even victories are not permanent; they are always at risk of being rolled back as the political winds change. One activist has received a great deal of attention for her work in high-profile, successful battles with the Port of Los Angeles, located next to her neighborhood, yet she has a hard time feeling celebratory:

> We were very cutting edge 10 years ago. We were the first ones to do a lawsuit. . . . It's perceived that we've had a lot of success. And I understand that perception, but I guess what I'm telling you is, as soon as you win, you lose, because as soon as you win, the effort is to try to make sure your win is minimized. I can't bring that point home enough.

Despite the environmental justice movement's many accomplishments since the 1980s, low-income communities and communities of color continue to live with a disproportionate burden of pollution, and changing this pattern would require vast policy changes on a scale much larger than any currently in play. Indeed, it would require a fundamental restructuring of American society and the economy in ways that erase deeply rooted race and class inequalities and neoliberal political ideologies on which capitalism depends. This is a daunting task—difficult to even imagine, much less bring about. As one activist says, "You have to have pretty close to a revolution to be acknowledged. That's a scary thought. And even then, you don't know what you're going to wind up with. Probably not good. History will tell us."

Assessing movement strategy and outcomes is difficult for a task this large. It draws as much on one's propensity to see things through the lens of "glass half empty" or "glass half full" as it does on actual movement outcomes. Yet these varying assessments of past strategy have material consequences, for they inform decisions about current strategy and the direction in which the movement should go. Some activists focus on how effective early, disruptive tactics were at preventing the construction of new hazardous waste incinerators and other polluting facilities and want to continue that type of activism. Others see how many problems remain despite those early successes and want to try new approaches. This type of divergence of opinion is not unique; it was also highly visible in the left's response to Donald Trump's election. Some activists doubled down on electoral politics to prevent the election of another such president, while others saw his election as a sign of the bankruptcy of an American political system that should be fundamentally remade.

Most environmental justice activists continue to try to bring about change, even when they don't achieve their biggest goals or even know how to achieve them. I asked one longtime activist what keeps her going, and she replied:

> One of the things that keeps me going is that when I'm on my deathbed, I can say to myself, "I didn't stick my head in the sand, I didn't just let it all happen." It might not have had the outcome I would have hoped for, but I know I tried. Once you're aware of something and your heart tells you it's not right, if you don't take action, you're going to have regrets. If you do take action and you fail, you'll be disappointed, heartbroken, but you won't have regrets. You won't hold it against yourself. So that's just really important to me, and I think that's sort of an activist thing, you know? It comes down to who you are as a person. Are you a person who can watch and say nothing, or are you a person who sees and has to do something, whether it's going to make a huge difference or not? You're never guaranteed anything, but you have to try.

In some ways, the story of the California environmental justice movement is a quintessential story of American social movements: a movement starts out with big demands and disruptive tactics, which are slowly moderated over time as the movement institutionalizes its organizational structure. But what are the effects of this shift? Scholars and activists are divided on the answer. People at one end of the spectrum view institutionalization and accompanying professionalization trends as a process of maturation and increasing sophistication that increases movement effectiveness. People at the other end of the spectrum view these trends as a process of co-optation by the state and industry, in which the social movement actors increasingly moderate their tactics and compromise on the needs of those most impacted by the effects of government decision-making and industry practice, eventually ceasing to be effective change agents. In making these divergent analyses, scholars and activists have different ideas of what counts as victory or failure and draw on different imaginaries for what might be possible in the future. The pro-institutionalization camp sees the limited gains of this approach as making concrete, if small, improvements to a system that seems to disallow dramatic change. The anti-institutionalization camp holds out for something bigger and sees more disruptive tactics as the likeliest way to achieve meaningful wins for the people that need them most. I chart a middle path through this debate, showing both what is gained and what is lost with the shift toward "insider" politics.

I have argued that the changes in the environmental justice movement can be better understood by placing them in the context of the larger historical changes in which they are enmeshed: the neoliberal ideologies that divert needs for direct regulation into voluntary practices and market-based reforms; the demographic changes in the United States, which open up some opportunities for environmental justice activists while foreclosing others; the continued generation of profits on the backs of the poor and of people of color through capitalism; the structural racism that persists even as overt expressions of individual racism decrease or go underground, only to pop up elsewhere; the slipperiness of polluters that put on a pleasant face, positioning themselves as allies rather than direct opponents; the efforts to change state policy that drive institutionalization into state structures; and the economic and technical requirements needed to sustain deep engagement in the policy process that both drive and respond to the movement's shift toward professionalization into nonprofit structures.

This context sheds light on how environmental justice activism has come to be where it is, but it does not decisively answer the fundamental question that activists face: How can we make deep, lasting improvements to the world we live in? This book shows that in their efforts to answer this question over the decades, environmental justice activists have tried multiple strategies to achieve broader social changes, but all of these strategies—the old and the new—fall short of the vision of environmental justice. These changing strategies and the changing political terrain in which they operate provide new challenges for activists. In this chapter, I summarize those challenges and reiterate the trade-offs inherent in the environmental justice movement's political evolution.

DILEMMAS
Disruptive Activism

Raucous, disruptive activism was ultimately very successful at preventing the construction of a slew of waste incinerators and other polluting facilities in California across the movement's lifetime, especially from the late 1980s through the 1990s. However, while some activists tried to work with other activist groups in other countries, this form of localized activism was not enough to prevent some such industries from simply moving abroad to places with lower wages and looser environmental regulations. It was also less effective at addressing forms of already existing pollution, especially pollution not emitted from single, discrete sources around which to rally opposition. Much early activism also depended on grassroots anger, some of which dissipated when relations with industry and government officials became less oppositional: officials moderated their racist, sexist, and classist treatment of residents and invited participation via advisory committees, while industries signed good neighbor agreements and hosted community tours of their facilities. While these new modes of interaction open up discursive space within the policy-making process, they can undercut the potential for more disruptive forms of protest.

The Expansion of the Environmental Justice Frame

Use of the term environmental justice has grown dramatically since it was first introduced in the 1980s. This success in promoting a justice-oriented frame for understanding environmental issues is one of the core achievements of the movement. But this accomplishment also has its drawbacks. As more nonprofits enter the arena of environmental justice work, they increase the competition for already limited funding—especially when the new groups are bigger and more professionalized, like the mainstream environmental groups. And as more organizations adopt the language of environmental justice to pursue their own goals, its meaning becomes increasingly diffuse. This allows the term to be used in ways (and by people) antithetical to the movement's founding principles, such as when government agencies and polluting industries use it to mean improvements in the openness of the processes of environmental decision-making, rather than improvements in the fairness of the outcomes of those decisions.

Institutionalization and Professionalization

Activists institutionalize into nonprofit structures in order to access financial resources to pursue their work. This is especially important for low-income activists, many of whom already work long hours with little extra time available for volunteer social change organizing. Nonprofits also sustain the movement in the downtimes between large campaigns that draw many people into the fight. And it is easier for formalized groups to gain access to and work with legal, scientific, and policy experts who support their cause.

However, institutionalization and professionalization comes with political trade-offs. Dependence on outside funding makes activists vulnerable to the political priorities of their funders and the tactics they find acceptable, and institutionalized groups are more likely to use insider, institutionalized policy advocacy and steer clear of direct action.[5] Institutionalization into nonprofits also concentrates power and authority in the hands of their staff, especially their leadership. As environmental justice activism professionalizes over time, some activists experience it less as a social movement and more as a diverse set of organizations working on loosely similar goals. The benefits of the increased funding, expertise, and institutional access that professionalization provides risk being offset by a loss of movement energy and community-level ownership of the movement itself.

Participation in Public Decision-Making

Environmental justice activists have long sought access and procedural improvements to environmental decision-making. They have gotten some of what they wanted: Spanish-language interpretation at public hearings is increasingly available, many work cordially with state agencies, and innumerable environmental justice advisory committees now exist at multiple levels of government. But these changes do not necessarily affect the outcomes of decision-making processes. When they do not, committee meetings use up valuable time, and activist participation can be used as a cover to deflect criticism of unpopular decisions. Of course, sometimes their participation does influence decisions made. But even when it does not, participation may yield other benefits. It can foster coalition building, as environmental justice activists who may not typically work closely come together in the same space. It can allow activists to watch the workings of government and learn who holds power and how it is shared; this knowledge can be useful in later campaigns. But it is hard to know in advance what kind of impact participation will make, if any.

Scaling Up: Policy Advocacy, Electoral Politics, and Co-optation into the State Apparatus

Activists have scaled up their work, hoping to improve conditions not just in individual communities but across the entire state. However, the scaling-up process presents new challenges. As activists pursue policy efforts that would impact people beyond the communities in which they are based, they begin to speak not for themselves but for others, thus increasing the possibility of intramovement conflict as communities are impacted by policy decisions made by organizations that do not necessarily have a base within them. Indeed, scaling up to work at the level of the state necessitates either a messy process of trying to make decisions across all state environmental justice organizations, or of making policy decisions that impact all group members without including all the groups in the decision-making process, which has proven divisive. This is complicated by the fact that policy victories typically require compromising many original goals. The more people are affected by these compromises, the harder it is to achieve consensus about when to compromise and when to draw the line.

Policy work at the state level also requires activists to work with politicians, who may support one group's cause and work against another's, causing tension within the movement itself. Activists employed within the state apparatus are also pressured to be "objective" and to remove their "activist hat" (although governance itself is always already political). As one environmental justice activist who transitioned into government puts it:

> On the outside, you're expected to push your agenda, whereas in the administration, in the agency world, you cannot be perceived in any way, shape, or form as pushing a particular agenda. The minute you're doing that, you're discredited. And so, if you have the moniker of environmental justice, you're automatically perceived as pushing that agenda. Once you step inside the administration, you really do have to take off your advocate hat, not because you don't still believe in the same things, but because you do have

to balance a lot of different things, and you don't have the flexibility to just take that one narrow viewpoint.

Perhaps this activist's comments explain why my email inbox recently contained *Los Angeles Times* coverage of a California environmental justice activist who had gone into public office and was now defending the permit extension of a contested power plant. Then again, perhaps this is an example of the co-optation of activism that can be brought on by incorporation into the state.

Ultimately, as environmental justice activists seek to influence governance, whether by policy advocacy, electoral politics, or taking jobs and offices within government, they must constantly work against the grain of capitalism, which shapes state action to its own ends.

Collaboration

Collaboration with state agencies can be productive: activists learn how to strategically promote their causes and connect with agency staff sympathetic to environmental justice concerns, fostering shared work toward common goals. On the other hand, environmental justice activists have historically defined themselves in opposition to both corporations and the state, and the "go along to get along" attitude rankles some activists. Collaboration with industry is perhaps more universally regarded with suspicion within the movement, although some activists do indeed engage in these efforts, often as part of a compromise in service of a particular goal.

If not approached with care, collaboration with state and industry entities can propel activists down a slippery slope toward co-optation.

Being "for Something" and DIY Projects

Activists are working toward proactive ways to solve environmental and social problems at their roots, rather than continually fighting defensive battles: to be "for something" rather than just "against something." But people are often more easily united around opposing polluters than around proactive solutions to complex social problems such as racism and classism.[6] And in seeking to be "for something," activists may fall into prevailing norms, espousing neoliberal "solutions" that rely on markets, individual action, and voluntarism and leaving behind potentially powerful confrontational tactics.[7]

The pressure to be "for something" may also nudge activists toward small-scale, ameliorative (rather than transformative) DIY local work, such as community gardening and promoting bicycle riding. Some scholars of the alternative food movement have described these types of tactics as apolitical and unlikely to significantly change low-income people's opportunities.[8] Environmental justice activists have shown it is wise not to assume these efforts are completely separate from their more explicitly political projects, and that each can enrich the other. However, if adopted in place of, rather than in addition to, older forms of environmental justice activism, they could siphon off activist labor from the constant, defensive vigilance required to protect old victories and fend off new threats, for as Rebecca Solnit writes, "Environmentalists like to say that defeats are permanent, victories temporary."[9]

CALIFORNIA IN THE NATION, CALIFORNIA IN THE WORLD

As this history of environmental justice activism in California has shown, California is an example of what can be achieved through activism; it is also a cautionary tale of how far we still must go to make real, substantive changes in health, equity, and the environment. California's state and local governments have consistently led the nation in environmental policy, and California is seen as something of a laboratory, testing out policies that can be pursued in other states or by the federal government. However, California still plays an enormous role in environmental degradation, and the environmental burden is still disproportionately borne by people of color and the poor. The state is a leading user of pesticides, and its cities consistently dominate the top ten spots in national lists of places with the highest levels of air pollution.[10] California is the nation's third or fourth largest oil-producing state, producing some of the dirtiest oil in North America; more than one million Californians do not have clean water coming out of their taps to drink and bathe in; and California ranks within the top quartile of states with the greatest levels of social inequality.[11] Indeed, despite California's high levels of economic growth at the state level, the agricultural San Joaquin Valley consistently ranks as one of the most impoverished regions of the country.[12]

Nonetheless, California's environmental regulations give environmental justice activists tools that activists in other states don't always have. This was brought home forcefully to me in 2013 when I spent two days in Los Angeles with environmental justice activists visiting from Houston, Texas. At the time, Houston was planning a port expansion project. The Houston activists were in town to learn from the Southern California activists who had won concessions from the ports of Long Beach and Los Angeles as they expanded during the 2000s. After suing the Port of Los Angeles, California activists were able to require ships in port at the China Shipping Container Terminal to run shipboard activities off of shore power provided via electricity cables rather than their own diesel engines, which pumped out damaging air pollutants. Lawsuits also forced the port to put funds into local mitigation projects.[13] When one of the Houston activists asked how they could achieve the same things, one of the California activists said that she doubted the same victories could be won in Houston; part of the California legal effort hinged on CEQA, the California Environmental Quality Act, which provided options for lawsuits that were not available to the Texas activists.[14]

California is neither completely unique nor completely representative of the rest of the country. At the state level in 2021, Democratic governors had been in power since the end of Arnold Schwarzenegger's term as governor in 2011, and even he was more open to environmental policymaking than many other Republican politicians on the national stage. National politics also make an impact. In response to the Republican Trump administration's attempts to roll back environmental regulations, California strengthened many of its own. For example, after the Trump administration rolled back Obama-era efforts to ban the use of chlorpyrifos, California and several other states banned them at the state level instead.[15] Indeed, California often has tighter environmental regulations than those of the federal government and has fought to be allowed to have some of its regulations supersede weaker federal regulations. But the state cannot operate entirely independently from the federal government.

While some California environmental victories "trickle up" to the federal government, others enter the global logics of capitalism: when regulations tighten, some industries leave first California and then the United States in search of cheaper labor and looser environmental regulations. Silicon Valley is perhaps the best example of this. As explained in chapter 1, activists in Silicon Valley fought several 1980s campaigns against the pollution created by electronics manufacturing, and as they won these battles, the industries slowly left the state, and then the nation.[16] Silicon Valley is still dominated by the electronics industry, but not electronics manufacturing; now, it primarily produces digital code and designs hardware and software. As the manufacturing and production phases were offshored, well-paid tech workers flooded in, and real estate prices skyrocketed. For forty years, Silicon Valley has been remaking the face of the San Francisco Bay Area in ways that harm the lower-income people and people of color who live there, whether through pollution or gentrification.

It is not only industrial manufacturing that has been offshored because of California policies; some other sources of pollution, too, have simply moved out of California rather than stopping or reducing their pollution levels. The forty-five-plus anti-incinerator victories of the California environmental justice movement raise questions about where the waste that would have been burned in them ultimately went. While some likely went to existing landfills, and some may have been accounted for by waste reduction measures, activists from the Global Anti-Incinerator Alliance suggest that anti-incinerator victories in the United States contributed to the growth of incinerator construction abroad.[17]

THINKING ABOUT WORKING WITH OR WITHIN THE STATE

This book has described the environmental justice movement's turn toward institutionalization over the years: how it took place, what influenced it, and how activists feel about it. But the real question is this: Has it been successful? As many of the interviews recorded here show, the answer is "in some ways yes, in other ways no." Several scholars have written about the limitations of the policy turn, and particularly the dangers of working with, rather than against, the state. As Laura Pulido, Ellen Kohl, Nicole Marie Cotton, and David Pellow remind us, the United States is a racial state operating within and for racial capitalism and is therefore deeply complicit with the histories of racism, classism, and violence that the environmental justice movement seeks to put right.[18] It is crucial that environmental justice activists recognize and name these ongoing problems even as they work toward incremental reforms and improvements. Scholars Michael Omi and Howard Winant point out the dangers of not recognizing this larger context by telling this story about Malcolm X: "A reporter once told Malcolm X that the passage of key pieces of civil rights legislation was clear proof that things were getting better for blacks. In response, Malcolm countered that it did not show improvement to stick a knife nine inches into someone, pull it out six inches, and call it progress. 'But some people,' Malcolm observed, 'don't even want to admit the knife is there.'"[19]

These cautionary notes serve to remind readers and activists of the continuing importance of understanding the state as an adversary rather than a friend. Pellow goes further, arguing that the state is a fundamental source of racial violence, and its power must therefore be curtailed. In his analysis of the overlap between environmental justice activism and Black Lives Matter activism, he argues that Black Lives Matter's work toward policy-driven reform in fact strengthens and legitimizes the state apparatus—a risky move when US government has so often used state power against Black people and other people of color. Drawing on anarchist thought, Pellow suggests that activists should not seek to expand and strengthen the state's enforcement powers in hopes that it will use them only against polluters; instead, he says, activists should work to shrink the state.[20]

These scholars make vital points about the way the state apparatus has drawn from and fomented racism to organize in the interests of power and profits at the expense of those with least power. They remind us to think beyond the limitations of the current moment and imagine, as the World Social Forums put it, that "A Better World is Possible." But at the time of this writing, the United States does not appear to be in a revolutionary moment, and the environmental justice movement, while broad, is not a mass movement. Certainly it is possible that some future world will be dramatically better—but what does a person do in the here and now, when their home is regularly invaded by pesticide drift or their children are bathing in contaminated water? And if activists succeed in shrinking the state (as neoliberals would also have it, though for different reasons), what source of power remains that might curtail the impacts of polluting industries?

The state and the people who run it have periodically been forced to make concessions that lessen the environmental degradation and multiple forms of social inequality that underpin capitalism: the end of slavery, the labor rights and social welfare victories of the 1930s, the civil rights victories of the 1960s, and the environmental policy victories of the 1970s all stand out. These victories went far beyond the scale of what environmental justice activists have yet been able to accomplish. And yet these too were all partial victories. Yes, slavery was ended, but the United States still lives in its long shadow, and multiple variants of white supremacy continue to thrive. Yes, the 1930s saw New Deal progressive victories in the areas of labor rights and social welfare, but many of these protections primarily benefited white people, as they were designed to do. The two occupations most likely held by Black people in the South, farmworker and domestic worker, were excluded from minimum wage requirements; they were also excluded from new protections against retaliation in response to union activities.[21] Yes, the civil rights movement of the 1950s and 1960s achieved crucial victories, improving voting rights and doing away with formal Jim Crow policies. But those victories, too, were blunted and undermined by ongoing white resistance. And as scholars have argued, these victories did not take account of socioeconomic status; the Black middle and upper classes benefited most, and the poorest were largely left behind.[22] Yes, many environmental laws were put in place in the 1970s, and as a result, some particularly toxic sites have been cleaned up and some particularly egregious violators have been stopped. But these laws have often stagnated or been walked back by industry and its friends in government. Racial capitalism continues to rule in the United States.

But even partial victories matter, and they are worth fighting hard for. When we situate the recent history of environmental justice activism against the longer history of struggles for justice in the United States, what we see is that, in Frederick Douglass's words, "without struggle there is no progress."[23] Most key moments of progress in the United States followed huge political upheavals, from mass strikes by workers, to civil disobedience and mass protest, and in the case of the abolition of slavery, war. While today's environmental justice activists struggle mightily, their work has not yet been supported by a mass movement strong enough to force the state and polluters into deep reforms. Indeed, the environmental justice movement started in the 1980s, at a moment when national politics were moving in the opposite direction, toward neoliberalism. Thus far, the movement has developed along the life course of neoliberalism—struggling against it, yet also being subtly influenced by it.

To my eye, activists and scholars must guard against being co-opted by the state, but they cannot give up on it either, for polluters are unlikely to do so; shrinking the state would give powerful transnational polluters free rein. We must seek to push the state in every way possible to protect the health and well-being of all its people through meaningful, strictly enforced regulation of polluters and equitably distributed public goods. Residents in polluted communities have asked for this over and over again, as Ester Guzman told the CalEPA, in Spanish: "Today I've come to demand that you make the regulations for locating new facilities stricter. My children are sick. One of them had to have sinus surgery at just two years old. You've sent around mobile asthma clinics that hand out Claritin and inhalers but the problem itself never goes away."[24] As this shows, even in California, that "model progressive state," sometimes state solutions are Band-Aids that treat the symptoms rather than the causes—a lesson that is perhaps even more true in the nation as a whole.

The limitations of both state-centered work and efforts to create solutions outside the state speak directly to the double bind in which activists find themselves. Activists who have dedicated their lives to the environmental justice movement need far more hands on deck to support them. We need sympathetic politicians, staff, and regulators on the inside to create stronger environmental policy, equitably implemented. We need mass movements on the outside that create enough political pressure to help turn activists' demands into reality. We need activists and scholars to remind us of the contradictions inherent in using state action to create social change. And we need to continue to dream—to hold out for something better while we seize what concessions we can in the here and now. In the face of skyrocketing income inequality, deep-seated racial capitalism, and the "spectacular racism" of the current moment, this is a tall order.[25] But as environmental justice activists have added friction to the wheels of racial capitalism, perhaps in the future they, or others inspired by them, can help apply the brakes.

Ultimately, social movements change, go through periods of decline, and sometimes show up again in new guises. It may be that the environmental justice movement will recede as a social movement, or that it will be built upon by other framings and people just as it borrowed from the social movements that preceded it.[26] I hope we can be nimble enough to go to the mat within the current political system for the things that matter, without losing the ability to work toward something better. Ultimately, all our victories are incomplete, but they remind us of what can be won and of the value of trying even when the odds seem stacked against us.

Appendix

Arguments for and against the
Environmental Justice Lawsuit Brought
against the California Air Resources Board

Environmental Critiques of the Lawsuit	Environmental Justice Responses
Cap-and-trade/offsets will not produce toxic hot spots.	Cap-and-trade/offsets likely will produce toxic hot spots, but even if they do not, cap-and-trade deprives communities living near industrial sources of pollution of the air quality improvements that would accrue from direct regulation or carbon fees.
Cap-and-trade, if done right, will reduce carbon emissions.	Cap-and-trade is likely to be gamed and not reduce carbon emissions.
Anything other than cap-and-trade is politically infeasible.	Better options are possible and should be fought for.
Carbon taxes will increase energy costs, which is bad for low-income people.	Proper design of a carbon tax could compensate for higher energy prices.
Compromise with industry is necessary to get things done.	Too much compromise with industry gets something that benefits industry more than the public.
Cap-and-trade in California can avoid the problems it has had elsewhere.	Cap-and-trade in California is likely to repeat the problems it has had elsewhere.
Climate change legislation should be used to reduce carbon emissions, not air pollution.	Climate change legislation should be used to achieve broad environmental benefits, and AB 32 specifically mandates a reduction of air pollution in addition to carbon.

Environmental Critiques of the Lawsuit	Environmental Justice Responses
AB 32 does not need to address air pollution because other laws already do so.	Existing air pollution laws are inadequate safeguards for low-income communities and communities of color.
Only 20 percent of the overall greenhouse gas reductions will be achieved through cap-and-trade measures.	The Scoping Plan intends cap-and-trade to be responsible for the vast majority of reductions among the industrial sources of greenhouse gas emissions that low-income communities and communities of color live close to.
Cap-and-trade is better than doing nothing.	"Doing something dysfunctional is not better than doing nothing at all."[*]

[*]Ejmatters.org, "Debunking the Myths of Cap-and-Trade," accessed April 5, 2021, https://web.archive.org/web/20100729080315/http://www.ejmatters.org/docs/GHG-Myths_FactsheetFINAL[1].pdf.

Notes

PREFACE

1. Krishnakumar and Kannan, "2020 California Fires Are the Worst Ever."

2. Baker et al., "Three Words."

3. Dillon and Sze, "Police Power and Particulate Matters"; Marbella, "Beginning of Freddie Gray's Life"; McCoy, "Freddie Gray's Life"; and Okorie, Hogan, and Effiong, "I Can't Breathe."

4. Beer, "Here Are the Police Officers and Other Public Employees Arrested"; and Westervelt, "Off-Duty Police Officers Investigated."

5. The contemporary and overt forms of racism that drew attention during the Trump administration are better thought of not as new phenomena but as an intensification of trends from the immediate past. To separate the societal racism of the Obama period from that of the Trump period is to underestimate the overt forms of racism of the former, as well as the way that the frames of "color-blind" rhetoric continued to percolate through the latter. Indeed, BLM protests against police brutality began under the Obama regime, and the racist backlash to his presidency that began as soon as his election was confirmed helped lead to Trump's election. As scholar Laura Pulido and her coauthors point out, Trump's overt racism created headlines because of its very transgressiveness; it punctured the still dominant, if shallow, norms of nonracism. Although racism, under Trump, became more overt and visible, the majority of the white American public still underestimates its presence, and color-blind rhetoric contributes to this outcome. Bonilla-Silva, "'Racists,' 'Class Anxieties,' Hegemonic Racism"; and Pulido et al., "Environmental Deregulation, Spectacular Racism, and White Nationalism."

6. "Obama's Full Remarks at Howard University Commencement Ceremony."

ACKNOWLEDGMENTS

1. Perkins, "Women's Pathways into Activism."
2. Perkins, Voices from the Valley.

INTRODUCTION

1. Cole and Foster, *From the Ground Up*.
2. Cole and Foster, *From the Ground Up*.
3. Blight, *Frederick Douglass*.
4. See Browning, Marshall, and Tabb, *Protest Is Not Enough*; Chafe, *Civilities and Civil Rights*; Dubofsky, *We Shall Be All*; Lackey, *Haverford Discussions*; Payne, *I've Got the Light of Freedom*; and Piven and Cloward, *Poor People's Movements*.
5. See Foreman, *Confessions of an Eco-Warrior*; Moore, *Confessions of a Greenpeace Dropout*; and Zelko, *Make It a Green Peace!*
6. Wayne Santoro and Gail McGuire call activists working within government spaces and using insider tactics "institutional activists" or "social movement participants who occupy formal statuses within the government and who pursue movement goals through conventional bureaucratic channels." Santoro and McGuire, "Social Movement Insiders," 504. My conception of the people who use insider tactics includes such institutional activists, as well as those who are not employed within the state itself but largely adhere to its official decision-making mechanisms (electoral politics, public hearings, advisory committees, etc.) in their efforts to promote environmental justice. Too, where Santoro and McGuire focus on the ability of social movement actors to work within the state apparatus to promote outsider goals, my research suggests it is also important to consider the possibility of movement co-optation through such hires, as well as the possibility that government bureaucracies and political cultures will shape such activists more than the activists are able to shape the state.
7. Szasz, *Ecopopulism*; Perkins, "Multiple People of Color Origins of the US Environmental Justice Movement"; and Perkins, "Women's Pathways into Activism." Some of the more radical tenets of early environmental justice activism can be seen in the "Principles of Environmental Justice" document adopted at the First National People of Color Environmental Leadership Summit held in Washington, D.C., in 1991. Little is written about how these principles were arrived at and drafted, and scholarship analyzing this history—who took leadership roles; what the areas of agreement and compromise consisted of; and how the group navigated diverse political, ideological, and racial backgrounds—would be an important contribution to environmental justice studies.
8. I see the environmental justice movement as traveling along a continuum from its roots to its current state rather than as divided into "before" and "after" periods. However, Eric Carter has conceptualized the movement in a

more binary way, referring to "1.0" and "2.0" versions of environmental justice activism. Carter, "Environmental Justice 2.0." See note 35 for more details.

9. This builds on Philip Selznick's definition of co-optation as "the process of absorbing new elements into the leadership or policy-determining structure of an organization as a means of averting threats to its stability or existence." Selznick, "Foundations of the Theory of Organization," 34. These new elements may be either people or ideas, such as when the concept of environmental justice is co-opted (and redefined) by countermovement actors, government officials, and some environmental justice activists themselves. Harrison, "Coopted Environmental Justice?"; and Harrison, *From the Inside Out*.

10. Selznick writes that co-optation is often unaddressed within movements, for "an open acknowledgement of capitulation to specific interests may itself undermine the sense of legitimacy of the [organization in question] within the community. Consequently, there is a positive pressure to refrain from explicit recognition of the relationship established." Selznick, "Foundations of the Theory of Organization," 35.

11. A small but growing amount of scholarship addresses tensions in particular places struggling with environmental injustice, showing that not all residents oppose the environmental threat in question and thus do not participate in environmental justice activism. Bell, *Fighting King Coal*; Bell and Braun, "Coal, Identity, and the Gendering of Environmental Justice Activism"; Malin, "When Is 'Yes to the Mill' Environmental Justice?" Fewer scholars have addressed the conflict and tensions *among* environmental justice activists. My work builds on the small body of literature that engages these themes. Laura Pulido, Ellen Kohl, and Nicole Marie Cotton acknowledge the diversity of political orientations among environmental justice activists and suggest that they may be splintering into liberal and radical factions, though this division is not the central focus of their study. Pulido, Kohl, and Cotton, "State Regulation and Environmental Justice." David Ciplet and Jill Harrison also identify three core tensions within the movement's efforts to create a "just transition" to sustainability, though their study is largely an analytic, theoretical intervention rather than an empirical or historical overview of intra-group tensions. Ciplet and Harrison, "Transition Tensions." Most relevant for this book, Michael Méndez usefully writes about internal environmental justice debates in his analysis of climate change policy advocacy in California, and Harrison discusses divisions among both activists and environmental justice government staff over how they conceptualize environmental justice and whether the regulatory or nonregulatory approach is the best way to achieve it. Méndez, *Climate Change from the Streets*; Harrison, "Coopted Environmental Justice?"; and Harrison *From the Inside Out*.

12. Eady, "Environmental Justice in State Policy Decisions"; Harrison, *From the Inside Out*; Harrison, *Pesticide Drift and the Pursuit of Environmental Justice*; Holifield, "Neoliberalism and Environmental Justice"; Jatkar and London, "From Testimony to Transformation"; Liévanos, "Certainty, Fairness, and Balance"; London et al., "Racing Climate Change"; London, Sze, and Liévanos, "Problems, Promise, Progress, and Perils"; Méndez, *Climate Change from the Streets*; Pastor et al., "Minding the Climate Gap; Pastor et al., "Risky Business";

Sadd, Hall, et al., "Ground-Truthing Validation to Assess the Effect of Facility Locational Error"; Sadd, Pastor, et al., "Playing It Safe"; and Shilling, London, and Liévanos, "Marginalization by Collaboration."

13. Overall, the bulk of environmental justice scholarship documents environmental inequality of various types.

14. Pellow, "Environmental Justice, Animal Rights, and Total Liberation"; Pellow, *What Is Critical Environmental Justice?*; Pulido and De Lara, "Reimagining 'Justice'"; and Pulido, Kohl, and Cotton, "State Regulation and Environmental Justice," 12.

15. Pulido and De Lara, "Reimagining 'Justice,'" 92.

16. McAdam, *Political Process and the Development of Black Insurgency*; Morris, "Black Southern Student Sit-In Movement"; and Morris, *The Origins of the Civil Rights Movement*. For a critique of political opportunity structure theory, which Pellow argues does not attend fully to race, the economy, and other factors that create and limit political opportunities, see Pellow, "Environmental Justice and the Political Process"; and Pellow, "Environmental Justice Movements and Political Opportunity Structures." Though it is not a central theme of this book, I also draw lightly on social movements scholars' insights on the role of emotion in activism through my analysis of how fear of hazardous waste strengthened activism in the early environmental justice movement and how resignation to seemingly intractable environmental risks hampered it later (see chapters 3 and 4). While the study of emotion is not typically considered a part of the political opportunity structure analyzed by social movement scholars, I gesture to it here because of the patterned way that emotions are produced at particular societal moments, which then facilitate or constrain activism. See Gould, *Moving Politics*; and Goodwin, Jasper, and Polletta, "Return of the Repressed."

17. McAdam, *Political Process and the Development of Black Insurgency*; Morris, "Black Southern Student Sit-In Movement"; and Morris, *The Origins of the Civil Rights Movement*.

18. Although many scholars see police violence and mass incarceration as being environmental justice matters, few self-identified environmental justice activists whom I interviewed work directly on them. Two California groups, the California Prison Moratorium Project and Valley Improvement Projects, are important exceptions. See Braz, "Joining Forces"; Dillon and Sze, "Police Power and Particulate Matters"; and Pellow, *What Is Critical Environmental Justice?*

19. Taylor, *Toxic Communities*.

20. Pulido, "Flint, Environmental Racism, and Racial Capitalism"; and Ranganathan, "Thinking with Flint."

21. For a discussion of the racial state, see Kurtz, "Acknowledging the Racial State"; for the racialized "treadmill of production," see Pellow, *Resisting Global Toxics*; for racial liberalism, see Ranganathan "Thinking with Flint"; for racial capitalism, see Robinson, *Black Marxism*, and Pulido, "Flint, Environmental Racism, and Racial Capitalism"; for racial neoliberalism in general, see Roberts and Mahtani, "Neoliberalizing Race, Racing Neoliberalism," and

Goldberg, *Threat of Race*; and for accounts of neoliberalism in food justice, see Sbicca and Myers, "Food Justice Racial Projects."

22. Pellow, *Resisting Global Toxics*.

23. For more on this type of erasure within environmental history, see also Finney, *Black Faces, White Spaces*; Taylor, *Rise of the American Conservation Movement*; and Gottlieb, *Forcing the Spring*.

24. Much of the early environmental justice movement focused on landfills, incinerators, and polluting industrial facilities. Other environmental threats, such as pesticide drift from agricultural fields into residential areas and occupational health threats, also primarily impacted low-income communities and communities of color, but they were not as prominent and/or not a focus among self-identified environmental justice activists in the early years.

25. Perkins, "Framing and the Politics of Environmental Justice Language."

26. Holifield, "Neoliberalism and Environmental Justice in the United States Environmental Protection Agency"; Liévanos, "Certainty, Fairness, and Balance"; and London, Sze, and Liévanos, "Problems, Promise, Progress, and Perils."

27. Park and Pellow, "Racial Formation, Environmental Racism, and the Emergence of Silicon Valley"; and Taylor, "Evolution of Environmental Justice Activism, Research, and Scholarship."

28. Perkins, "Multiple People of Color Origins of the US Environmental Justice Movement."

29. Alkon, Cortez, and Sze, "What Is in a Name?"

30. Perkins, "Multiple People of Color Origins of the US Environmental Justice Movement."

31. Bryant and Hockman, "A Brief Comparison of the Civil Rights Movement and the Environmental Justice Movement"; Cable, Mix, and Hastings, "Mission Impossible?"; Chavis, Foreword; Pellow and Brulle, "Power, Justice, and the Environment"; Pezzullo, "Performing Critical Interruptions"; Szasz, *Ecopopulism*; and Taylor, "Rise of the Environmental Justice Paradigm."

32. McGurtry, *Transforming Environmentalism*.

33. Perkins, "Multiple People of Color Origins of the US Environmental Justice Movement" (overly simplistic); Chavis and Lee, *Toxic Wastes and Race in the United States*; and US General Accounting Office, *Siting of Hazardous Landfills* (relationship between race and waste disposal).

34. See Agyeman et al., "Trends and Directions in Environmental Justice"; Carter, "Environmental Justice 2.0"; Harrison, "Coopted Environmental Justice?"; Harrison, *From the Inside Out*; Méndez, *Climate Change from the Streets*; Schlosberg, "Theorising Environmental Justice"; Schlosberg and Collins, "From Environmental to Climate Justice"; Sze and London, "Environmental Justice at the Crossroads"; and Taylor, "Evolution of Environmental Justice Activism, Research, and Scholarship."

35. See Agyeman et al., "Trends and Directions in Environmental Justice"; Schlosberg "Theorising Environmental Justice"; Schlosberg and Collins, "From Environmental to Climate Justice"; and Sze and London, "Environmental Justice at the Crossroads." Carter's "Environmental Justice 2.0" is a significant exception to this trend. He argues that a new wave of Latinx environmentalism

is distinct from the environmental justice activism that came before it, because it focuses not on reducing pollution but on the creation of nature in the city. It retreats from regulatory politics and forges citywide networks that include new types of Latinx "environmental entrepreneurs." My research suggests that Carter is right to note the shifting nature of activism at the intersection of race, justice, and the environment in Los Angeles and to chart the impact of neoliberalism and Latinx political incorporation on such changes. However, my interviews suggest that his findings are relevant to a particular group of environmental actors, not the environmental justice movement in general. Indeed, part of the difference in our findings seems to stem from the very partial overlap in the people we interviewed. The people at the center of my research are identified as environmental justice activists by their peers and themselves, and most have ties to long-standing environmental justice organizations. Carter notes that his interviewees do not necessarily identify as environmental justice activists. My approach helps analyze the trajectory of the early environmental justice movement, while Carter's approach documents newer work on race and the environment that is less well integrated into older environmental justice networks. We both describe the impact of neoliberalism on activism and note that the growing interest in gardens and other such "do it yourself" (DIY) practices can be linked to neoliberal trends. We both document the new emphasis on the production of environmental amenities, which is billed as leading activism toward purported "win-win" solutions that involve collaboration with industry, though I am more skeptical than Carter that these tactics are improvements. But my work, unlike Carter's, documents activists' significant shift *toward* the state rather than away from it. Another fundamental difference is how we see the movement's trajectory: I do not conceptualize current environmental justice activism as a "2.0" version of what came before, because there are important continuities that bind them. Finally, while both of us describe new tactics that activists are experimenting with in attempts to address the limitations of earlier approaches, I also point to the ongoing value of earlier disruptive approaches to environmental justice activism.

36. This is sometimes the case in more popular depictions of environmental history as well. See, for example, the movie *A Fierce Green Fire: The Battle for a Living Planet* (dir. Mark Kitchell).

37. Eady, "Environmental Justice in State Policy Decisions"; Harrison, *From the Inside Out*; Harrison, *Pesticide Drift and the Pursuit of Environmental Justice*; Holifield, "Neoliberalism and Environmental Justice"; Jatkar and London, "From Testimony to Transformation"; Liévanos, "Certainty, Fairness, and Balance"; London et al., "Racing Climate Change"; London, Sze, and Liévanos, "Problems, Promise, Progress, and Perils"; Méndez, *Climate Change from the Streets*; Pastor et al., *Minding the Climate Gap*; Pastor et al., "Risky Business"; Rechtschaffen, Guana, and O'Neill, *Environmental Justice*; Sadd et al., "Ground-Truthing Validation to Assess the Effect of Facility Locational Error"; Sadd et al., "Playing It Safe"; and Shilling, London, and Liévanos, "Marginalization by Collaboration."

38. I had more exposure to environmental justice activism in the San Joaquin Valley than elsewhere due to my prior research in that region. My public-facing

work, such as the Voices from the Valley project, which was guided by an advisory committee of activists active in the San Joaquin Valley, also put me in greater touch with activists from that region. I also served on the board of directors for Greenaction for Health and Environmental Justice from 2011 to 2015, which works with community groups across California and much of the western United States.

39. Interviewees were identified through snowball sampling: I began with activists suggested by movement leaders, and then at the end of each interview asked for suggestions of who else to interview. Interviews lasted from thirty minutes to three hours, with interview lengths of one to two hours being most common. Interviews took place at a location of the interviewee's choice, most often in their home or office, with a few taking place in restaurants, community centers, or before or after meetings hosted on the premises of supportive NGOs. I conducted ten interviews in Spanish and the rest in English, though many English-speaking interviewees were bi- or multilingual. Interviewees included both "grassroots" activists, whose efforts were largely unpaid, and "grasstips" and "professional" activists doing paid work from inside nonprofit or state institutions. (There was often overlap between these two categories, with some activists starting in one category before moving to the other, or moving back and forth across them over time.) While I did not collect formal demographic data, the interviewees ranged from teenagers to the elderly, with the majority being between their twenties and sixties. Explicit and implicit self-presentation suggests an interview pool that was majority female, with a significant minority of men and one person who spoke to their gender ambiguity and change during the time we stayed in touch after the interview took place. The majority identified as people of color, with a significant minority of white people. Among the people of color, Latinx dominated, though Black, Asian Pacific American, and Indigenous activists were also interviewed, and many participants crossed several racial categories. (I follow the convention used by some academics and activists of using the term "Latinx" in order to avoid using the male form "Latinos" to represent men, women, and nonbinary people. However, I use the male and female singular forms "Latino" and "Latina" to talk about individual people, in deference to how they gender themselves and/or were gendered by others at the time of our interview.) In the subgroup of twenty-two interviews conducted with participants in the Ward Valley anti–nuclear waste campaign, Indigenous activists from the region along the lower Colorado River dominated. These included people from the Fort Mojave, Chemehuevi, Quechan, Cocopah, and the Colorado River Indian Tribes. All interviews were recorded via audio-recorders and then transcribed. Transcription was done by professional transcribers or by student research assistants at UC Santa Cruz and Howard University. Most of the students were undergraduates who worked under my guidance as a way to learn more about the research process through semester-long independent study classes, though several were also paid graduate student research assistants. Spanish-language interviews were transcribed and then translated by professional translators. In addition to the audio-recording, some of the Ward Valley interviews were also recorded via video for an archival repository and public-facing storytelling project. In some of these cases, I conducted the interviews and recorded the video simultaneously;

in others, Howard University MA student Jesse DiValli (at the time, Jesse Card) did the recording. Analysis of interview transcripts took place through coding via NVivo and later Dedoose. At various stages of the project, I had assistance in coding the interviews from undergraduate research assistants at UC Santa Cruz and Howard University. Preliminary codes (sometimes called "a-priori" or "pre-set" codes) were created before beginning coding from the themes discussed in the interviews. These were refined, and more codes and subcodes were added upon reviewing the transcripts (often called "emergent" codes). For more detailed methodological information about the interviews conducted with women activists from the San Joaquin Valley, see my 2012 article, "Women's Pathways into Activism: Rethinking the Women's Environmental Justice Narrative in California's San Joaquin Valley." For insight into one component of my participant observation, see my 2015 book chapter, "On Becoming a Public Sociologist: Amplifying Women's Voices in the Quest for Environmental Justice." In addition to this book, these interviews resulted in the following articles and websites: Perkins, "The Environmental Justice Legacy of the United Farm Workers of America"; Perkins, "The Multiple People of Color Origins of the US Environmental Justice Movement"; Perkins, "On Becoming a Public Sociologist; Perkins, Voices from the Valley; Perkins, "Women's Pathways into Activism"; Perkins and Soto-Karlin, "Situating Global Policies within Local Realities"; and Perkins and Sze, "Images from the Central Valley." The interviews also contributed indirectly to Perkins and Dillon, "Gonzales."

40. In some cases I have changed names to preserve anonymity.

41. For analysis of Northern California Indigenous involvement in water politics among the Winnemem Wintu, Pit River Tribe, and the Maidu Summit, see Dallman et al., "Political Ecology of Emotion and Sacred Space"; Middleton-Manning, Gali, and Houck, "Holding the Headwaters"; Shilling, London, and Liévanos, "Marginalization by Collaboration"; and Ramsden and Slattery, Thirsty for Justice. For a literature review of environmental justice scholarship on Indigenous peoples, see Vickery and Hunter, "Native Americans"; for an introduction to the environmental injustices experienced by Indigenous peoples and their fight for environmental justice, see Gilio-Whitaker, As Long as Grass Grows.

42. See McGurtry, Transforming Environmentalism.

43. For a description of the 1988 march, see Montague, "Great Louisiana Toxics March Sets Pace for the Movement"; and Schmich, "They March to Clean Up a State's Act"; for a description of a later bus tour, see Spears, " 'Freedom Buses' Roll along Cancer Alley."

44. Pellow, Resisting Global Toxics; and Kitchell, Fierce Green Fire.

45. Baldassare et al., PPIC Statewide Survey; Hertsgaard, "Latinos Are Ready to Fight Climate Change"; Sahagun, "Latinos, Asians More Worried about Environment Than Whites, Poll Finds"; Sierra Club, National Survey of Hispanic Voters on Environmental Issues; and Sierra Club and National Council of La Raza, 2012 National Latinos and the Environment Survey.

46. See, for example, Hanemann's description of California's pioneering fuel efficiency standards in "How California Came to Pass AB 32"; or Vogel, California Greenin'.

47. Pastor, *State of Resistance*, 3.

48. Cole and Foster, *From the Ground Up*; Avila, "Magdalena Avila Tells How Hispanic Farmworkers Stopped an Incinerator"; California Rural Legal Assistance, "Small Community Derails Toxic Incinerator"; and Center for Health, Environment and Justice, "25 Years of Action."

CHAPTER 1. EMERGENCE OF THE DISRUPTIVE ENVIRONMENTAL JUSTICE MOVEMENT

1. For information about the other factors that led to what was called the "landfill crisis" of this time, see Blumberg and Gottlieb, *War on Waste*; Gould, Schnaiberg, and Weinberg, *Local Environmental Struggles*; and Pellow, "Environmental Inequality Formation."

2. California Waste Management Board, "Waste-to-Energy Update March 1986."

3. For discussions of the societal conditions that gave rise to the incinerator industry, see Ali et al., "Waste Incineration in California and Impacts to Waste Hierarchy"; Blumberg and Gottlieb, *War on Waste*; Pellow, *Garbage Wars*; and Tangri, *Waste Incineration*.

4. Similar critiques apply to the incinerators proposed in the 1980s and those proposed today. Ciplet, *Industry Blowing Smoke*; Costner and Thornton, *Playing with Fire*; "Garbage Incineration: What a Waste"; Perkins and Dillon, "Gonzales"; and Tangri, *Waste Incineration*.

5. Pardo, "Mexican American Women Grassroots Community Activists."

6. Reynolds, "LANCER and the Vernon Incinerator," 96.

7. A California group formed in the mid-1980s called the Toxics Coordinating Project (TCP) came before CCAT, but I do not see TCP as an environmental justice project: it had fewer grassroots community group participants, and it did not emphasize racial inequality. CCAT was made up explicitly of community-based activists, and it used both class and race framing to explain and call attention to the toxic hazards faced by low-income white communities and communities of color. For more on TCP, see Stammer, "70 Groups Unite in Battle against Pollution"; and Santa Clara Center for Occupational Safety and Health (SCCOSH) and Silicon Valley Toxics Coalition (SVTC), Records, Series I.

8. Blumberg and Gottlieb, *War on Waste*; and Winton, "Concerned Citizens." LANCER stands for Los Angeles City Energy Recovery Project.

9. Brown, *Laying Waste*; and Sarathy, "Legacies of Environmental Justice in Inland Southern California."

10. Tompkins, "Cancer Valley, California."

11. Park and Pellow, "Racial Formation, Environmental Racism, and the Emergence of Silicon Valley"; and Smith, "Pioneer Activist for Environmental Justice in Silicon Valley, 1967–2000."

12. "Henry Clark and Ahmadia Thomas," 5.

13. Lopez, "11 Arrested in Protest Near Toxic Waste Site."

14. Angel, *Toxic Threat to Indian Lands*.

15. Two of these three were still in operation in 2021. Rosengren, "After Its First WTE Facility Closes." These numbers come from personal communications

with Mike Ewall, executive director of Energy Justice Network, September 3, 2018, and Bradley Angel, executive director of Greenaction for Health and Environmental Justice, March 26, 2021. Although no new commercial municipal waste incinerators have been built in the time indicated, several incinerators have been retrofitted, expanded, or built on the same site as existing incinerators since 1995. In addition, in 2017 a small, noncommercial-scale gasification incinerator was built at Army Garrison Fort Hunter Liggett in Monterey County, California. There are also two medical waste incinerators operating in California, in Paramount and Hesperian. Here I follow the activist convention of calling these modern facilities incinerators, whereas the waste industry calls them waste-to-energy facilities that "superheat" waste rather than burn it. Greenaction for Health and Environmental Justice and Global Alliance for Incinerator Alternatives, "Incinerators in Disguise."

16. I came to this number through interviews and the following sources: Blumberg and Gottlieb, *War on Waste;* California Waste Management Board, "Waste-to-Energy Update March 1986"; Global Alliance for Incinerator Alternatives, "Incinerators Blocked/Closed." This number does not disambiguate between incinerator proposals that were defeated in one location and then moved to another; in this way this list may overrepresent incinerators that might realistically have been built. However, the California Waste Management Board report of 1986 lists thirty-four discrete proposed incinerators, and many, many more were proposed after 1986.

17. Angel, *Toxic Threat to Indian Lands,* 1.

18. Elsewhere I compare the origins of the California environmental justice movement with the better-known story of the national environmental justice movement's connection to activism in Warren County, highlighting regional and racial variation in the preexisting political formations that gave rise to local expressions of environmental justice activism. Perkins, "Multiple People of Color Origins of the US Environmental Justice Movement."

19. Communities for a Better Environment transitioned from being a predominantly white to a predominantly people of color organization over the decades. Concerned Neighbors in Action (CAN) and the Center for Community Action and Environmental Justice, CNA's successor organization, shifted demographics too, with participants and leadership moving from predominantly white to predominantly Latina over time. Sarathy, "Legacies of Environmental Justice." The predominantly white Silicon Valley Toxics Coalition also had changes in the makeup of its staff over time, and starting in 2006 was led by Black woman Sheila Davis. However, SVTC broadened its focus from local to global as electronics manufacturing left California and the United States for other countries. As a result, it is no longer considered a core organization within California-focused environmental justice networks. National Toxics Coalition, which began as a predominantly white organization, tried to hire more people of color into staff positions and the board of directors, but it eventually collapsed, in part because of ongoing racial and gender tensions within the organization. Burke, "Poisoning the National Toxics Campaign"; and Hinds et al., *National Toxics Campaign.*

20. Tangri, *Waste Incineration.*

21. Gottlieb, *Forcing the Spring*; and Sandler and Pezzullo, eds., *Environmental Justice and Environmentalism* (most were male). Jerome Ringo became the first Black chair of the National Wildlife Federation in 2005.

22. Gottlieb, *Forcing the Spring*.

23. McGurtry, *Transforming Environmentalism*, 124–25.

24. Radical environmental groups such as Earth First! also eschewed the tactics of the Big 10 environmental groups, preferring direct-action instead. However, these radical groups were predominantly white and typically focused on wilderness and wildlife preservation rather than the health-threatening pollution in low-income white communities and communities of color. Greenpeace was one significant exception to this trend, as it ran a national toxics program that supported many antitoxics and environmental justice efforts in low-income white communities and communities of color on the West Coast during the late 1980s and throughout much of the 1990s.

25. Gutiérrez, "Mothers of East Los Angeles Strike Back," 231.

26. Mayer, *Blue-Green Coalitions*.

27. "North Carolina: Part 2."

28. Angel later formed Greenaction for Health and Environmental Justice.

29. Montague, "Violence in Indian Country over Waste."

30. Burwell and Cole, "Environmental Justice Comes Full Circle," 17–18.

31. McGurtry, *Transforming Environmentalism*.

32. "Toxics Activist's Home Is Torched."

33. I have merged the reflections of two people I interviewed here into one passage. For other accounts of this campaign, see Henry, "Protesters Take to Tents to Blockade Sludge Plant"; Henry, "EPA Seeks Help in Removal of Sludge"; and Montague, "Violence in Indian Country over Waste."

34. *How to Win at Public Hearings*.

35. Almeida, "Network for Environmental and Economic Justice in the Southwest."

36. For a discussion of this trend across social movements, see Brooker and Meyer, "Coalitions and the Organization of Collective Action."

37. Szasz, *Ecopopulism*.

38. Szasz, *Ecopopulism*, 14.

39. US Environmental Protection Agency, "Penny Newman," 3, 2.

40. US General Accounting Office, *How to Dispose of Hazardous Waste*, 69, 71.

41. Burwell and Cole, "Environmental Justice Comes Full Circle," 12–13.

42. Comptroller General of the United States, *EPA's Inventory of Potential Hazardous Waste Sites Is Incomplete*.

43. Magnuson et al., "Problem That Cannot Be Buried."

44. Burwell and Cole, "Environmental Justice Comes Full Circle," 13.

45. Cole and Foster, *From the Ground Up*.

46. Almeida, "Network for Environmental and Economic Justice," 178.

47. Blumberg and Gottlieb, *War on Waste*.

48. Blumberg and Gottlieb, *War on Waste*, 71.

49. See note 15.

50. Blumberg and Gottlieb, *War on Waste*.

51. Almeida, "Network for Environmental and Economic Justice"; Pellow, *Garbage Wars*; Pellow and Park, *Silicon Valley of Dreams*; and Pellow, *Resisting Global Toxics*.

52. Wang et al., "Community Pressure and the Spatial Redistribution of Pollution."

CHAPTER 2. THE INSTITUTIONALIZATION OF THE ENVIRONMENTAL JUSTICE MOVEMENT

1. Emiliano Mataka's absence is deeply felt in the many community networks to which he contributed. Valley Improvement Projects continues its work and has named an award in honor of Emiliano's life and service.

2. For more about Ralph Abascal and his many legal victories on behalf of farmworkers and the poor, see his obituaries in the *New York Times* and the *Los Angeles Times*, Golden, "Ralph S. Abascal, 62, Dies," and "Ralph Abascal," as well as some of his own writings, for example, Abascal, "California Rural Legal Assistance and Environmental Justice"; and Abascal and Cole, "Struggle for Environmental Justice."

3. Moore and Head, "Acknowledging the Past, Confronting the Present," 121.

4. Salcido, "Reviving the Environmental Justice Agenda."

5. Roberts and Toffolon-Weiss, *Chronicles from the Environmental Justice Frontlines*; and Gross and Stretesky, "Environmental Justice in the Court."

6. Clinton, "Executive Order 12898."

7. Harris, "Witness to Environmental Justice over 20 Years."

8. Almeida, "Network for Environmental and Economic Justice in the Southwest," 183.

9. Almeida, "Network for Environmental and Economic Justice in the Southwest," 183.

10. Roberts and Toffolon-Weiss, *Chronicles from the Environmental Justice Frontlines*, 193.

11. McQuaid, "Calling in Help Risks 'Outsider' Label," as cited in Roberts and Toffolon-Weiss, *Chronicles from the Environmental Justice Frontlines*, 194.

12. Roberts and Toffolon-Weiss, *Chronicles from the Environmental Justice Frontlines*, 192. For an excellent overview of the mixed Black responses to the first Earth Day of 1970 and environmentalism of that era more generally, see also Washington, "Ball of Confusion."

13. Salcido, "Reviving the Environmental Justice Agenda"; and Roberts and Toffolon-Weiss, *Chronicles from the Environmental Justice Frontlines*.

14. Whitman, "EPA's Commitment to Environmental Justice," 2 ("justice for *all* communities"; (emphasis added); and US Environmental Protection Agency, *Toolkit for Assessing Potential Allegations of Environmental Injustice*, 9.

15. Peter, "Implementing Environmental Justice."

16. Bills requiring that racial data be reported, or that included language specifying "fair treatment of people, regardless of race, culture or income level"

(Peter, "Implementing Environmental Justice," 545), were consistently vetoed until 1999. For example, in 1998 the California legislature passed AB 2237, which only required the state to identify places that had "disproportionately high and adverse effects on human health and the environment" (547). As Peter writes, "In the last staff analysis in the Legislature, it was noted that the bill was race and income neutral and that the bill did not require, but appeared to steer, the state agencies towards the goal of awarding loans and grants in a manner that is equitable and commensurate with the threats that communities face" (547–48). Nonetheless, Governor Wilson vetoed even this moderate bill. In his words, Wilson objected to the inclusion of "so-called 'environmental racism' or 'environmental justice' issues in their selection criteria for environmental loans and grants" (548).

17. Peter, "Implementing Environmental Justice"; and Abel, Salazar, and Robert, "States of Environmental Justice."

18. Cole and Foster, *From the Ground Up*.

19. Activists who work in 501(c)(3) nonprofit organizations are careful to do this political work on their own time in order to not jeopardize the tax-exempt status of their organizations.

20. Almeida, "Network for Environmental and Economic Justice," 167–68.

21. The six core members of CEJA are Asian Pacific Environmental Network, Communities for a Better Environment, Center for Community Action and Environmental Justice, Environmental Health Coalition, People Organizing to Demand Environmental and Economic Rights, and the Center on Race, Poverty and the Environment. CEJA began when four of the current six core member organizations began working together within the California Alliance, which had begun in 2003 as a group of locally based organizations meeting to organize low-income residents statewide and had grown to focus on larger get-out-the-vote efforts. In 2009, this group rebranded as California Calls. The environmental groups in the network spun off into their own organization, which ultimately became CEJA. CEJA later added nonmember organizations in the form of partners, which in 2021 included Central Coast Alliance United for a Sustainable Economy, Leadership Counsel for Justice and Accountability, Physicians for Social Responsibility—Los Angeles, and Strategic Concepts in Organizing and Policy Education. In 2010, the network hired two full-time staff to coordinate members' policy efforts, which substantially increased its activities. CEJA hired more staff over time, and by 2021 had three offices and sixteen staff members.

22. Coe, "Calif. Trash-to-Energy Plants May Labor for Renewable Status."

23. Perkins and Dillon, "Gonzales." Industry proponents insist that in what they call modern "waste-to-energy facilities," such as the one proposed in Gonzales, waste is "super-heated," not burned. Activists insist these facilities are simply "incinerators in disguise." Greenaction for Health and Environmental Justice and Global Alliance for Incinerator Alternatives, "Incinerators in Disguise."

24. "Henry Clark and Ahmadia Thomas," 37.

25. "Henry Clark and Ahmadia Thomas," 37.

26. Ottinger, *Refining Expertise*.

27. "Q & A: A Conversation with Dr. Henry Clark."

28. Eventually, CEJA's efforts helped pass AB 693 in 2015, which created the Multifamily Affordable Housing Renewable Energy Program. The program funds rooftop solar panels on the homes of low-income renters, aiming to reduce reliance on fossil fuels and thereby lower air pollution levels, while also reducing electricity bills for low-income people.

29. Gould and Lewis, *Green Gentrification*.

30. Walker, McQuarrie, and Lee, "Rising Participation and Declining Democracy," 7.

31. Walker, McQuarrie, and Lee, "Rising Participation and Declining Democracy," 7–12.

32. Skocpol, *Diminished Democracy*.

33. Brulle and Jenkins, "Foundations and the Environmental Movement"; and Jenkins et al., "Foundation Funding of the Environmental Movement."

34. Jenkins, "Resource Mobilization Theory and the Study of Social Movements"; Jenkins et al., "Foundation Funding of the Environmental Movement"; McCarthy and Zald, "Resource Mobilization and Social Movements"; and McCarthy and Zald, *Trend of Social Movements in America*.

35. "Henry Clark and Ahmadia Thomas," 37.

36. Roelofs, *Foundations and Public Policy*; Arnove, *Philanthropy and Cultural Imperialism*; Incite! Women of Color Against Violence, *Revolution Will Not Be Funded*; Brulle, *Agency, Democracy, and Nature*; and Brulle and Jenkins, "Foundations and the Environmental Movement."

37. There are many other documented cases of this kind of pressure from funders. Brulle and Jenkins write that during the early years of the Natural Resources Defense Council (NRDC), "the Ford Foundation pressured the organization to abandon an aggressive legal strategy of suing corporations, which resulted in the firing of several of the legal staff and the creation of a screening board controlled by the Ford Foundation for any lawsuits undertaken by the NRDC." Brulle and Jenkins, "Foundations and the Environmental Movement," 162. Similarly, Aldon Morris and Megan Francis describe how the Student Nonviolent Coordinating Committee (SNCC) and the National Association for the Advancement of Colored People (NAACP) both moderated their tactics in response to foundation preferences. Taylor, *From #BlackLivesMatter to Black Liberation*, 178, 179–80.

38. Even the budgets of these relatively "large" environmental justice groups still pale in comparison to the budgets of the largest groups from the broader environmental movement, which regularly top $100 million. *Forbes*, "200 Largest U.S. Charities: Environment/Animal."

39. Harrison, "Bureaucrats' Tacit Understandings and Social Movement Policy Implementation"; and Harrison, "Coopted Environmental Justice?"

40. Some social movement scholars note that police responses to Black protesters are often an exception to the shift from "escalated force" to "negotiated management." Davenport, Soule, and Armstrong II, "Protesting While Black?" Other scholars point to changes in the general trend away from "escalated force" to "negotiated management" policing tactics by suggesting tightened phases of policing protest stem from the disruptive protests at the 1999 World

Trade Organization meeting in Seattle and the terrorist attacks on New York of September 11, 2001.

41. McPhail, Schweingruber, and McCarthy, "Policing Protest in the United States."

42. Yoder, "Tale of Two (Occupied) Cities," 598.

43. Mitchell and Staeheli, "Permitting Protest," 805.

44. Mitchell and Staeheli, "Permitting Protest," 797. Here, they draw on Marx, "Afterword: Some Reflections on the Democratic Policing of Demonstrations."

45. Piven and Cloward, *Poor People's Movements*.

46. Piven and Cloward, "Collective Protest," 452.

CHAPTER 3. EXPLAINING THE CHANGES IN ENVIRONMENTAL JUSTICE ACTIVISM

1. Early collective behavior scholars used a "natural history" approach to argue that social movements typically progress through a series of stages toward institutionalization. Some contemporary social movement scholars argue that these classical theories of social movement stages underestimate the variations within the general trend. Staggenborg, "Consequences of Professionalization and Formalization in the Pro-Choice Movement." Others enrich the standard narrative by placing movement institutionalization within its historical context. Skocpol, for example, situates this trend within the broader decline of membership organizations. Skocpol, *Diminished Democracy*. Here I focus on the historical context's facilitation of social movement institutionalization, which between the 1960s and the 2010s moved toward institutionalization and professionalization, with some clear exceptions.

2. Kline, *First Along the River*; and McDonnell, "'Rubble Rousers' Fight Dump."

3. Bacon, "Immigrants: The Mountain of Concrete."

4. Loh, "Where Do We Go from Here?"

5 Some nonprofits seek to lessen hierarchy within their ranks, and several California environmental justice NGOs have experimented with a model of two codirectors rather than a single executive director.

6. Romero, *As California Goes, So Goes the Nation?*

7. National Association of Latino Elected and Appointed Officials Educational Fund, *Profile of Latino Elected Officials in the United States and Their Progress since 1996*.

8. Baldassare et al., *PPIC Statewide Survey*; Hertsgaard, "Latinos Are Ready to Fight Climate Change"; Sahagun, "Latinos, Asians More Worried about Environment Than Whites"; Sierra Club, *National Survey of Hispanic Voters on Environmental Issues*; and Sierra Club and National Council of La Raza, *2012 National Latinos and the Environment Survey*. In California, Latinx and Asian Pacific Americans reported worrying more about global warming, soil and water contamination, and air pollution than whites. Another study finds that Latinx and Black people are more concerned about air pollution than other racialized groups. Black people are the most likely to think the federal and state

governments are not doing enough to combat air pollution, followed by Latinx, Asian Pacific Americans, and then whites. Baldassare et al., *PPIC Statewide Survey*.

9. Cervas, "Legislature Should Stand Up for Environmental Justice."

10. Between 1996 and 2007, the number of Latinx elected officials in California grew by 67.8 percent, to 1,163 people. Nationally, Latinx elected officials grew by 52.0 percent during the same time period at the federal level. National Association of Latino Elected and Appointed Officials Educational Fund, *Profile of Latino Elected Officials in the United States and Their Progress since 1996*.

11. Gutiérrez, "Mothers of East Los Angeles Strike Back," 229.

12. Not all of these bills were signed into law by the governor. Peter, "Implementing Environmental Justice"; and Matsuoka, *Building Healthy Communities from the Ground Up*.

13. Méndez, *Climate Change from the Streets*. At the time of this writing, the Latino Caucus is made up of seven senators and twenty-one assembly members, with five auxiliary members from other positions in state government. Their members have held positions including the president pro tempore of the Senate, the Assembly majority whip, the Assembly majority floor leader, the attorney general, the secretary of state, and the chairs of many committees relevant to environmental justice policymaking.

14. Pastor, *State of Resistance*, 14.

15. Bonilla-Silva, *Racism without Racists*, 4th ed., 310.

16. Bacon, "Immigrants: The Mountain of Concrete."

17. Phillips, *Brown Is the New White*, 149, 150.

18. League of Conservation Voters, *2016 National Environmental Scorecard*.

19. Demographic change and the upward mobility of some people of color after the civil rights victories of the mid-nineteenth century have shaped the way that class structures are racialized. In *Black Bourgeoisie*, sociologist Franklin E. Frazier, the first Black president of the American Sociological Association, wrote a piercing critique of the mid-century Black middle class. He argued that their aspirations for upward mobility within white society made them willing participants in capitalist class inequality even as whites continued to reject them. Frazier, *Black Bourgeoisie*. Writer Margo Jefferson describes how during her childhood, upper- and middle-class Black children were trained to distance themselves from working-class and poor Black children—a theme echoed by others writing about contemporary Black life. Jefferson, *Negroland*; and Lacy, *Blue-Chip Black*. For information on Black and Latinx upward class mobility, see Black Demographics, "African American Income"; and Clark, *Immigration and Hispanic Middle Class*. For information on the changing racial makeup of the US middle class, see Reeves and Busette, "Middle Class Is Becoming Race-Plural."

20. Exposure to environmental pollutants is both raced and classed. People of color at all income levels are more likely to live near a greenhouse gas–emitting facility (and the co-pollutants it emits) than their white counterparts at the equivalent income level, but the likelihood of living near a greenhouse gas–emitting facility also decreases with increasing income. Pastor et al., "Minding the Climate Gap."

21. Baldassare et al., *PPIC Statewide Survey*. Given predictions that both the US population and the middle class will be made up of a majority of people of color by the early 2040s, it is more important than ever to analyze the intersection of race and class politics.

22. Bonilla-Silva, *Racism without Racists*, 5th ed., 188; and López, *Dog Whistle Politics*.

23. Anderson, *White Rage*.

24. Gross and Stretesky, "Environmental Justice in the Court."

25. Deloitte Consulting, *Evaluation of the EPA Office of Civil Rights*; and US Commission on Civil Rights, *Environmental Justice*.

26. Center on Race, Poverty and the Environment, *Right without a Remedy*.

27. Holifield, "Neoliberalism and Environmental Justice in the United States Environmental Protection Agency"; Liévanos, "Certainty, Fairness, and Balance"; and London, Sze, and Liévanos, "Problems, Promise, Progress, and Perils."

28. Most of my interviews took place before the uptick in white supremacist hate crimes that accompanied the Trump presidency, so I do not know what interviewees' experiences of racism were during that time.

29. Harrison, "'We Do Ecology, Not Sociology,'" 206.

30. Scholar Jill Harrison interviewed government staffers active in environmental justice issues across the country about their experiences inside the halls of government. She found that "smiling" racism is pervasive in the state institutions that most directly impact environmental justice work, as purportedly "color-blind" staffers assert that there is no pattern of racism and thus no need to do anything about it. However, when racism is brought up, these "smiling," "color-blind" people fight back: they bully the victims of racism, deny the severity of the environmental problems in communities of color, and actively ignore environmental justice staff and their contributions. Harrison, "'We Do Ecology, Not Sociology.'"

31. Bogado, "What This California Department's Racist Emails Could Mean."

32. McGreevy, "Toxics Agency Chief Condemns Racially Charged Emails."

33. Harvey, *Brief History of Neoliberalism*, 2.

34. Pulido, "Flint, Environmental Racism, and Racial Capitalism," 1. See also Robinson, *Black Marxism*.

35. Gilens, *Why Americans Hate Welfare*; and Wiltz, "Racial Generation Gap Looms Large for States." Political attacks on social safety nets such as welfare are highly racialized. Reagan made an art of this with his racially coded "dog whistle" speeches, which implicitly communicated racial resentment to his white voters. For example, his speeches about "welfare queens" who supposedly cheat the system by having multiple children out of wedlock and using public dollars to buy Cadillacs imply (but do not explicitly say) that those who "cheat the system" are Black. López, *Dog Whistle Politics*.

36. For example, Ira Katznelson argues persuasively that the 1930s-era policies of the New Deal funneled public support differentially to whites—what he calls affirmative action for whites, although the term affirmative action did not appear in American politics until the 1960s (and then was used in reference

to Black people as its proposed beneficiaries). Katznelson, *When Affirmative Action Was White*. As Katznelson shows, support for K–12 public schools is one vivid example of this trend: as public schools were racially integrated, many white people pulled their children out and placed them instead in private schools. As a result, over time political support among whites for funding public schools declined, and today's schools are even more racially segregated than they were in the 1950s. The white desire to not invest in public goods that may also go to people of color can increase in the face of demographic shifts; in the 1990s California saw a wave of anti-immigrant sentiment and legislation. Prop 187 (1994), also known as the "Save Our State" initiative, restricted access to state services for undocumented residents; it was later declared unconstitutional. In 1996, Prop 209 ended the affirmative action programs in the state's flagship system of higher education, and in 1998, Prop 227 ended bilingual education in the state's public schools.

37. Andrews, *Managing the Environment, Managing Ourselves.*

38. Murphy, "Uncertain Exposures and the Privilege of Imperception," 272.

39. Holifield, "Neoliberalism and Environmental Justice."

40. Harrison, "Coopted Environmental Justice?"

41. Harrison attributes this outcome to two factors. CalEPA has a supportive policy environment, within which staffers can pursue programming aligned with environmental justice goals; in addition, their decision-makers are political appointees rather than staff. According to Harrison, appointees are far less susceptible to outside influence; staffers may be influenced by threats to their jobs, but appointees' jobs are inherently term limited. While Harrison finds that CalEPA environmental justice grants are less neoliberal than most, the San Francisco EJ Grants Program, which she describes as neoliberal, is an exception to these California findings. Harrison, "Coopted Environmental Justice?"

42. Kenney et al., *Evaluating the Use of Good Neighbor Agreements.*

43. Jatkar and London, "From Testimony to Transformation."

44. Wall, Rotkin-Ellman, and Solomon, *Uneven Shield*, 16.

45. Wall, Rotkin-Ellman, and Solomon, *Uneven Shield.*

46. Filter, *2009 Environmental Justice Enforcement Initiative Report*, 5.

47. Filter, *2009 Environmental Justice Enforcement Initiative Report*, 7.

48. These online reporting networks now exist in Imperial Valley, Kern County, Fresno, Coachella Valley, Wilmington, Bayview-Hunters Point, and Kings County. For more information see Jatkar and London, "From Testimony to Transformation."

49. Jatkar and London, "From Testimony to Transformation."

50. Huynh, "Evaluating the Innovation Value Access Network (IVAN) Model," as cited in Jatkar and London, "From Testimony to Transformation," 7.

51. Jatkar and London, "From Testimony to Transformation."

52. Fox, "The Uncertain Relationship between Transparency and Accountability."

53. Environmental Enforcement Watch, *Congressional Report Card* (violations may be underreported by up to 85 percent); and Fredrickson et al., *Sheep in the Closet* (lowest level since the EPA began recording inspections in 1994).

54. Kelderman, Schaeffer, Pelton, Phillips, and Bernhardt, *The Thin Green Line.*

55. Environmental Enforcement Watch, *Congressional Report Card.*

56. Environmental Enforcement Watch, *Congressional Report Card.*

57. Environmental Enforcement Watch, *Congressional Report Card.*

58. Environmental Enforcement Watch, *Congressional Report Card.*

59. For a description of how funders prioritize these approaches in California's Central Valley, see Kohl-Arenas, "Governing Poverty amidst Plenty."

60. Gottlieb, *Forcing the Spring,* 10.

61. Costco pays higher hourly wages and has better benefits than competitors such as Walmart, and some Costco workers are unionized.

62. Dillon, "Breathers of Bayview Hill"; and Dillon, "Race, Waste, and Space."

63. Checker, "Wiped Out by the 'Greenwave,'" 216; and Gould and Lewis, *Green Gentrification.*

64. Mares and Alkon, "Mapping the Food Movement"; and Guthman, "Neoliberalism and the Making of Food Politics in California."

65. Nembhard, *Collective Courage*; and White, *Freedom Farmers.*

66. Szasz, *Ecopopulsim.*

67. Harrison, *Pesticide Drift*; and Perkins, *In Her Own Words.*

68. Perkins, "Voices."

69. Jain, *Malignant,* 13. Sociologist Javier Auyero and anthropologist Débora Swistun, too, show how long-term exposure can habituate people to toxic contamination in ways that undermine the potential for collective action. Auyero and Swistun, *Flammable.*

70. See note 15 in chapter 1.

71. Brooker and Meyer, "Coalitions and the Organization of Collective Action."

CHAPTER 4. KETTLEMAN CITY

1. The landfill is managed by Chemical Waste Management, Inc., a subsidiary of Waste Management. Speakers use variations of both names (Chemical Waste, Chem Waste, and Waste Management), usually to refer to the local managers of the landfill.

2. US Bureau of the Census, "ACS Demographic and Housing Estimates" (Latinx population); US Bureau of the Census, "Educational Attainment" (education); and US Bureau of the Census, "Selected Economic Characteristics" (income).

3. Cole and Foster, *From the Ground Up*; and Bullard, *Confronting Environmental Racism.*

4. See chapter 1, note 15.

5. Pellow, "Environmental Inequality Formation"; and Gould, Schnaiberg, and Weinberg, *Local Environmental Struggles.*

6. Baptista and Perovich, *U.S. Municipal Solid Waste Incinerators;* Costner and Thornton, *Playing with Fire*; and White, "Hazardous Waste Incineration and Minority Communities."

7. Cole and Foster, *From the Ground Up.*

8. The Cerrell Report itself does not specify race as a category by which locations for incinerators should be chosen, but many of the proposed locations were nonetheless in communities of color. Powell, *Political Difficulties Facing Waste-to-Energy Conversion Plant Siting.*

9. Perkins, "Voices."

10. Perkins, "Multiple People of Color Origins of the US Environmental Justice Movement"; and Perkins, "Women's Pathways into Activism."

11. Cole, "Environmental Justice Litigation."

12. Cole and Foster, *From the Ground Up.*

13. Cole and Foster, *From the Ground Up.*

14. Cole and Foster, *From the Ground Up*, 7.

15. Perkins, "Voices."

16. Cole and Foster, *From the Ground Up.*

17. Morello-Frosch, Zuk, et al., "Understanding the Cumulative Impacts of Inequalities in Environmental Health."

18. Nidever, "Sludge Composting Plant Starts Up."

19. Boxer, "Boxer Asks Bodman."

20. Perkins, "Voices."

21. Perkins, "Voices."

22. El Pueblo Para El Aire y Agua Limpio, "Is There a Toxic Monster in Kettleman City?"

23. California Environmental Protection Agency and California Department of Public Health, "Investigation of Birth Defects and Community Exposures in Kettleman City."

24. While the overall cumulative health risk was not addressed, the cumulative exposure to multiple pesticides was considered in the study.

25. El Pueblo Para El Aire y Agua Limpio, "Is There a Toxic Monster in Kettleman City?"

26. Richter, "Constructing Insignificance."

27. Brown and Mikkelsen, *No Safe Place*; Morello-Frosch, Pastor, et al., "Citizens, Science, and Data Judo"; and Scammell and Howard, *Is a Health Study Right for Your Community?*

28. Richter, "Constructing Insignificance."

29. Richter, "Constructing Insignificance," 116.

30. California Department of Toxic Substances Control, "CWM Kettleman Hills Facility RCRA/TSCA Inspections 1983–Present."

31. California Department of Public Health, *Birth Defects in Kettleman City and Surrounding Areas.*

32. Nidever, "Sludge Composting Plant Starts Up."

33. As of April 30, 2019, Kings County's nonattainment of air pollution standards was "extreme" for the eight-hour ozone National Ambient Air Quality Standards (NAAQS). Kings County, where Kettleman City is located, was also out of attainment with PM 2.5 NAAQS. US Environmental Protection Agency, "Current Nonattainment Counties for All Criteria Pollutants."

34. US Environmental Protection Agency, *Kettleman City Residential Sampling.*

35. Hull, "Big Air Quality Win for Enviros in 9th Circuit"; and Center for Biological Diversity, "Federal Court Strikes Down Illegal Permit for Avenal Power Plant in California."

36. Harrison, "Coopted Environmental Justice."

37. Naturally occurring arsenic in some regions and underfunded water districts with poorly maintained pipes and other water infrastructure also contribute to drinking water contamination across the San Joaquin Valley. Balazs et al., "Social Disparities in Nitrate Contaminated Drinking Water"; Balazs et al., "Environmental Justice Implications of Arsenic Contamination"; and Balazs and Ray, "Drinking Water Disparities Framework."

38. Forbes, "#458 Waste Management."

39. Abramsky, "T Is for Toxic."

40. Nidever, "Kettleman Hopes Bottled Water Continues."

41. Cohn, "Small Community Is One of Many Grappling with Big Water Problems."

42. State of California Assembly Bill 1329, Hazardous Waste, passed September 25, 2013.

43. Alexeeff et al., *Cumulative Impacts*; and Goss and Kroeger, *White Paper on Potential Control Strategies.*

44. In Kettleman City, these PR efforts include, among other things, providing T-shirts for the local soccer team and inviting local schoolchildren to tour the landfill as a class field trip.

45. Valley fever is a fungal infection endemic to the San Joaquin Valley and other parts of the arid West. It can cause fever, chest pain, coughing, aching joints, and chronic fatigue, and in the worst cases can lead to meningitis and chronic pneumonia.

46. For a broader discussion of the limitations of environmental consumerism as a response to environmental threats, see Szasz, *Shopping Our Way to Safety.*

CHAPTER 5. CALIFORNIA CLIMATE CHANGE BILL AB 32

1. The ARB is governed by a sixteen-member board appointed by the governor and/or the state senate and assembly. Of these sixteen, two represent environmental justice communities. ARB manages thirty-five local and regional air pollution control districts across California; these local boards manage industrial pollution, issue permits, and develop air plans for their areas. California Environmental Protection Agency Air Resources Board, "History of Air Resources Board." This chapter builds on my prior analysis of efforts to tie California's carbon market to offsets in Chiapas, Mexico. Perkins and Soto-Karlin, "Situating Global Policies within Local Realities." It also builds on existing research covering climate politics in California, in particular by Alice Kaswan, Julie Sze, Jonathan London, Michael Méndez, and their coauthors. Like them, I also highlight the conflict over market-based policy versus direct regulation, the shortcomings of advisory committees, and the importance of scalar thinking and racism to understanding environmental justice activists' concerns. One difference between our approaches is the larger pool of environmental justice

activists my work draws on, and conversely, the small number of people I interviewed who work within the state government or mainstream environmental organizations, as well as the lack of interviews with people representing industry. Thus, my research provides broader insights into the perspectives of environmental justice activists, while sacrificing some of the perspectives of people in these other categories beyond what I gleaned from public documents, the news, and other scholarship (including those sources already listed). This chapter, as part of the larger book, also places environmental justice activists' engagement with California climate politics in the context of their many other concerns. It also locates the fights over AB 32 within the changing historical context of the California environmental justice movement. This historical context includes demographic change, the impact of neoliberal political ideology on climate policy, and long-standing efforts of California environmental justice activists to participate in environmental decision-making, all described by the previously mentioned scholars. To these issues I add the context of the long history of racial capitalism as it intertwines with neoliberalism, a critical assessment of the institutionalization of much environmental justice activism within the nonprofit form, the entrenchment of "color-blind" racism, and the decline of more disruptive forms of environmental justice protest. Kaswan, "Climate Change and Environmental Justice"; London, Karner, et al, "Racing Climate Change"; Méndez, *Climate Change from the Streets*; and Sze et al., "Best in Show?"

2. Gnerre, "Fletcher Oil Fire."

3. Jaffe, "Above the Surface and Below"; Srebotnjak and Rotkin-Ellman, *Drilling in California*; and Natural Resources Defense Council, "Fracking Threatens Health of Los Angeles County Communities."

4. Shonkoff et al., "Minding the Climate Gap."

5. Park, *Everybody's Movement*.

6. Park, *Everybody's Movement*, 28.

7. Sze et al., "Best in Show?," 183.

8. Hanemann, "How California Came to Pass AB 32."

9. Bigger, "'We Couldn't Have Done It Without You Guys.'"

10. Méndez, *Climate Change from the Streets*; and Perkins and Soto-Karlin, "Situating Global Policies within Local Realities."

11. Pastor et al., "Minding the Climate Gap"; Pastor et al., "Risky Business"; and Shonkoff et al., "Minding the Climate Gap." AB 32 regulates the following greenhouse gases: carbon dioxide, methane, nitrous oxide, hydrofluorocarbons, perfluorocarbons, and sulfur hexafluoride. When these gases are concentrated (as they are in the workplace), there are health consequences to exposure. Exposure to more dilute forms, such as the levels in the outdoors from the sources at issue here, is much less dangerous. Most advocates and regulators focus on carbon dioxide since it is the largest single contributor to climate change.

12. Sze et al., "Best in Show?"; and Méndez, *Climate Change from the Streets*.

13. Ejmatters.org, "Factsheet: The Cap and Trade Charade for Climate Change"; McAllister, "Overallocation Problem in Cap-and-Trade"; and Wara and Victor, "Realistic Policy on International Carbon Offsets." Though environmental justice advocates remain supportive of a state-level climate change

policy in general, others have raised concerns about the efficacy of *any* non-global efforts to slow climate change. For example, researchers find that greenhouse gas emissions have declined in developed countries in part by offshoring industry to poorer countries, which changes the distribution of global greenhouse gas emissions without actually reducing them. Peters et al., "Growth in Emission Transfers."

14. Taylor, "Letter to Senator Darrell Steinberg and Speaker John A. Perez."

15. Hull, "13 Things to Know about California's Cap-and-Trade Program."

16. Hanemann, "How California Came to Pass AB 32"; and Sze et al., "Best in Show?"

17. Martin, "Núñez Slams Governor on Emission Law."

18. State of California Assembly Bill 32, Chapter 488, Section 38570.

19. Morello-Frosch, Pastor, and Sadd, "Environmental Justice and Southern California's 'Riskscape'"; Rechtschaffen, Guana, and O'Neill, *Environmental Justice.*

20. State of California Assembly Bill 32, ch. 488, § 38591.

21. State of California Assembly Bill 32, ch. 488, § 38562 ("disproportionately impact low-income communities"); and State of California Assembly Bill 32, ch. 488, § 38565 ("most disadvantaged communities in California").

22. Environmental Justice Advisory Committee on the Implementation of the Global Warming Solutions Act of 2006, "Recommendation and Comments."

23. Taylor, *Toxic Communities*; and Pulido, "Critical Review of the Methodology."

24. Environmental Justice Advisory Committee on the Implementation of the Global Warming Solutions Act of 2006, "Recommendation and Comments." See also London, Karner, et al., "Racing Climate Change," for a conceptualization of how market and state optimism and pessimism impacted the battle over cap-and-trade in AB 32.

25. "Global Warming I."

26. Environmental Justice Advisory Committee on the Implementation of the Global Warming Solutions Act of 2006, "Recommendation and Comments."

27. Farrell, "Just Transition," 58.

28. The plaintiffs included the Association of Irritated Residents, CCAT, Communities for a Better Environment, Coalition for a Safe Environment, Society of Positive Action, West County Toxics Coalition, and advisory committee members or alternates Angela Johnson Meszaros, Caroline Farrell, Henry Clark, Jesse N. Marquez, Martha Dina Arguello, Shabaka Heru, and Tom Frantz. They were represented by lawyers at the Center on Race, Poverty and the Environment and Communities for a Better Environment.

29. NRDC, the other key mainstream organization that supported AB 32, did not try to intervene in the suit against the environmental justice advocates, although it supported the inclusion of cap-and-trade within the Scoping Plan. Eberhard, "Air Board Should Move Ahead with AB 32 Scoping Plan."

30. Krupp and Horn, *Earth, the Sequel*; Krupp, "EDF and the Third Wave of Environmentalism"; and Ruta, "Environmental Defense Fund."

31. Newell, "Climate Justice."

32. Pooley, "In Defense of Unlikely Partnerships."

33. Hauter, "Environmental Defense Fund."

34. Park, *Everybody's Movement*.

35. Fimrite, "Sierra Club Wants Landmark Climate Law Altered"; and Magavern, "Re: Need to Re-Evaluate AB 32 Cap-and-Trade Rule."

36. Association of Irritated Residents v. California Air Resources Board (Cal. Ct. App., 2012).

37. Magavern, "Re: Need to Re-Evaluate AB 32 Cap-and-Trade Rule"; and Activist San Diego et al., "Re: Climate Change Policy."

38. The judge did support one of their claims in this section of the case. While assessing the claim that the ARB did not evaluate the potential health effects of its proposed plan for the agricultural sector, Judge Goldsmith writes: "An examination of the Agricultural Working Group's document 'The Agriculture Sector Summary and Analysis' reveals that the health evaluation merely consists of two sentences. . . . In the analysis of voluntary and incentivized measures for the agricultural sector, the record does not demonstrate that ARB used the best available models as required by AB 32." Association of Irritated Residents v. California Air Resources Board (Cal. Super. Ct., 2011). However, Judge Goldsmith does not refer to this point again, nor does he require the problem be remedied.

39. Association of Irritated Residents v. California Air Resources Board (Cal. Ct. App., 2012).

40. Corburn, *Street Science*; Minkler and Wallerstein, *Community-Based Participatory Research for Health*; Morello-Frosch, Pastor, et al., "Citizens, Science, and Data Judo"; and Oreskes and Conway, *Merchants of Doubt*.

41. Association of Irritated Residents v. California Air Resources Board (Cal. Super. Ct., 2011).

42. Kaswan, "Climate Change and Environmental Justice," 13.

43. California Rural Legal Assistance Foundation et al., "Re: Comments on U.S. Environmental Protection Agency Draft Policy Papers."

44. Kaswan, "Climate Change and Environmental Justice."

45. Zagofsky, "Process Evaluation."

46. Hecht, "California Environmental Justice Advocates Sue Air Resources Board."

47. When this speaker references Spanish speakers getting "twice as much" time to speak at public hearings, they are alluding to environmental justice activists' successful efforts to ensure that the time used to translate monolingual Spanish speakers' comments into English at public hearings is not counted against the overall time they are allowed to speak.

48. Other committees had more impact. Bigger analyzes the role of financial actors in the creation of AB 32, whose efforts on the Economy and Allocation Advisory Committee had a much different outcome than the EJAC's, writing that they had "enormous clout in shaping the central epistemic framework" of AB 32. Bigger, "'We Couldn't Have Done It without You Guys,'" 7. Part of the power of the committees that Bigger describes comes from the fact that "regulators cannot accomplish their mandate without the participation of financial capital," 15.

49. Hemphill, "Justice in Fighting Prop 23."

50. See Méndez, *Climate Change from the Streets,* for more details on the policy history of SB 535.

51. Méndez, *Climate Change from the Streets.*

52. California Environmental Justice Alliance, "Environmental Justice Groups Disappointed by the Speakers' Actions."

53. Currie, "Air Resources Board Elevates Environmental Justice to Executive Level."

54. California Air Resources Board, "California Climate Investments Legislative Guidance."

55. Cart, "They Come Hat in Hand."

56. Stark, "Newsom Catches Heat for Using Climate Funds on Drinking Water Plan."

57. Haya, "AB 398's Use of Excess Carbon Credits Instead of Real Reductions"; Haya et al., "RE: Public Comments on Methods"; and Taylor, *Cap-and-Trade Extension.*

58. Aronoff, "California Gov. Jerry Brown Was a Climate Leader."

59. California Environmental Justice Alliance, "CEJA Announces Opposition to AB 398 and ACA 1."

60. Cervas and Vanderwarker, "Justice Deferred."

61. Fowlie, Walker, and Wooley, "Climate Policy, Environmental Justice, and Local Air Pollution."

62. London, Nguyen, et al., *Community Engagement in AB 617.*

63. Fowlie, Walker, and Wooley, "Climate Policy, Environmental Justice, and Local Air Pollution."

64. Cervas and Vanderwarker, "Justice Deferred."

65. Goodman, "'Climate Capitalism Is Killing Our Communities'"; and California Environmental Justice Alliance, "Community Solutions Take Center Stage."

66. This builds on the original goal of 20 percent by 2020 (set in 2002). Now the targets are 50 percent by 2026, 60 percent by 2030, and 100 percent carbon free (but not necessarily renewable) by 2045.

67. Roberts, "California Gov. Jerry Brown Casually Unveils History's Most Ambitious Climate Target"; and Brown "Executive Order B-55-18 to Achieve Carbon Neutrality."

68. Mishak, "Big Oil's Grip on California."

69. Aronoff, "California Gov. Jerry Brown Was a Climate Leader."

70. In some recent cases, California has worked to block further fossil fuel development in the state. In response to the Trump administration's announcement that offshore waters of the Pacific Ocean would be opened for oil drilling, the California legislature passed two bills in 2018 preventing the new drilling by blocking the construction of the necessary transportation infrastructure on state lands. Phillips, "Trump Fracking Plan Targets over 1 Million Acres in California."

71. Horn, "As Indigenous Peoples Protest, California Approves Global Cap-And-Trade Plan"; and Greenleaf, "California Polluters May Soon Buy Carbon 'Offsets' from the Amazon."

72. Hudson et al., "Re: EPA Administrator Appointment."

73. Instead of Nichols, Michael Regan, the head of the North Carolina Department of Environmental Quality, was nominated as the federal EPA administrator. Regan is the first Black man to head the agency. He prioritized some environmental justice concerns during his tenure in North Carolina, though he too faces criticism from some North Carolinians who have suffered environmental harms during his leadership of the state's environmental decision-making. Kahn, "California Environmentalists Quietly Seethe at Activists over Nichols Losing EPA Job"; California Environmental Justice Alliance, "Statement on the Nomination of Michael Regan for EPA Administrator."

74. Cushing, Blaustein-Retjo, et al., "Carbon Trading, Co-Pollutants, and Environmental Equity"; Cushing, Wander, et al., *A Preliminary Environmental Equity Assessment of California's Cap-and-Trade Program*; and Johnson, "Biggest Fight over Cap and Trade Isn't about What You Think It Is."

75. Hernandez-Cortes and Meng, "Do Environmental Markets Cause Environmental Injustice?"

76. Cullenward and Valenzuela, "Critique of 'Do Environmental Markets Cause Environmental Injustice?'"; and Hansen, "State Officials Dispute Cap-and-Trade Study Conclusions."

77. Cushing, Blaustein-Retjo, et al., "Carbon Trading, Co-Pollutants, and Environmental Equity"; and Cullenward, Inman, and Mastrandrea, "California's Climate Emissions Are Falling."

78. Perkins and Dillon, "Gonzales" ("renewable energy" in California); and Mulvaney, *Solar Power* (Indigenous lands in the California deserts).

CONCLUSION

1. Bullard et al., *Toxic Wastes and Race at Twenty*.

2. Californians for Pesticide Reform, "Pesticide Use in California Remains at Record High, New Data Show." For more details, see California Department of Pesticide Regulation, "Summary of Pesticide Use Report Data—2018."

3. Alexeeff et al., *Cumulative Impacts*; Capitman and Tyner, *Impacts of Short-Term Changes in Air Quality on Emergency Room and Hospital Use*; Morello-Frosch, Pastor, and Sadd, "Environmental Justice and Southern California's 'Riskscape'"; and Morello-Frosch, Zuk, et al., "Understanding the Cumulative Impacts of Inequalities in Environmental Health."

4. Ard, "Trends in Exposure to Industrial Air Toxins"; Bullock, Ard, and Saalman, "Measuring the Relationship between State Environmental Justice Action and Air Pollution Inequality"; Currie, Voorheis, and Walker, "What Caused Racial Disparities in Particulate Exposure to Fall?"; Kravitz-Wirtz et al., "Long-Term Dynamics of Racial/Ethnic Inequality"; and Salazar et al., "Race, Income, and Environmental Inequality in the U.S. States."

5. Piven and Cloward, *Poor People's Movements*; and Staggenborg, "Consequences of Professionalization and Formalization." As a counterexample, Greenpeace worked with environmental justice activists in the 1980s and 1990s, showing that some formal NGOs can promote direct-action techniques.

6. Brooker and Meyer, "Coalitions and the Organization of Collective Action."

7. Harrison, "Abandoned Bodies and Spaces of Sacrifice."

8. Guthman, "Neoliberalism and the Making of Food Politics in California"; and Mares and Alkon, "Mapping the Food Movement."

9. Solnit, *Hope in the Dark*, 60.

10. *State of the Air 2019*; and Harrison, *Pesticide Drift*.

11. Wolf and Siegel, *Oil Stain*; and US Energy Information Administration, "California" (dirtiest oil). One recent study estimated that in the next seventy years, more than fifteen thousand cases of cancer could be related to drinking water contamination in California. Nichols, "TRUE"; and Stoiber et al., "Applying a Cumulative Risk Framework to Drinking Water Assessment."

12. Sommeiller and Price, *The New Gilded Age* (economic growth at the state level); Cowan, *California's San Joaquin Valley*; "Down on the Farms"; and Martinez, "Poverty Plagues 'New Appalachia.'"

13. Matsuoka et al., *Global Trade Impacts*.

14. CEQA was passed in 1970, shortly after its federal equivalent, the National Environmental Protection Act (NEPA). CEQA is stronger than NEPA and stronger than most equivalent policies in the states that have them. Texas does not have its own state environmental version of NEPA.

15. Egelko, "California to Block Food Pesticide."

16. Smith, Sonnenfeld, and Pellow, eds., *Challenging the Chip*; Pellow and Park, *Silicon Valley of Dreams*; and Pellow, *Resisting Global Toxics*.

17. Pellow, *Resisting Global Toxics*.

18. Pellow, *What Is Critical Environmental Justice?*; and Pulido, Kohl, and Cotton, "State Regulation and Environmental Justice."

19. Omi and Winant, *Racial Formation in the United States*, 1, citing Lipsitz, *Possessive Investment in Whiteness*.

20. Pellow, *What Is Critical Environmental Justice?*

21. Farhang and Katznelson, "Southern Imposition." Ira Katznelson has described many of the victories of this period as "affirmative action for whites." Katznelson, *When Affirmative Action Was White*. Other scholars are more optimistic about the Progressive Era, arguing that the 1930s were a turning point that later led to meaningful racial reforms. See Sitkoff, *New Deal for Blacks*.

22. Allen, *Black Awakening in Capitalist America*; and Marable, *How Capitalism Underdeveloped Black America*.

23. Douglass, *The Life and Writings of Frederick Douglass*, 437.

24. "Share the Burden."

25. Pulido et al., "Environmental Deregulation, Spectacular Racism, and White Nationalism."

26. Perkins, "Multiple People of Color Origins of the US Environmental Justice Movement."

Bibliography

Abascal, Ralph Santiago. "California Rural Legal Assistance and Environmental Justice." *Chicano-Latino Law Review* 14, no. 1 (1994): 44–47.

Abascal, Ralph Santiago, and Luke W. Cole. "The Struggle for Environmental Justice: Legal Services Advocates Tackle Environmental Poverty Law." *Clearinghouse Review* 24, no. 4 (1995): 459–63.

Abel, Troy D., Debra J. Salazar, and Patricia Robert. "States of Environmental Justice: Redistributive Politics across the United States, 1993–2004." *Review of Policy Research* 32, no. 2 (2015): 200–225. https://doi.org/10.1111/ropr.12119.

Abramsky, Sasha. "T Is for Toxic: Danger Lurking in California School Drinking Fountains." Water Deeply, July 5, 2017. www.newsdeeply.com/water/articles/2017/07/05/t-is-for-toxic-danger-lurking-in-california-school-drinking-fountains.

Activist San Diego et al. "Re: Climate Change Policy—International Forest Offsets in California's Cap and Trade." July 10, 2012. https://1bps6437gg8c169ioy1drtgz-wpengine.netdna-ssl.com/wp-content/uploads/2018/10/Letter_to_Governor_and_ARB_re_CA_REDD_final.pdf.

Agyeman, Julian, David Schlosberg, Luke Craven, and Caitlin Matthews. "Trends and Directions in Environmental Justice: From Inequity to Everyday Life, Community, and Just Sustainabilities." *Annual Review of Environment and Resources* 41 (2016): 6.1–6.20. https://doi.org/10.1146/annurev-environ-110615-090052.

Alexeeff, George, John Faust, Laura Meehan August, Carmen Milanes, Karen Randles, and Lauren Zeise. *Cumulative Impacts: Building a Scientific*

Foundation. Sacramento: California Environmental Protection Agency, 2010.

Ali, Bezait, Dylan Avatar-Arnold, Anthy Alexiades, and David Shugar. "Waste Incineration in California and Impacts to Waste Hierarchy." U.S.-Denmark Summer Workshop on Renewable Energy, Technical University of Denmark, Lyngby, Denmark, July–August 2013.

Alkon, Alison Hope, Marisol Cortez, and Julie Sze. "What Is in a Name? Language, Framing and Environmental Justice Activism in California's Central Valley." *Local Environment* 18, no. 10 (2013): 1167–83. https://doi.org/10.1080/13549839.2013.788483.

Allen, Robert L. *Black Awakening in Capitalist America: An Analytic History.* Trenton, NJ: Africa World Press, 1990.

Almeida, Paul. "The Network for Environmental and Economic Justice in the Southwest: An Interview with Richard Moore." In *Struggle for Ecological Democracy: Environmental Justice Movements in the United States*, edited by Daniel Faber, 159–87. New York: Guilford Press, 1998.

Anderson, Carol. *White Rage: The Unspoken Truth of Our Racial Divide.* New York: Bloomsbury, 2016.

Andrews, Richard N. L. *Managing the Environment, Managing Ourselves: A History of American Environmental Policy.* New Haven, CT: Yale University Press, 2006.

Angel, Bradley. *The Toxic Threat to Indian Lands: A Greenpeace Report.* San Francisco: Greenpeace, 1991. www.ejnet.org/ej/toxicthreattoindianlands.pdf.

Ard, Kerry. "Trends in Exposure to Industrial Air Toxins for Different Racial and Socioeconomic Groups: A Spatial and Temporal Examination of Environmental Inequality in the U.S. from 1995 to 2004." *Social Science Research* 53 (September 2015): 375–90. https://doi.org/10.1016/j.ssresearch.2015.06.019.

Arnove, Robert F., ed. *Philanthropy and Cultural Imperialism.* Boston: G. K. Hall, 1980.

Aronoff, Kate. "California Gov. Jerry Brown Was a Climate Leader, But His Vision Had a Fatal Flaw." The Intercept, November 28, 2018. https://theintercept.com/2018/11/28/california-jerry-brown-climate-legacy/.

Association of Irritated Residents v. California Air Resources Board (Cal. Super. Ct., 2011).

Association of Irritated Residents v. California Air Resources Board (Cal. Ct. App., 2012).

Auyero, Javier, and Débora Alejandra Swistun. *Flammable: Environmental Suffering in an Argentine Shantytown.* New York: Oxford University Press, 2009.

Avila, Magdalena. "Magdalena Avila Tells How Hispanic Farmworkers Stopped an Incinerator." In *Green Versus Gold: Sources in California's Environmental History*, edited by Carolyn Merchant, 445–48. Covelo, CA: Island Press, 1998.

Bacon, David. "Immigrants: The Mountain of Concrete." David Bacon: Stories & Photographs, December 28, 1994. http://dbacon.igc.org/Imgrants/08mount.html.

Baker, Mike, Jennifer Valentino-DeVries, Manny Fernandez, and Michael LaForgia. "Three Words, 70 Cases: The Tragic History of 'I Can't Breathe.'"

New York Times, June 29, 2020. www.nytimes.com/interactive/2020/06/28
/us/i-cant-breathe-police-arrest.html.

Balazs, Carolina, Rachel Morello-Frosch, Alan Hubbard, and Isha Ray. "Social Disparities in Nitrate Contaminated Drinking Water in California's San Joaquin Valley." *Environmental Health Perspectives* 119, no. 9 (2011): 1272–78. https://doi.org/10.1289/ehp.1002878.

Balazs, Carolina L., Rachel Morello-Frosch, Alan E. Hubbard, and Isha Ray. "Environmental Justice Implications of Arsenic Contamination in California's San Joaquin Valley: A Cross-Sectional, Cluster-Design Examining Exposure and Compliance in Community Drinking Water Systems." *Environmental Health* 11 (2012): 84. https://doi.org/10.1186/1476-069X-11-84.

Balazs, Carolina L., and Isha Ray. "The Drinking Water Disparities Framework: On the Origins and Persistence of Inequities in Exposure." *American Journal of Public Health* 104, no. 4 (2014): 603–11. https://doi.org/10.2105 /AJPH.2013.301664.

Baldassare, Mark, Dean Bonner, Sonja Petek, and Jui Shrestha. *PPIC Statewide Survey: Californians and the Environment*. San Francisco: Public Policy Institute of California, 2012. www.ppic.org/content/pubs/survey/S _712MBS.pdf.

Baptista, Ana Isabel, and Adrienne Perovich. *U.S. Municipal Solid Waste Incinerators: An Industry in Decline*. New York: Tishman Environment and Design Center at the New School, 2019.

Beer, Tommy. "Here Are the Police Officers and Other Public Employees Arrested in Connection to Capitol Riot." *Forbes*, January 18, 2021. www .forbes.com/sites/tommybeer/2021/01/18/here-are-the-police-officers-and -other-public-employees-arrested-in-connection-to-capitol-riot/?sh=5fba 5d863c45.

Bell, Shannon Elizabeth. *Fighting King Coal: The Challenges to Micromobilization in Central Appalachia*. Cambridge, MA: MIT Press, 2016.

Bell, Shannon Elizabeth, and Yvonne A. Braun. "Coal, Identity, and the Gendering of Environmental Justice Activism in Central Appalachia." *Gender & Society* 24, no. 6 (December 2010): 794–813. https://doi.org/10.1177 /0891243210387277.

Bigger, Patrick. "'We Couldn't Have Done It without You Guys': Enrolling Finance in Environmental Governance (and Vise-Versa)." Paper presented at the Annual Meeting of the American Association of Geographers, Tampa, FL, April 2014.

Black Demographics. "African American Income." Accessed March 21, 2019. https://blackdemographics.com/households/african-american-income/.

Blight, David W. *Frederick Douglass: Prophet of Freedom*. New York: Simon & Schuster, 2018.

Blumberg, Louis, and Robert Gottlieb. *War on Waste: Can American Win Its Battle with Garbage?* Covelo, CA: Island Press, 1989.

Bogado, Aura. "What This California Department's Racist Emails Could Mean for the Communities It's Supposed to Protect." Grist, December 23, 2015. http://grist.org/politics/what-this-california-departments-racist-emails-could -mean-for-the-communities-its-supposed-to-protect/.

Bonilla-Silva, Eduardo. *Racism without Racists: Color-Blind Racism and the Persistence of Racial Inequality in America.* 4th ed. Lanham, MD: Rowman & Littlefield, 2014.

———. *Racism without Racists: Color-Blind Racism and the Persistence of Racial Inequality in the United States.* 5th ed. Lanham, MD: Rowman & Littlefield, 2018.

———. "'Racists,' 'Class Anxieties,' Hegemonic Racism, and Democracy in Trump's America." *Social Currents* 6, no. 1 (February 2019): 14–31. https://doi.org/10.1177/2329496518804558.

Boxer, Barbara. "Boxer Asks Bodman about Dump of Rocketydyne Waste in Kettleman Hills." November 3, 2006. https://web.archive.org/web/201509 10131128/https://www.boxer.senate.gov/press/release/boxer-asks-bodman -about-dump-of-rocketdyne-waste-in-kettleman-hills/.

Braz, R. "Joining Forces: Prisons and Environmental Justice in Recent California Organizing." *Radical History Review*, no. 96 (2006): 95–111. https://doi .org/10.1215/01636545-2006-006.

Brooker, Megan E., and David S. Meyer. "Coalitions and the Organization of Collective Action." In *The Wiley Blackwell Companion to Social Movements*, edited by David A. Snow, Sarah A. Soule, Hanspeter Kriesi, and Holly J. McCammon, 252–68. Oxford: John Wiley & Sons, 2019.

Brown, Edmund G., Jr. "Executive Order B-55-18 to Achieve Carbon Neutrality." September 10, 2018. www.ca.gov/archive/gov39/wp-content/uploads /2018/09/9.10.18-Executive-Order.pdf.

Brown, Michael. *Laying Waste: The Poisoning of America by Toxic Chemicals.* New York: Pantheon Books, 1979.

Brown, Phil, and Edwin J. Mikkelsen. *No Safe Place: Toxic Waste, Leukemia, and Community Action.* Berkeley: University of California Press, 1997.

———. "Towards Domestic Fair Trade? Farm Labor, Food Localism, and the 'Family Scale' Farm." *GeoJournal* 73, no. 1 (September 2008): 11–22. https://doi.org/10.1007/s10708-008-9192-2.

Browning, Rufus P., Dale Rogers Marshall, and David H. Tabb. *Protest Is Not Enough: The Struggle of Blacks and Hispanics for Equality in Urban Politics.* Berkeley: University of California Press, 1984.

Brulle, Robert J. *Agency, Democracy, and Nature: The U.S. Environmental Movement from a Critical Theory Perspective.* Boston: MIT Press, 2000.

Brulle, Robert J., and Craig J. Jenkins. "Foundations and the Environmental Movement: Priorities, Strategies and Impact." In *Foundations for Social Change: Critical Perspectives on Philanthropy and Popular Movements*, edited by Daniel Faber and Debra McCarthy, 151–73. Oxford: Rowman & Littlefield, 2005.

Bryant, Bunyan, and Elaine Hockman. "A Brief Comparison of the Civil Rights Movement and the Environmental Justice Movement." In *Power, Justice, and the Environment: A Critical Appraisal of the Environmental Justice Movement*, edited by David Naguib Pellow and Robert J. Brulle, 23–36. Cambridge, MA: MIT Press, 2005.

Bullard, Robert D., ed. *Confronting Environmental Racism: Voices from the Grassroots.* Boston: South End Press, 1993.

Bullard, Robert D., Paul Mohai, Robin Saha, and Beverly Wright. *Toxic Wastes and Race at Twenty: 1987–2007.* Cleveland, OH: United Church of Christ Justice and Witness Ministries, 2007. http://d3n8a8pro7vhmx.cloudfront .net/unitedchurchofchrist/legacy_url/7987/toxic-wastes-and-race-at-twenty -1987-2007.pdf?1418432785.

Bullock, Clair, Kerry Ard, and Grace Saalman. "Measuring the Relationship between State Environmental Justice Action and Air Pollution Inequality, 1990–2009." *Review of Policy Research* 35, no. 3 (May 2018): 466–90. https://doi.org/10.1111/ropr.12292.

Burke, W. K. "Poisoning the National Toxics Campaign." *In These Times,* October 28, 1992.

Burwell, Dollie, and Luke W. Cole. "Environmental Justice Comes Full Circle: Warren County Before and After." *Golden Gate University Law Journal* 1, no. 1 (2007): 9–40.

Cable, Sherry, Tamara Mix, and Donald Hastings. "Mission Impossible? Environmental Justice Activists' Collaborations with Professional Environmentalists and with Academics." In *Power, Justice, and the Environment: A Critical Appraisal of the Environmental Justice Movement,* edited by David Naguib Pellow and Robert J. Brulle, 55–75. Cambridge, MA: MIT Press, 2005.

California Air Resources Board. "California Climate Investments Legislative Guidance." Accessed February 5, 2021. https://ww2.arb.ca.gov/resources /documents/california-climate-investments-legislative-guidance.

California Department of Pesticide Regulation. "Summary of Pesticide Use Report Data—2018." Sacramento, 2018. www.cdpr.ca.gov/docs/pur/pur18 rep/18sum.htm.

California Department of Public Health. *Birth Defects in Kettleman City and Surrounding Areas: 2009–2011 Update.* Sacramento, CA, 2012. www.cdph .ca.gov/Programs/CCDPHP/DEODC/EHIB/EES/CDPH%20Document%20 Library/MO-CBDMP-BirthDefectinKC-English-2009-11.pdf#search=Birth% 20Defects%20in%20Kettleman%20City%20and%20Surrounding%20Areas.

California Department of Toxic Substances Control. "CWM Kettleman Hills Facility RCRA/TSCA Inspections: 1983–Present." 2012.

California Environmental Justice Alliance. "CEJA Announces Opposition to AB 398 and ACA 1." July 17, 2017. https://caleja.org/2017/07/ceja-announces -opposition-to-ab-398-and-aca-1/.

———. "Community Solutions Take Center Stage during Climate Justice Mobilizations in San Francisco!" October 2018. https://caleja.org/2018/10 /community-solutions-take-center-stage-during-climate-justice-mobilizations -in-san-francisco/.

———. "Environmental Justice Groups Disappointed by the Speakers' Actions to Replace CARB Member." News release, June 5, 2018. https://caleja.org /wp-content/uploads/2018/06/CEJA-statement-on-ARB-appt.pdf.

———. "Statement on the Nomination of Michael Regan for EPA Administrator." December 17, 2020. https://caleja.org/2020/12/statement-on-nomination -of-michael-regan-for-epa-administrator/.

California Environmental Protection Agency and California Department of Public Health. "Investigation of Birth Defects and Community Exposures in

Kettleman City, CA: Public Review Draft." November 2010. www.countyof kings.com/home/showdocument?id=826.

California Environmental Protection Agency Air Resources Board. "History of Air Resources Board." Accessed January 25, 2015. www.arb.ca.gov/know zone/history.htm.

California Rural Legal Assistance. "Small Community Derails Toxic Incinerator." *Noticiero* 1, no. 2 (1992): 1, 8.

California Rural Legal Assistance Foundation et al. "Re: Comments on U.S. Environmental Protection Agency Draft Policy Papers, *Title VI of the Civil Rights Act of 1964: Adversity and Compliance with Environmental Health-Based Standards* (Released Jan. 24, 2013); *Title VI of the Civil Rights Act of 1964: Draft Role of Complainants and Recipients in the Title VI Complaints and Resolution Process* (Released Jan. 25, 2013)." March 20, 2013.

California Waste Management Board. "Waste-to-Energy Update March 1986." 1986.

Californians for Pesticide Reform. "Pesticide Use in California Remains at Record High, New Data Show." January 21, 2021. www.pesticidereform .org/pesticide-use-in-california-remains-at-record-high-new-data-show/.

Capitman, John Amson, and Tim R. Tyner. *The Impacts of Short-Term Changes in Air Quality on Emergency Room and Hospital Use in California's San Joaquin Valley*. Fresno: Central Valley Health Policy Institute, California State University, Fresno, June 2011.

Cart, Julie. "They Come Hat in Hand for California's 'Green' Money." Cal-Matters, September 5, 2017. https://calmatters.org/environment/2017/09 /come-hat-hand-californias-green-money/.

Carter, Eric. "Environmental Justice 2.0: New Latino Environmentalism in Los Angeles." *Local Environment: The International Journal of Justice and Sustainability* 21, no. 1 (2016): 3–23. https://doi.org/10.1080/13549839.2014 .912622.

Center for Biological Diversity. "Federal Court Strikes Down Illegal Permit for Avenal Power Plant in California." News release, August 12, 2014. www .biologicaldiversity.org/news/press_releases/2014/avenal-power-plant-08-12 -2014.html.

Center for Health Environment and Justice. "25 Years of Action." *Everyone's Backyard: The Journal of the Grassroots Environmental Movement* 24, no. 1 (2006): 8–13, 16, 18–21.

Center on Race, Poverty, and the Environment. *A Right without a Remedy: How the EPA Failed to Protect the Civil Rights of Latino Schoolchildren*. Delano, CA, 2016. https://crpe-ej.org/wp-content/uploads/2016/12/Right -without-a-Remedy-FINAL.pdf.

Cervas, Strela. "Legislature Should Stand Up for Environmental Justice." *Sacramento Bee*, January 27, 2015. www.sacbee.com/opinion/op-ed/soapbox /article8413050.html.

Cervas, Strela, and Amy Vanderwarker. "Justice Deferred: A Break Down of California's Cap & Trade Bill from the Environmental Justice Perspective." Medium, July 25, 2017. https://cejapower.medium.com/justice-deferred-a-break-down -of-californias-cap-trade-bill-from-the-environmental-justice-fbc35f87b6db.

Chafe, William H. *Civilities and Civil Rights: Greensboro, North Carolina, and the Black Struggle for Freedom*. Oxford: Oxford University Press, 1981.

Chavis, Benjamin F., Jr. Foreword to *Confronting Environmental Racism: Voices from the Grassroots*, edited by Robert D. Bullard, 3–5. Boston: South End Press, 1993.

Chavis, Benjamin F., Jr., and Charles Lee. *Toxic Wastes and Race in the United States: A National Report on the Racial and Socio-Economic Characteristics of Communities with Hazardous Waste Sites*. New York: United Church of Christ Commission for Racial Justice, 1987.

Checker, Melissa. "Wiped Out by the 'Greenwave': Environmental Gentrification and the Paradoxical Politics of Urban Sustainability." *City & Society* 23, no. 2 (December 2011): 210–29. https://doi.org/10.1111/j.1548-744X.2011.01063.x.

Ciplet, David. *An Industry Blowing Smoke: 10 Reasons Why Gasification, Pyrolysis & Plasma Incineration Are Not "Green Solutions"*. Berkeley, CA: GAIA, 2009.

Ciplet, David, and Jill Lindsey Harrison. "Transition Tensions: Mapping Conflicts in Movements for a Just and Sustainable Transition." *Environmental Politics* 29, no. 3 (2020): 435–56. https://doi.org/10.1080/09644016.2019.1595883.

Clark, Henry and Ahmadia Thomas. "Henry Fighting Toxic Emissions in Richmond, California, 1984–2000." An oral history conducted in 1999 and 2000 by Carl Wilmsen. Regional Oral History Office, The Bancroft Library, University of California, Berkeley, 2003. https://ia802307.us.archive.org/34/items/toxicemissionsooclarrich/toxicemissionsooclarrich.pdf.

Clark, William A. V. *Immigration and Hispanic Middle Class*. Washington, DC: Center for Immigration Studies, April 1, 2001. https://cis.org/Report/Immigration-and-Hispanic-Middle-Class.

Clinton, William J. "Executive Order 12898." *Federal Register: Presidential Documents* 59, no. 32 (February 1994): 1–5. www.archives.gov/files/federal-register/executive-orders/pdf/12898.pdf.

Coe, Erin. "Calif. Trash-to-Energy Plants May Labor for Renewable Status." Law360, June 14, 2012. www.law360.com/articles/350251/calif-trash-to-energy-plants-may-labor-for-renewable-status.

Cohn, Scott. "Small Community Is One of Many Grappling with Big Water Problems." Marketplace, February 22, 2017. www.marketplace.org/2017/02/22/sustainability/small-community-one-many-grappling-big-water-problems/.

Cole, Luke W. "Environmental Justice Litigation: Another Stone in David's Sling." *Fordham Urban Law Journal* 21, no. 3 (1993): 523–45.

Cole, Luke W., and Sheila Foster. *From the Ground Up: Environmental Racism and the Rise of the Environmental Justice Movement*. New York: New York University Press, 2001.

Comptroller General of the United States. *EPA's Inventory of Potential Hazardous Waste Sites Is Incomplete*. Washington, DC: General Accounting Office, March 26, 1985. www.gao.gov/assets/rced-85-75.pdf.

Corburn, Jason. *Street Science: Community Knowledge and Environmental Health Justice*. Cambridge, MA: MIT Press, 2005.

Costner, Pat, and Joe Thornton. *Playing with Fire: Hazardous Waste Incineration*. Washington, DC: Greenpeace USA, 1990.

Cowan, Tadlock. *California's San Joaquin Valley: A Region in Transition*. Washington, DC: Congressional Research Service, December 12, 2005. www .cdfa.ca.gov/agvision/files/California/California_CRSReportforCongressSan JoaquinValley-ARegioninTransition.pdf.

Cullenward, Danny, Mason Inman, and Michael Mastrandrea. "California's Climate Emissions Are Falling, but Cap-and-Trade Is Not the Cause." Near Zero, November 10, 2017. http://wp.nearzero.org/wp-content/uploads /2017/11/Near-Zero-2016-MRR-Research-Note.pdf.

Cullenward, Danny, and Katie Valenzuela. "A Critique of 'Do Environmental Markets Cause Environmental Injustice? Evidence from California's Carbon Market,' a 2020 NBER Working Paper by Danae Hernández-Cortés and Kyle C. Meng." Climate Policy: Danny Cullenward on the Law and Economics of Climate Change Policy, December 1, 2020. www.ghgpolicy.org /writing/hcm-error.

Currie, Janet, John Voorheis, and Reed Walker. "What Caused Racial Disparities in Particulate Exposure to Fall? New Evidence from the Clean Air Act and Satellite-Based Measures of Air Quality." Working Paper 26659, National Bureau of Economic Research, Cambridge, MA, January 20, 2020. https://doi.org/10.3386/w26659.

Currie, Melanie. "Air Resources Board Elevates Environmental Justice to Executive Level." *Streetsblog California*, January 21, 2021. https://cal.streetsblog .org/2021/01/21/air-resources-board-elevates-environmental-justice-to -executive-level/.

Cushing, Lara, Dan Blaustein-Rejto, Madeline Wander, Manuel Pastor, James Sadd, Allen Zhu, and Rachel Morello-Frosch. "Carbon Trading, Co-Pollutants, and Environmental Equity: Evidence from California's Cap-and-Trade Program (2011–2015)." *PLOS Medicine* 15, no. 7 (2018): e1002604. https://doi.org/10.1371/journal.pmed.1002604.

Cushing, Lara J., Madeline Wander, Rachel Morello-Frosch, Manuel Pastor, Allen Zhu, and James Sadd. *A Preliminary Environmental Equity Assessment of California's Cap-and-Trade Program*. Program for Environmental and Regional Equity, University of Southern California, Los Angeles, 2016. https://dornsife.usc.edu/assets/sites/242/docs/Climate_Equity_Brief_CA _Cap_and_Trade_Sept2016_FINAL2.pdf.

Dallman, Suzanne, Mary Ngo, Paul Laris, and Deborah Thien. "Political Ecology of Emotion and Sacred Space: The Winnemem Wintu Struggles with California Water Policy." *Emotion, Space and Society* 6 (February 2013): 33–43. https://doi.org/10.1016/j.emospa.2011.10.006.

Davenport, Christian, Sarah A. Soule, and David A. Armstrong II. "Protesting While Black? The Differential Policing of American Activism, 1960 to 1990." *American Sociological Review* 76, no. 1 (2011): 152–78. https://doi .org/10.1177/0003122410395370.

Deloitte Consulting. *Evaluation of the EPA Office of Civil Rights*. Washington, DC, March 21, 2011. https://archive.epa.gov/epahome/ocr-statement/web /pdf/epa-ocr_20110321_finalreport.pdf.

Dillon, Lindsey. "The Breathers of Bayview Hill: Redevelopment and Environmental Justice in Southeast San Francisco." *Hastings Environmental Law Journal* 24, no. 2 (2018): 227–36.

———. "Race, Waste, and Space: Brownfield Redevelopment and Environmental Justice at the Hunters Point Shipyard." *Antipode* 46, no. 5 (2014): 1205–21. https://doi.org/10.1111/anti.12009.

Dillon, Lindsey, and Julie Sze. "Police Power and Particulate Matters: Environmental Justice and the Spatialities of In/Securities in U.S. Cities." *English Language Notes* 54, no. 2 (2016): 13–23. https://doi.org/10.1215/00138282 -54.2.13.

Douglass, Frederick. *The Life and Writings of Frederick Douglass.* 5 vols. Edited by Philip S. Foner. New York: International Publishers, 1950.

"Down on the Farms." *Economist*, August 3, 2013. www.economist.com /united-states/2013/08/03/down-on-the-farms.

Dubofsky, Melvyn. *We Shall Be All: A History of the Industrial Workers of the World.* Chicago: Quadrangle Books, 1969.

Eady, Veronica. 2003. "Environmental Justice in State Policy Decisions." In *Just Sustainabilities: Development in an Unequal World*, edited by Julian Agyeman, Robert D. Bullard, and Bob Evans, 168–82. Cambridge, MA: MIT Press.

Eberhard, Kristin. "Air Board Should Move Ahead with AB 32 Scoping Plan: California's Blueprint for Transitioning to a Clean Energy Economy." *Switchboard: Natural Resources Defense Council Staff Blog*, August 24, 2011. http://switchboard.nrdc.org/blogs/kgrenfell/air_board_should_move _ahead_wi.html.

Egelko, Bob. "California to Block Food Pesticide That Trump's EPA Saved from Nationwide Ban." *San Francisco Chronicle*, May 8, 2019. www.sfchronicle .com/science/article/California-moves-to-ban-pesticide-widely-used-by-138 29656.php?psid=651B1.

Ejmatters.org. "Debunking the Myths of Cap-and-Trade." Accessed April 5, 2021. https://web.archive.org/web/20100729080315/http://www.ejmatters .org/docs/GHG-Myths_FactsheetFINAL[1].pdf.

———. "Factsheet: The Cap and Trade Charade for Climate Change." 2006. www.ejmatters.org/docs/Cap-Trade_FACTSHEET.pdf.

El Pueblo Para El Aire y Agua Limpio/People for Clean Air and Water and Greenaction for Health and Environmental Justice. "Is There a Toxic Monster in Kettleman City? Why the State of California's Draft Report and Investigation of Kettleman City Birth Defects are Incomplete, Flawed and Misleading." December 2, 2010. https://web.archive.org/web/20101 222193226/http://greenaction.org/incinerators/kettleman/documents /ElPuebloGreenactionReportOnKettlemanCityInvestigation.pdf.

Environmental Enforcement Watch. *Congressional Report Card.* March 18, 2021.

Environmental Justice Advisory Committee on the Implementation of the Global Warming Solutions Act of 2006. "Recommendation and Comments of the Environmental Justice Advisory Committee on the Implementation of the Global Warming Solutions Act of 2006 (AB 32) on the Draft Scoping Plan." October 1, 2008.

Farhang, Sean, and Ira Katznelson. "The Southern Imposition: Congress and Labor in the New Deal and Fair Deal." *Studies in American Political Development* 19, no. 1 (2005): 1–30. https://doi.org/https://doi.org/10.1017/S0898588X05000015.

Farrell, Caroline. "A Just Transition: Lessons Learned from the Environmental Justice Movement." *Duke Forum for Law & Social Change* 4 (2012): 45–63.

Filter, Gale. *2009 Environmental Justice Enforcement Initiative Report*. Sacramento: California Environmental Protection Agency, 2009.

Fimrite, Peter. "Sierra Club Wants Landmark Climate Law Altered." *San Francisco Chronicle*, May 12, 2011. www.sfgate.com/default/article/Sierra-Club-wants-landmark-climate-law-altered-2371978.php.

Finney, Carolyn. *Black Faces, White Spaces: Reimagining the Relationship of African Americans to the Great Outdoors*. Chapel Hill: University of North Carolina Press, 2014.

Forbes. "#458 Waste Management." n.d. www.forbes.com/companies/waste-management/#59d9b3cf31d6.

———. "The 200 Largest U.S. Charities: Environment/Animal." n.d. www.forbes.com/lists/top-charities/#4011cebc5f50.

Foreman, Dave. *Confessions of an Eco-Warrior*. New York: Crown Trade Paperbacks, 1991.

Fowlie, Meredith, Reed Walker, and David Wooley. "Climate Policy, Environmental Justice, and Local Air Pollution." *Brookings Economic Studies*, October 20, 2020. www.brookings.edu/research/climate-policy-environmental-justice-and-local-air-pollution/.

Fox, Jonathan. "The Uncertain Relationship between Transparency and Accountability." *Development in Practice* 17, nos. 4–5 (2007): 663–71. https://doi.org/10.1080/09614520701469955.

Frazier, E. Franklin. *Black Bourgeoisie*. New York: Free Press, 1957.

Fredrickson, Leif, Marianne Sullivan, Christopher Sellers, Jennifer Ohayon, Ellen Kohl, Sarah Lamdan, Alissa Cordner, et al. *A Sheep in the Closet: The Erosion of Enforcement at the EPA*. Environmental Data & Governance Initiative, May 31, 2019. https://envirodatagov.org/wp-content/uploads/2018/11/Sheep-in-the-Closet.pdf.

Gilens, Martin. *Why Americans Hate Welfare: Race, Media, and the Politics of Antipoverty Policy*. Chicago: Chicago University Press, 1999.

Gilio-Whitaker, Dina. *As Long as Grass Grows: The Indigenous Fight for Environmental Justice, from Colonization to Standing Rock*. Boston: Beacon Press, 2019.

Global Alliance for Incinerator Alternatives. "Garbage Incineration: What a Waste." September 2017. www.no-burn.org/wp-content/uploads/Garbage-Incineration-What-a-Waste-factsheet.pdf.

———. "Incinerators Blocked/Closed, U.S. & Canada, 2012–2017." Accessed September 18, 2018. www.no-burn.org/incinerators-blocked-closed-u-s-canada-2012-2016-2/.

"Global Warming I: Developing Cap and Trade Programs to Reduce Greenhouse Gas Emissions." *Environmental Law News* 16, no. 1 (2007): 34–43.

Gnerre, Sam. "The Fletcher Oil Fire." *South Bay Daily Breeze*, July 7, 2010. http://blogs.dailybreeze.com/history/2010/07/07/the-fletcher-oil-fire/.

Goldberg, David Theo. *The Threat of Race: Reflections on Racial Neoliberalism*. Malden, MA: Wiley-Blackwell, 2009.

Golden, Tim. "Ralph S. Abascal, 62, Dies; Leading Lawyer for the Poor." *New York Times*, March 19, 1997. www.nytimes.com/1997/03/19/us/ralph-s -abascal-62-dies-leading-lawyer-for-the-poor.html.

Goodman, Amy. "'Climate Capitalism Is Killing Our Communities': Protesters Disrupt Gov. Brown's SF Climate Summit." Democracy Now!, September 14, 2018. www.democracynow.org/2018/9/14/climate_capitalism_is _killing_our_communities.

Goodwin, Jeff, James Jasper, and Francesca Polletta. "The Return of the Repressed: The Fall and Rise of Emotions in Social Movement Theory." *Mobilization* 5, no. 1 (2000): 65–83. https://doi.org/10.17813/maiq.5.1 .74u39102m1078748.

Goss, Tracy A., and Amy Kroeger. *White Paper on Potential Control Strategies to Address Cumulative Impacts from Air Pollution*. South Coast Air Quality Management District, August, 2003.

Gottlieb, Robert. *Forcing the Spring: The Transformation of the American Environmental Movement*. 2nd ed. Washington, DC: Island Press, 2005.

Gould, Deborah B. *Moving Politics: Emotion and ACT UP's Fight against AIDS*. Chicago: University of Chicago Press, 2009.

Gould, Kenneth, Allan Schnaiberg, and Adam Weinberg. *Local Environmental Struggles: Citizen Activism in the Treadmill of Production*. Cambridge: Cambridge University Press, 1996.

Gould, Kenneth A., and Tammy L. Lewis. *Green Gentrification: Urban Sustainability and the Struggle for Environmental Justice*. New York: Routledge, 2017.

Greenaction for Health and Environmental Justice and Global Alliance for Incinerator Alternatives. "Incinerators in Disguise: Case Studies of Gasification, Pyrolysis, and Plasma in Europe, Asia, and the United States." June 2006. www.no-burn.org/incinerators-in-disguise-case-studies-of-gasification -pyrolysis-and-plasma-in-europe-asia-and-the-united-states/.

Greenleaf, Maron. "California Polluters May Soon Buy Carbon 'Offsets' from the Amazon—Is That Ethical?" The Conversation, September 26, 2019. https://theconversation.com/california-polluters-may-soon-buy-carbon -offsets-from-the-amazon-is-that-ethical-123738.

Gross, Elizabeth, and Paul Stretesky. "Environmental Justice in the Court." In *Failed Promises: Evaluating the Federal Government's Response to Environmental Justice*, edited by David M. Konisky, 205–31. Cambridge, MA: MIT Press, 2015.

Guthman, Julie. "Neoliberalism and the Making of Food Politics in California." *Geoforum* 39, no. 3 (May 2008): 1171–83. https://doi.org/10.1016/j .geoforum.2006.09.002.

Gutiérrez, Gabriel. "Mothers of East Los Angeles Strike Back." In *Unequal Protection: Environmental Justice and Communities of Color*, edited by Robert D. Bullard, 220–33. San Francisco: Sierra Club Books, 1994.

Hanemann, W. Michael. "How California Came to Pass AB 32, the Global Warming Solutions Act of 2006." Working Paper no. 1040, University of California, Berkeley, Department of Agricultural and Resource Economics, March 1, 2007.

Hansen, Todd R. "State Officials Dispute Cap-and-Trade Study Conclusions." *Daily Republic*, July 12, 2018. www.dailyrepublic.com/all-dr-news/solano -news/fairfield/state-officials-dispute-cap-and-trade-study-conclusions/.

Harris, Rita. "A Witness to Environmental Justice over 20 Years." Sierra Club, February 26, 2014. www.sierraclub.org/compass/2014/02/witness -environmental-justice-over-20-years.

Harrison, Jill. "Abandoned Bodies and Spaces of Sacrifice: Pesticide Drift Activism and the Contestation of Neoliberal Environmental Politics in California." *Geoforum* 39, no. 3 (May 2008): 1197–1214. https://doi.org/10.1016 /j.geoforum.2007.02.012.

Harrison, Jill Lindsey. "Bureaucrats' Tacit Understandings and Social Movement Policy Implementation: Unpacking the Deviation of Agency Environmental Justice Programs from EJ Movement Priorities." *Social Problems* 63, no. 4 (2016): 534–53. https://doi.org/10.1093/socpro/spw024.

———. "Coopted Environmental Justice? Activists' Roles in Shaping EJ Policy Implementation." *Environmental Sociology* 1, no. 4 (2015): 241–55. https:// doi.org/10.1080/23251042.2015.1084682.

———. *From the Inside Out: The Fight for Environmental Justice within Government Agencies.* Cambridge, MA: MIT Press, 2019.

———. *Pesticide Drift and the Pursuit of Environmental Justice.* Cambridge, MA: MIT Press, 2011.

———. "'We Do Ecology, Not Sociology': Interactions among Bureaucrats and the Undermining of Regulatory Agencies' Environmental Justice Efforts." *Environmental Sociology* 3, no. 3 (2017): 197–212. https://doi.org/https:// doi.org/10.1080/23251042.2017.1344918.

Harvey, David. *A Brief History of Neoliberalism.* New York: Oxford University Press, 2005.

Hauter, Wenonah. "Environmental Defense Fund: Stop Your Sell-Out to the Gas Industry." *Huffington Post*, August 28, 2012. www.huffingtonpost.com /wenonah-hauter/environmental-defense-fun_b_1834029.html.

Haya, Barbara. "AB 398's Use of Excess Carbon Credits Instead of Real Reductions." Berkeley Energy and Climate Institute, University of California, July 17, 2017.

Haya, Barbara, Lara Cushing, Rachel Morello-Frosch, Manuel Pastor, Michael Wara, and David Wooley. "RE: Public Comments on Methods for Determining Whether Offset Projects Result in Direct Environmental Benefits in the State (DEBS)." July 20, 2018. www.arb.ca.gov/lists/com-attach/39-ct-6 -21-18-wkshp-ws-BnZXJFY1AzwGaVMw.pdf.

Hecht, Sean. "California Environmental Justice Advocates Sue Air Resources Board over Climate Scoping Plan." *Legal Planet: The Environmental Law and Policy Blog*, June 10, 2009. http://legal-planet.org/2009/06/10/california -environmental-justice-advocates-sue-air-resources-board-over-climate -scoping-plan/.

Hemphill, Bonnie Frye. "The Justice in Fighting Prop 23." May 2, 2012. http://cairnwords.files.wordpress.com/2012/08/justice-in-fighting-prop-23-bonnie-frye-hemphill.pdf.

Henry, Mark. "EPA Seeks Help in Removal of Sludge." *Press-Enterprise*, October 20, 1994.

———. "Protesters Take to Tents to Blockade Sludge Plant." *Press-Enterprise*, October 18, 1994.

Hernandez-Cortes, Danae, and Kyle C. Meng. "Do Environmental Markets Cause Environmental Injustice? Evidence from California's Carbon Market." Working Paper 27205, National Bureau of Economic Research, Cambridge, MA, May 2020. https://doi.org/10.3386/w27205.

Hertsgaard, Mark. "Latinos Are Ready to Fight Climate Change—Are Green Groups Ready for Them?" *Nation*, December 5, 2012. www.thenation.com/article/171617/latinos-are-ready-fight-climate-change-are-green-groups-ready-them#.

Hinds, Cathy, Heeten Kalan, Jane McAlevey, Baldemar Velasquez, Diane Takvorian, Pam Tau Lee, and Anthony Thigpenn. *The National Toxics Campaign: Some Reflections, Thoughts for the Movement.* N.p., 1992. http://www.ejnet.org/ej/ntcf.pdf.

Holifield, Ryan. "Neoliberalism and Environmental Justice in the United States Environmental Protection Agency: Translating Policy into Managerial Practice in Hazardous Waste Remediation." *Geoforum* 35, no. 3 (May 2004): 285–97. https://doi.org/10.1016/j.geoforum.2003.11.003.

Horn, Steve. "As Indigenous Peoples Protest, California Approves Global Cap-and-Trade Plan." Real News Network, September 23, 2019. https://therealnews.com/as-indigenous-peoples-protest-california-approves-global-cap-and-trade-plan.

How to Win at Public Hearings. Falls Church, VA: Center for Health, Environment & Justice, 2009.

Hudson, Drew, et al. "Re: EPA Administrator Appointment." December 2, 2020.

Hull, Dana. "13 Things to Know about California's Cap-and-Trade Program." *San Jose Mercury News*, February 22, 2013. www.mercurynews.com/ci_22092533/13-things-know-about-california-cap-trade-program.

Hull, Tim. "Big Air Quality Win for Enviros in 9th Circuit." Courthouse News Service, August 12, 2014. www.courthousenews.com/Big-Air-Quality-Win-for-Enviros-in-9th-Circuit-/.

Huynh, Dan K. "Evaluating the Innovation Value Access Network (IVAN) Model as a Tool for Environmental Reporting and Enforcement in California Communities." Master's thesis, University of California, Los Angeles, 2013.

Incite! Women of Color Against Violence. *The Revolution Will Not Be Funded: Beyond the Non-profit Industrial Complex.* Cambridge, MA: INCITE! and South End Press Collective, 2007.

Jaffe, Matt. "Above the Surface and Below, L.A. Is Still an Oil Town." *Los Angeles Magazine*, February 5, 2018. www.lamag.com/citythinkblog/surface-l-still-oil-town/.

Jain, S. Lochlann. *Malignant: How Cancer Becomes Us*. Berkeley: University of California Press, 2013.

Jatkar, Shrayas, and Jonathan London. "From Testimony to Transformation: The Identifying Violations Affecting Neighborhoods (IVAN) Program in California." Davis Center for Regional Change, University of California, June 6, 2015.

Jefferson, Margo. *Negroland: A Memoir*. New York: Vintage Books, 2015.

Jenkins, J. Craig. "Resource Mobilization Theory and the Study of Social Movements." *Annual Review of Sociology*, no. 9 (1983): 527–53.

Jenkins, J. Craig, Jason T. Carmichael, Robert J. Brulle, and Heather Boughton. "Foundation Funding of the Environmental Movement." *American Behavioral Scientist* 61, no. 13 (2018): 1640–57.

Johnson, Nathanael. "The Biggest Fight over Cap and Trade Isn't about What You Think It Is." Grist, October 19, 2020. https://grist.org/climate/the-biggest-fight-over-cap-and-trade-isnt-about-what-you-think-it-is/.

Kahn, Debra. "California Environmentalists Quietly Seethe at Activists over Nichols Losing EPA Job." Politico, December 17, 2020. www.politico.com/states/california/story/2020/12/17/california-environmentalists-quietly-angry-at-activists-over-nichols-losing-epa-job-1348317.

Kaswan, Alice. "Climate Change and Environmental Justice: Lessons from the California Lawsuits." *San Diego Journal of Climate & Energy Law* 5, no. 1 (2014): 1–42.

Katznelson, Ira. *When Affirmative Action Was White: An Untold History of Racial Inequality in Twentieth Century America*. New York: W. W. Norton, 2005.

Kelderman, Keene, Eric Schaeffer, Tom Pelton, Ari Phillips, and Courtney Bernhardt. *The Thin Green Line: Cuts to State Pollution Control Agencies Threaten Public Health*. Environmental Integrity Project, December 5, 2019. www.environmentalintegrity.org/wp-content/uploads/2019/12/The-Thin-Green-Line-report-12.5.19.pdf.

Kenney, Douglas S., Miriam Stohs, Jessica Chavez, Anne Fitzgerald, and Teresa Erickson. *Evaluating the Use of Good Neighbor Agreements for Environmental and Community Protection*. Boulder, CO: Natural Resource Law Center, University of Colorado School of Law, 2004.

Kitchell, Mark, dir. *A Fierce Green Fire: The Battle for a Living Planet*. Oley, PA: Bullfrog Films, 2012.

Kline, Benjamin. *First Along the River: A Brief History of the U.S. Environmental Movement*. 4th ed. Lanham, MD: Rowman & Littlefield, 2011.

Kohl-Arenas, Erica. "Governing Poverty amidst Plenty: Participatory Development and Private Philanthropy." *Geography Compass* 5, no. 11 (November 2011): 811–24. https://doi.org/10.1111/j.1749-8198.2011.00453.x.

Kravitz-Wirtz, Nicole, Kyle Crowder, Anjum Hajat, and Victoria Sass. "The Long-Term Dynamics of Racial/Ethnic Inequality in Neighborhood Air Pollution Exposure, 1990–2009." *Du Bois Review* 13, no. 2 (2016): 237–59. https://doi.org/10.1017/S1742058X16000205.

Krishnakumar, Priya, and Swetha Kannan. "2020 California Fires Are the Worst Ever: Again." *Los Angeles Times*, September 15, 2020. www.latimes.com/projects/california-fires-damage-climate-change-analysis/.

Krupp, Fred. "EDF and the Third Wave of Environmentalism." *Pulp and Paper*, July 1994.

Krupp, Fred, and Miriam Horn. *Earth, the Sequel: The Race to Reinvent Energy and Stop Global Warming*. New York: W. W. Norton, 2008.

Kurtz, Hilda E. "Acknowledging the Racial State: An Agenda for Environmental Justice Research." *Antipode* 41, no. 4 (2009): 684–704. https://doi.org/10.1111/j.1467-8330.2009.00694.x.

Lackey, Michael, ed. *The Haverford Discussions: A Black Integrationist Manifesto for Racial Justice*. Charlottesville: University of Virginia Press, 2013.

Lacy, Karyn R. *Blue-Chip Black: Race, Class, and Status in the New Black Middle Class*. Berkeley: University of California Press, 2007.

League of Conservation Voters. *2016 National Environmental Scorecard: Report on Congressional Caucuses of Color*. Washington, DC, 2017. www.lcv.org/2016-scorecard-caucuses-of-color/.

Liévanos, Raoul S. "Certainty, Fairness, and Balance: State Resonance and Environmental Justice Policy Implementation." *Sociological Forum* 27, no. 2 (June 2012): 481–503. https://doi.org/https://doi.org/10.1111/j.1573-7861.2012.01327.x.

Lipsitz, George. *The Possessive Investment in Whiteness: How White People Profit from Identity Politics*. Philadelphia: Temple University Press, 1998.

Loh, Penn. "Where Do We Go from Here? 'We Must All Be Accountable in a Grassroots Movement.'" *Race, Poverty and the Environment* 10, no. 1 (2003). www.reimaginerpe.org/20years/loh.

London, Jonathan, Ganlin Huang, and Tara Zagofsky. "Land of Risk/Land of Opportunity: Cumulative Environmental Vulnerabilities in California's San Joaquin Valley." November 2011. UC Davis Center for Regional Change. https://regionalchange.ucdavis.edu/sites/g/files/dgvnsk986/files/inline-files/FINAL-Land%20of%20Risk-Land%20of%20Opportunity%20-2.pdf.

London, Jonathan, Alex Karner, Julie Sze, Dana Rowan, Gerardo Gambirazzio, and Deb Niemeier. "Racing Climate Change: Collaboration and Conflict in California's Global Climate Change Policy Arena." *Global Environmental Change* 23, no. 4 (2013): 791–99. https://doi.org/10.1016/j.gloenvcha.2013.03.001.

London, Jonathan K., Peter Nguyen, Mia Dawson, and Katrina Manrique. *Community Engagement in AB 617: An Evaluation of Challenges, Successes, Lessons Learned and Recommendations for the Future*. Davis: University of California, June 2020. https://ww2.arb.ca.gov/sites/default/files/2020-10/17RD035-English-AB 617 UC Davis Report Final for distribution.pdf.

London, Jonathan K., Julie Sze, and Raoul S. Liévanos. "Problems, Promise, Progress, and Perils: Critical Reflections on Environmental Justice Policy Implementation in California." *UCLA Journal of Environmental Law and Policy* 26, no. 2 (2008): 255–89.

López, Ian Haney. *Dog Whistle Politics: How Coded Racial Appeals Have Reinvented Racism and Wrecked the Middle Class*. New York: Oxford University Press, 2014.

Lopez, Patricia. "11 Arrested in Protest Near Toxic Waste Site." *Los Angeles Times*, August 13, 1985. http://articles.latimes.com/1985-08-13/news/mn -1361_1_toxic-waste.

Magavern, Bill. "Re: Need to Re-Evaluate AB 32 Cap-and-Trade Rule." Sierra Club California, May 9, 2011.

Magnuson, Ed, J. Madeleine Nash, Peter Stoler, and John E. Yang. "A Problem That Cannot Be Buried: The Poisoning of America Continues." *Time*, October 14, 1985.

Malin, Stephanie. "When Is 'Yes to the Mill' Environmental Justice? Interrogating Sites of Acceptance in Response to Energy Development." *Analyse und Kritik* 36, no. 2 (2014): 263–85. https://doi.org/10.1515/auk-2014-0205.

Marable, Manning. *How Capitalism Underdeveloped Black America: Problems in Race, Political Economy, and Society*. Chicago: Haymarket Books, 2015.

Marbella, Jean. "Beginning of Freddie Gray's Life as Sad as Its End, Court Case Shows." *Baltimore Sun*, April 23, 2015. www.baltimoresun.com/maryland /baltimore-city/bs-md-freddie-gray-lead-paint-20150423-story.html.

Mares, Teresa Marie, and Alison Hope Alkon. "Mapping the Food Movement: Addressing Inequality and Neoliberalism." *Environment and Society: Advances in Research* 2, no. 1 (2011): 68–86. https://doi.org/10.3167/ares .2011.020105.

Martin, Mark. "Núñez Slams Governor on Emission Law." *San Francisco Chronicle*, October 17, 2006. www.sfgate.com/green/article/SACRAMENTO-N -ez-slams-governor-on-emission-2485726.php.

Martinez, Michael. "Poverty Plagues 'New Appalachia.'" *Chicago Tribune*, September 18, 2006. www.chicagotribune.com/news/ct-xpm-2006-09-18-0609 180188-story.html.

Marx, Gary T. "Afterword: Some Reflections on the Democratic Policing of Demonstrations." In *Policing Protest: The Control of Mass Demonstrations in Western Democracies*, 253–69. Minneapolis: University of Minnesota Press, 1998.

Matsuoka, Martha. *Building Healthy Communities from the Ground Up: Environmental Justice in California*. September 2003. www.reimaginerpe.org /files/healthy-communities.pdf.

Matsuoka, Martha, Andrea Hricko, Robert Gottlieb, and Juan DeLara. *Global Trade Impacts: Addressing the Health, Social and Environmental Consequences of Moving International Freight through Our Communities*. Occidental College and University of Southern California, Los Angeles, 2011.

Mayer, Brian. *Blue-Green Coalitions: Fighting for Safe Workplaces and Healthy Communities*. Ithaca, NY: Cornell University Press, 2009.

McAdam, Douglas. *Political Process and the Development of Black Insurgency, 1930–1970*. Chicago: University of Chicago Press, 1982.

McAllister, Lesley K. "The Overallocation Problem in Cap-and-Trade: Moving Toward Stringency." *Columbia Journal of Environmental Law* 34, no. 2 (2009): 395–445.

McCarthy, John D., and Mayer N. Zald. "Resource Mobilization and Social Movements: A Partial Theory." *American Journal of Sociology*, no. 82 (1977): 1212–41.

———. *The Trend of Social Movements in America: Professionalization and Resource Mobilization.* Morristown, NJ: General Learning Press, 1973.

McCoy, Terrence. "Freddie Gray's Life a Study on the Effects of Lead Paint on Poor Blacks." *Washington Post*, April 29, 2015. www.washingtonpost.com /local/freddie-grays-life-a-study-in-the-sad-effects-of-lead-paint-on-poor -blacks/2015/04/29/0be898e6-eea8-11e4-8abc-d6aa3bad79dd_story.html.

McDonnell, Patrick J. "'Rubble Rousers' Fight Dump." *Los Angeles Times*, March 17, 1996. http://articles.latimes.com/1996-03-17/local/me-48072_1 _cottage-street.

McGreevy, Patrick. "Toxics Agency Chief Condemns Racially Charged Emails." *Los Angeles Times*, December 9, 2015. www.latimes.com/politics/la-me-pc -toxics-agency-chief-condemns-racially-charged-emails-20151209-story.html.

McGurtry, Eileen. *Transforming Environmentalism: Warren County, PCBs, and the Origins of Environmental Justice.* New Brunswick, NJ: Rutgers University Press, 2007.

McPhail, Clark, David Schweingruber, and John McCarthy. "Policing Protest in the United States: 1960–1995." In *Policing Protest: The Control of Mass Demonstrations in Western Democracies*, edited by Donatella Della Porta and Herbert Reiter, 49–69. Minneapolis: University of Minnesota Press, 1998.

McQuaid, John. "Calling in Help Risks 'Outsider' Label." *New Orleans Times-Picayune*, May 22, 2000. www.nola.com/news/politics/article_8df94ed4 -7aa5-5e39-b887-3231d3544cf1.html https://www.nola.com/politics/2000 /05/calling_in_help_risks_outsider.html.

Méndez, Michael. *Climate Change from the Streets: How Conflict and Collaboration Strengthen the Environmental Justice Movement.* New Haven, CT: Yale University Press, 2020.

Middleton-Manning, Beth Rose, Morning Star Gali, and Darcie Houck. "Holding the Headwaters: Northern California Indian Resistance to State and Corporate Water Development." *Decolonization: Indigeneity, Education & Society* 7, no. 1 (2018): 174–98.

Minkler, Meredith, and Nina Wallerstein, eds. *Community-Based Participatory Research for Health: From Process to Outcomes.* San Francisco: Jossey-Bass, 2011.

Mishak, Michael J. "Big Oil's Grip on California." Center for Public Integrity, February 13, 2017. https://publicintegrity.org/environment/big-oils-grip-on -california/.

Mitchell, Don, and Lynn A. Staeheli. "Permitting Protest: Parsing the Fine Geography of Dissent in America." *International Journal of Urban and Regional Research* 29, no. 4 (2005): 796–813. https://doi.org/10.1111/j.1468-2427 .2005.00622.x.

Montague, Peter. "Great Louisiana Toxics March Sets Pace for the Movement." *Rachel's Democracy & Health News*, no. 101, October 30, 1988. https://rachelsdemocracyandhealthnews.wordpress.com/2013/10/26/rachels -101-great-louisiana-toxics-march-sets-the-pace-for-the-movement/.

———. "Violence in Indian Country over Waste." *Rachel's Environment & Health Weekly*, no. 404, August 24, 1994. https://www.ejnet.org/rachel /rehw404.htm.

Moore, Patrick. *Confessions of a Greenpeace Dropout: The Making of a Sensible Environmentalist*. Vancouver, BC: Beatty Street Publishing, 2013.

Moore, Richard, and Louis Head. "Acknowledging the Past, Confronting the Present: Environmental Justice in the 1990s." In *Toxic Struggles: The Theory and Practice of Environmental Justice*, edited by Richard Hofrichter, 118–27. Philadelphia: New Society Publishers, 1993.

Morello-Frosch, Rachel, Manuel Pastor, and James Sadd. "Environmental Justice and Southern California's 'Riskscape': The Distribution of Air Toxics Exposures and Health Risks among Diverse Communities." *Urban Affairs Review* 36, no. 4 (March 1, 2001): 551–78. https://doi.org/10.1177/10780870122184993.

Morello-Frosch, Rachel, Manuel Pastor, James L. Sadd, Carlos Porras, and Michele Prichard. "Citizens, Science, and Data Judo: Leveraging Secondary Data Analysis to Build a Community-Academic Collaborative for Environmental Justice in Southern California." In *Methods in Community-Based Participatory Research for Health*, edited by Barbara A. Israel, Eugenia Eng, Amy J. Schulz, and Edith A. Parker, 371–92. San Francisco: John Wiley and Sons, 2005.

Morello-Frosch, Rachel, Miriam Zuk, Michael Jerrett, Bhavna Shamasunder, and Amy D. Kyle. "Understanding the Cumulative Impacts of Inequalities in Environmental Health: Implications for Policy." *Health Affairs* 30, no. 5 (2011): 879–87. https://doi.org/10.1377/hlthaff.2011.0153.

Morris, Aldon. "Black Southern Student Sit-In Movement: An Analysis of Internal Organization." *American Sociological Review* 46, no. 6 (1981): 744–67.

———. *The Origins of the Civil Rights Movement: Black Communities Organizing for Change*. New York: Free Press, 1984.

Mulvaney, Dustin. *Solar Power: Innovation, Sustainability, and Environmental Justice*. Berkeley: University of California Press, 2019.

Murphy, Michelle. "Uncertain Exposures and the Privilege of Imperception: Activist Scientists and Race at the U.S. Environmental Protection Agency." *Osiris* 19, no. 1 (2004): 266–82.

National Association of Latino Elected and Appointed Officials Educational Fund. *A Profile of Latino Elected Officials in the United States and Their Progress since 1996*. Los Angeles: NALEO Educational Fund, 2007.

Natural Resources Defense Council. "Fracking Threatens Health of Los Angeles County Communities Already Overburdened with Pollution." NRDC Fact Sheet, September 2014. www.nrdc.org/sites/default/files/california-fracking-risks-LA-FS.pdf.

Nembhard, Jessica Gordon. *Collective Courage: A History of African American Cooperative Economic Thought and Practice*. University Park, PA: Penn State University Press, 2014.

Newell, Brent. "Climate Justice: Global Climate Disruption and the Struggle for Environmental Justice." Talk given at the Environmental Studies Department, University of California, Santa Cruz, April 4, 2011.

Nichols, Chris. "TRUE: 'More than a Million Californians' Don't Have Clean Drinking Water . . . It Could Be Higher." Politifact California, February 14,

2019. www.politifact.com/california/statements/2019/feb/14/gavin-newsom/true-more-million-californians-dont-have-clean-dri/.

Nidever, Seth. "Kettleman Hopes Bottled Water Continues." *Hanford Sentinel*, July 5, 2017. https://hanfordsentinel.com/news/local/kettleman-hopes-bottled-water-continues/article_2c91a998-5af9-5d42-9504-78b465584c25.html.

———. "Sludge Composting Plant Starts Up." *Hanford Sentinel*, May 11, 2016. https://hanfordsentinel.com/news/local/sludge-composting-plant-starts-up/article_97bd3268-167a-55bb-b83a-a8e68cb3958e.html.

"North Carolina: Part 2." *Waste Not*, no. 164, September 12, 1991. http://www.americanhealthstudies.org/wastenot/wn164.htm.

"Obama's Full Remarks at Howard University Commencement Ceremony." Politico, May 7, 2016. www.politico.com/story/2016/05/obamas-howard-commencement-transcript-222931.

Okorie, Obasi, Ekemini Hogan, and Utibe Effiong. "I Can't Breathe: Asthma, Black Men and the Police." *Scientific American*, October 14, 2020. www.scientificamerican.com/article/i-cant-breathe-asthma-black-men-and-the-police/.

Omi, Michael, and Howard Winant. *Racial Formation in the United States.* 3rd ed. New York: Routledge, 2015.

Oreskes, Naomi, and Erik M. Conway. *Merchants of Doubt: How a Handful of Scientists Obscured the Truth on Issues from Tobacco Smoke to Global Warming.* New York: Bloomsbury, 2010.

Ottinger, Gwen. *Refining Expertise: How Responsible Engineers Subvert Environmental Justice Challenges.* New York: New York University Press, 2013.

Pardo, Mary. "Mexican American Women Grassroots Community Activists: 'Mothers of East Los Angeles.'" *Frontiers: A Journal of Women Studies* 11, no. 1 (1990): 1–7. https://doi.org/https://doi.org/10.2307/3346696.

Park, Angela. *Everybody's Movement: Environmental Justice and Climate Change.* Washington, DC: Environmental Support Center, December 2009. https://kresge.org/sites/default/files/Everybodys-movement-climate-social-justice.pdf.

Park, Lisa Sun-Hee, and David Pellow. "Racial Formation, Environmental Racism, and the Emergence of Silicon Valley." *Ethnicities* 4, no. 3 (2004): 403–24. https://doi.org/https://doi.org/10.1177/1468796804045241.

Pastor, Manuel. *State of Resistance: What California's Dizzying Descent and Remarkable Resurgence Mean for America's Future.* New York: New Press, 2018.

Pastor, Manuel, Rachel Morello-Frosch, James Sadd, and Justin Scoggins. "Minding the Climate Gap: What's at Stake If California's Climate Law Isn't Done Right and Right Away." Program for Environmental and Regional Equity, University of Southern California, Los Angeles, 2010.

———. "Risky Business: Cap-and-Trade, Public Health, and Environmental Justice." In *Urbanization and Sustainability: Linking Urban Ecology, Environmental Justice and Global Environmental Change,* edited by Christopher G. Boone and Michail Fragkias, 75–94. New York: Springer, 2013.

Payne, Charles M. *I've Got the Light of Freedom: The Organizing Tradition and the Mississippi Freedom Struggle.* Berkeley: University of California Press, 2007.

Pellow, David N. "Environmental Inequality Formation: Toward a Theory of Environmental Injustice." *American Behavioral Scientist* 43, no. 4 (2000): 581–601. https://doi.org/10.1177/0002764200043004004.

———. "Environmental Justice and the Political Process: Movements, Corporations, and the State." *Sociological Quarterly* 42, no. 1 (2001): 47–67. https://doi.org/10.1111/j.1533-8525.2001.tb02374.x.

———. "Environmental Justice, Animal Rights, and Total Liberation: From Conflict and Distance to Points of Common Focus." In *Routledge International Handbook of Green Criminology*, edited by Nigel South and Avi Brisman, 331–46. New York: Routledge, 2013.

———. "Environmental Justice Movements and Political Opportunity Structures." In *The Routledge Handbook of Environmental Justice*, edited by Ryan Holifield, Jayajit Chakraborty, and Gordon Walker, 37–49. New York: Routledge, 2017.

———. *Garbage Wars: The Struggle for Environmental Justice in Chicago.* Cambridge, MA: MIT Press, 2002.

———. *Resisting Global Toxics: Transnational Movements for Environmental Justice.* Cambridge, MA: MIT Press, 2007.

Pellow, David N., and Lisa Sun-Hee Park. *The Silicon Valley of Dreams: Environmental Injustice, Immigrant Workers, and the High-Tech Global Economy.* New York: New York University Press, 2002.

Pellow, David Naguib. *What Is Critical Environmental Justice?* Cambridge, UK: Polity Press, 2018.

Pellow, David Naguib, and Robert J. Brulle. "Power, Justice, and the Environment: Toward Critical Environmental Justice Studies." In *Power, Justice, and the Environment: A Critical Appraisal of the Environmental Justice Movement*, edited by David Naguib Pellow and Robert J. Brulle, 1–21. Cambridge, MA: MIT Press, 2005.

Perkins, Tracy. "The Environmental Justice Legacy of the United Farm Workers of America: Stories from the Birthplace of Industrial Agriculture." Humanities for the Environment, August 10, 2014. https://hfe-observatories.org/stories/the-environmental-justice-legacy-of-the-united-farm-workers-of-america-stories-from-the-birthplace-of-industrial-agriculture/.

———. "Framing and the Politics of Environmental Justice Language: A Typology of Uses." Paper presented at the Annual Meeting of the American Sociological Association, New York, August 2019.

———. "In Her Own Words: Remembering Teresa De Anda, Pesticides Activist (1959–2014)." 2015. www.rememberingteresa.org.

———. "The Multiple People of Color Origins of the US Environmental Justice Movement: Social Movement Spillover and Regional Racial Projects in California." *Environmental Sociology* 7, no. 2 (2021): 147–59. https://doi.org/10.1080/23251042.2020.1848502.

———. "On Becoming a Public Sociologist: Amplifying Women's Voices in the Quest for Environmental Justice." In *Sociologists in Action: Race, Class, Gender, and Sexuality*, edited by Shelley White, Kathleen Odell Korgen, and Jonathan White, 88–92. Los Angeles: SAGE Publications, 2015.

————. "Origin Stories of the Environmental Justice Movement." Paper presented at the Bridging the Gap: Race and the Environment Mini-Conference, Annual Meeting of the American Sociological Association, Philadelphia, PA, 2018.

————. "Research Trip to Los Angeles." TracyPerkins.org, November 23, 2013. https://tracyperkins.org/2013/11/23/field-trip-to-los-angeles/.

————. "Slideshow: Environmental Justice Coalition Founding Conference. TracyPerkins.org, November 9, 2014. https://tracyperkins.org/2014/11/09/slideshow-california-environmental-justice-coalition-founding-conference/.

————. "Slideshow: Happy People's Earth Day!" TracyPerkins.org, April 22, 2013. https://tracyperkins.org/2013/04/22/slideshow-happy-peoples-earth-day/.

————. "Slideshow: The Faces of Public Participation." TracyPerkins.org, December 19, 2013. https://tracyperkins.org/2013/12/19/slideshow-the-faces-of-public-participation/.

————. "Voices." Voices from the Valley: Environmental Justice in California's San Joaquin Valley, 2008. www.voicesfromthevalley.org/voices/.

————. Voices from the Valley: Environmental Justice in California's San Joaquin Valley, 2008. www.voicesfromthevalley.org.

————. "Women's Pathways into Activism: Rethinking the Women's Environmental Justice Narrative in California's San Joaquin Valley." *Organization & Environment* 25, no. 1 (2012): 76–94. https://doi.org/https://doi.org/10.1177/1086026612445390.

Perkins, Tracy, and Lindsey Dillon. "Gonzales." Critical Sustainabilities: Competing Discourses of Urban Development in California, 2015. https://critical-sustainabilities.ucsc.edu/gonzales-ca/.

Perkins, Tracy, and Aaron Soto-Karlin. "Situating Global Policies within Local Realities: Climate Conflict from California to Latin America." In *Sustainability: Approaches to Environmental Justice and Social Power*, edited by Julie Sze, 102–23. New York: New York University Press, 2018.

Perkins, Tracy, and Julie Sze. "Images from the Central Valley." *Boom: A Journal of California* 1, no. 1 (2011): 70–80. https://doi.org/10.1525/boom.2011.1.1.71.

Pesticide Action Network North America. "New Rule Puts Limits on Pesticide Use Near Schools." News release, November 7, 2017. www.panna.org/press-release/new-rule-puts-limits-pesticide-use-near-schools

Peter, Ellen M. "Implementing Environmental Justice: The New Agenda for California State Agencies." *Golden Gate University Law Review* 31, no. 4 (2001): 529–91.

Peters, Glen P., Jan C. Minx, Christopher L. Weber, and Ottmar Edenhofer. "Growth in Emission Transfers via International Trade from 1990 to 2008." *Proceedings of the National Academy of Sciences of the United States of America* 108, no. 21 (May 24, 2011): 8903–8. https://doi.org/10.1073/pnas.1006388108.

Pezzullo, Phaedra C. "Performing Critical Interruptions: Stories, Rhetorical Invention, and the Environmental Justice Movement." *Western Journal of*

Communication 65, no. 1 (2001): 1–25. https://doi.org/10.1080/10570310 109374689.

Phillips, Anna M. "Trump Fracking Plan Targets over 1 Million Acres in California." *Los Angeles Times*, April 25, 2019. www.latimes.com/politics/la-na -pol-trump-fracking-oil-gas-california-20190425-story.html.

Phillips, Steve. *Brown Is the New White: How the Demographic Revolution Has Created a New American Majority.* New York: New Press, 2016.

Piven, Frances Fox, and Richard A. Cloward. "Collective Protest: A Critique of Resource Mobilization Theory." *International Journal of Politics, Culture, and Society* 4, no. 4 (1991): 435–58.

———. *Poor People's Movements: Why They Succeed, How They Fail.* New York: Pantheon Books, 1977.

Pooley, Eric. "In Defense of Unlikely Partnerships." *Climate 411* (blog), Environmental Defense Fund, May 20, 2011. http://blogs.edf.org/climate411 /2011/05/20/in-defense-of-unlikely-partnerships/.

Powell, Stephen J. *Political Difficulties Facing Waste-to-Energy Conversion Plant Siting.* Los Angeles: Cerrell Associates, 1984.

"The Principles of Environmental Justice." In *The First National People of Color Environmental Leadership Summit*, xii–xiv. Washington, DC, United Church of Christ Commission for Racial Justice, October 1991.

Pulido, Laura. "A Critical Review of the Methodology of Environmental Racism Research." *Antipode* 28, no. 2 (1996): 142–59. https://doi.org/https:// doi.org/10.1111/j.1467-8330.1996.tb00519.x.

———. "Flint, Environmental Racism, and Racial Capitalism." *Capitalism Nature Socialism* 27, no. 3 (2016): 1–16. https://doi.org/10.1080/10455752 .2016.1213013.

Pulido, Laura, Tianna Bruno, Cristina Faiver-Serna, and Cassandra Galentine. "Environmental Deregulation, Spectacular Racism, and White Nationalism in the Trump Era." *Annals of the American Association of Geographers* 109, no. 2 (2019): 520–32. https://doi.org/10.1080/24694452.2018.1549473.

Pulido, Laura, and Juan De Lara. "Reimagining 'Justice' in Environmental Justice: Radical Ecologies, Decolonial Thought, and the Black Radical Tradition." *Environment and Planning E: Nature and Space* 1, nos. 1–2 (2018): 76–98. https://doi.org/10.1177/2514848618770363.

Pulido, Laura, Ellen Kohl, and Nicole Marie Cotton. "State Regulation and Environmental Justice: The Need for Strategy Reassessment." *Capitalism Nature Socialism* 27, no. 2 (2016): 12–31. https://doi.org/10.1080/104 55752.2016.1146782.

"Q & A: A Conversation with Dr. Henry Clark, Environmental Activist." *Richmond Today: Richmond Refinery Newsletter*, December 2017.

"Ralph Abascal: Lawyer Was Advocate for Poor." *Los Angeles Times*, March 20, 1997.

Ramsden, Lindi, and Ian Slattery, dirs. *Thirsty for Justice: The Struggle for the Human Right to Water.* Sacramento: The Unitarian Universalist Justice Ministry of California; Environmental Justice Coalition for Water; Unitarian Universalist Service Committee, 2014.

Ranganathan, Malini. "Thinking with Flint: Racial Liberalism and the Roots of an American Water Tragedy." *Capitalism Nature Socialism* 27, no. 3 (2016): 17–33. https://doi.org/10.1080/10455752.2016.1206583.

Rechtschaffen, Clifford, Eileen Guana, and Catherine A. O'Neill. *Environmental Justice: Law, Policy, and Regulation.* Durham, NC: Carolina Academic Press, 2009.

Reeves, Richard V., and Camille Busette. "The Middle Class Is Becoming Race-Plural, Just Like the Rest of America." *Social Mobility Memos,* February 27, 2018. www.brookings.edu/blog/social-mobility-memos/2018/02/27/the-middle-class-is-becoming-race-plural-just-like-the-rest-of-america/.

Reynolds, Joel R. "LANCER and the Vernon Incinerator: Protecting Communities from the Projects That 'Have to Go Somewhere . . . .'" In *Everyday Heroes Protect the Air We Breathe, the Water We Drink, and the Natural Areas We Prize: Thirty-Five Years of the California Environmental Quality Act,* 95–96. Sacramento: Planning and Conservation League Foundation and the California League of Conservation Voters, 2005.

Richter, Lauren. "Constructing Insignificance: Critical Race Perspectives on Institutional Failure in Environmental Justice Communities." *Environmental Sociology* 4, no. 1 (2018): 107–21. https://doi.org/10.1080/23251042.2017.1410988.

Roberts, David. "California Gov. Jerry Brown Casually Unveils History's Most Ambitious Climate Target." Vox, September 12, 2018. www.vox.com/energy-and-environment/2018/9/11/17844896/california-jerry-brown-carbon-neutral-2045-climate-change.

Roberts, David J., and Minelle Mahtani. "Neoliberalizing Race, Racing Neoliberalism: Placing 'Race' in Neoliberal Discourses." *Antipode* 42, no. 2 (2010): 248–57. https://doi.org/10.1111/j.1467-8330.2009.00747.x.

Roberts, J. Timmons, and Melissa M. Toffolon-Weiss. *Chronicles from the Environmental Justice Frontlines.* Cambridge: Cambridge University Press, 2001.

Robinson, Cedric. *Black Marxism.* 2nd ed. Chapel Hill: University of North Carolina Press, 2005.

Roelofs, J. *Foundations and Public Policy: The Mask of Pluralism.* Albany: State University of New York Press, 2003.

Romero, Mindy. *As California Goes, So Goes the Nation? U.S. Demographic Change and the Latino Vote.* Davis: California Civic Engagement Project, 2016. https://regionalchange.ucdavis.edu/sites/g/files/dgvnsk986/files/inline-files/ucdavisccepjan2016report.pdf.

Rosengren, Cole. "After Its First WTE Closes, California Down to 2." *Wastedive,* August 2, 2018. www.wastedive.com/news/california-first-wte-facility-closes/529164/.

Ruta, Gwen. "Environmental Defense Fund." In *Good Cop/Bad Cop: Environmental NGOs and Their Strategies toward Business,* edited by Thomas P. Lyon, 184–94. Washington, DC: RFF Press, 2010.

Sadd, J. L., E. S. Hall, M. Pastor, R. A. Morello-Frosch, D. Lowe-Liang, J. Hayes, and C. Swanson. "Ground-Truthing Validation to Assess the Effect of Facility

Locational Error on Cumulative Impacts Screening Tools." *Geography Journal* 2015 (August 31, 2015): 1–8. https://doi.org/10.1155/2015/324683.

Sadd, James L., Manuel Pastor, Rachel Morello-Frosch, Justin Scoggins, and Bill Jesdale. "Playing It Safe: Assessing Cumulative Impact and Social Vulnerability through an Environmental Justice Screening Method in the South Coast Air Basin, California." *International Journal of Environmental Research and Public Health* 8, no. 5 (May 2011): 1441–59. https://doi.org/10.3390/ijerph8051441.

Sahagun, Louis. "Latinos, Asians More Worried about Environment Than Whites, Poll Finds." *Los Angeles Times*, November 20, 2010. http://articles.latimes.com/2010/nov/20/local/la-me-poll-environment-20101120.

Salazar, Debra J., Stacy Clauson, Troy D. Abel, and Aran Clauson. "Race, Income, and Environmental Inequality in the U.S. States, 1990–2014." *Social Science Quarterly* 100, no. 3 (May 2019): 592–603. https://doi.org/10.1111/ssqu.12608.

Salcido, Rachael. "Reviving the Environmental Justice Agenda." *Chicago-Kent Law Review* 91, no. 1 (2016): 115–37.

Sandler, Ronald, and Phaedra C. Pezzullo, eds. *Environmental Justice and Environmentalism: The Social Justice Challenge to the Environmental Movement.* Cambridge, MA: MIT Press, 2007.

Santa Clara Center for Occupational Safety and Health (SCCOSH) and Silicon Valley Toxics Coalition (SVTC). Records, Series I: SCCOSH, Activism 1976–2003, Series Scope and Content Summary. Accessed September 17, 2018. https://oac.cdlib.org/findaid/ark:/13030/kt2b69r7hf/dsc/.

Santoro, Wayne A., and Gail M. McGuire. "Social Movement Insiders: The Impact of Institutional Activists on Affirmative Action and Comparable Worth Policies." *Social Problems* 44, no. 4 (1997): 503–19. https://doi.org/10.2307/3097220.

Sarathy, Brinda. "Legacies of Environmental Justice in Inland Southern California." *Race, Gender & Class* 2, no. 4 (2013): 254–68.

Sbicca, Joshua, and Justin Sean Myers. "Food Justice Racial Projects: Fighting Racial Neoliberalism from the Bay to the Big Apple." *Environmental Sociology* 3, no. 1 (2017): 30–41. https://doi.org/10.1080/23251042.2016.1227229.

Scammell, Madeleine Kangsen, and Gregory J. Howard. *Is a Health Study Right for Your Community? A Guide for Making Informed Decisions.* Boston: Boston University School of Public Health, 2015.

Schlosberg, David. "Theorising Environmental Justice: The Expanding Sphere of a Discourse." *Environmental Politics* 22, no. 1 (2013): 37–55. https://doi.org/10.1080/09644016.2013.755387.

Schlosberg, David, and Lisette B. Collins. "From Environmental to Climate Justice: Climate Change and the Discourse of Environmental Justice." *WIREs Climate Change* 5, no. 3 (2014): 359–74. https://doi.org/10.1002/wcc.275.

Schmich, Mary T. "They March to Clean Up a State's Act." *Chicago Tribune*, November 20, 1988. http://articles.chicagotribune.com/1988-11-20/news/8802170889_1_mississippi-river-bridge-greenpeace-marchers_.

Selznick, Philip. "Foundations of the Theory of Organization." *American Sociological Review* 13, no. 1 (1948): 25–35.

"Share the Burden." Living on Earth, October 2003. www.loe.org/shows /segmentprint.html?programID=03-P13-00043&segmentID=1.

Shilling, Fraser M., Jonathan K. London, and Raoul S. Liévanos. "Marginalization by Collaboration: Environmental Justice as a Third Party in and beyond CALFED." *Environmental Science & Policy* 12, no. 6 (October 2009): 694–709. https://doi.org/10.1016/j.envsci.2009.03.003.

Shonkoff, Seth B., Rachel Morello-Frosch, Manuel Pastor, and James Sadd. "Minding the Climate Gap: Environmental Health and Equity Implications of Climate Change Mitigation Policies in California." *Environmental Justice* 2, no. 4 (2009): 173–77. https://doi.org/10.1089/env.2009.0030.

Sierra Club. *National Survey of Hispanic Voters on Environmental Issues.* 2008. https://vault.sierraclub.org/ecocentro/survey/Executive%20Summary.pdf.

Sierra Club and National Council of La Raza. *2012 National Latinos and the Environment Survey: Executive Summary.* 2012. https://vault.sierraclub.org /ecocentro/survey/2012 Latinos and the Environment Survey_Exec Summary_English.pdf.

Sitkoff, Harvard. *A New Deal for Blacks: The Emergence of Civil Rights as a National Issue; The Depression Decade.* 30th anniversary ed. Oxford: Oxford University Press, 2009.

Skocpol, Theda. *Diminished Democracy: From Membership to Management in American Civic Life.* Norman: University of Oklahoma Press, 2003.

Smith, Ted. "Pioneer Activist for Environmental Justice in Silicon Valley, 1967–2000." An oral history conducted in 1999 by Carl Wilmsen. Regional Oral History Office, The Bancroft Library, University of California, Berkeley, 2003. https://digitalassets.lib.berkeley.edu/rohoia/ucb/text /pioneeractivistsiloosmitrich.pdf.

Smith, Ted, David A. Sonnenfeld, and David Naguib Pellow, eds. *Challenging the Chip: Labor Rights and Environmental Justice in the Global Electronics Industry.* Philadelphia: Temple University Press, 2006.

Solnit, Rebecca. *Hope in the Dark: Untold Histories, Wild Possibilities.* New York: Nation Books, 2004.

Sommeiller, Estelle, and Mark Price. *The New Gilded Age: Income Inequality in the U.S. by State, Metropolitan Area, and County.* Washington, DC: Economic Policy Institute, 2018. www.epi.org/files/pdf/147963.pdf.

SouthWest Organizing Project. "Letter to Jay D. Hair." Albuquerque, NM, March 16, 1990. www.ejnet.org/ej/swop.pdf.

Spears, Ellen. "'Freedom Buses' Roll along Cancer Alley." *Southern Changes: The Journal of the Southern Regional Council* 15, no. 1 (1993): 1–11.

Srebotnjak, Tanja, and Miriam Rotkin-Ellman. *Drilling in California: Who's at Risk?* New York: Natural Resources Defense Council, October 2014. www .nrdc.org/sites/default/files/california-fracking-risks-report.pdf.

Staggenborg, Suzanne. "The Consequences of Professionalization and Formalization in the Pro-Choice Movement." *American Sociological Review* 53, no. 4 (1998): 585–605.

Stammer, Larry B. "70 Groups Unite in Battle against Pollution." *Los Angeles Times*, February 19, 1986.

Stark, Kevin. "Newsom Catches Heat for Using Climate Funds on Drinking Water Plan." KQED, June 19, 2019. www.kqed.org/science/1943578/climate-funds-for-clean-water-democrats-enviro-groups-are-split.

State of California Assembly Bill 32, Chapter 488. Approved September 27, 2006. www.leginfo.ca.gov/pub/05-06/bill/asm/ab_0001-0050/ab_32_bill_20060927_chaptered.pdf.

State of California Assembly Bill 1329 Hazardous Waste. Passed September 25, 2013. http://leginfo.legislature.ca.gov/faces/billNavClient.xhtml?bill_id=201320140AB1329.

State of the Air 2019. Chicago: American Lung Association, 2019. www.lung.org/assets/documents/healthy-air/state-of-the-air/sota-2019-full.pdf.

Stoiber, Tasha, Alexis Temkin, David Andrews, Chris Campbell, and Olga V. Naidenko. "Applying a Cumulative Risk Framework to Drinking Water Assessment: A Commentary." *Environmental Health* 18 (2019): 37. https://doi.org/10.1186/s12940-019-0475-5.

Szasz, Andrew. *Ecopopulism: Toxic Waste and the Movement for Environmental Justice*. Minneapolis: University of Minnesota Press, 1994.

———. *Shopping Our Way to Safety: How We Changed from Protecting the Environment to Protecting Ourselves*. Minneapolis: University of Minnesota Press, 2009.

Sze, Julie, Gerardo Gambirazzio, Alex Karner, Dana Rowan, Jonathan London, and Deb Niemeier. "Best in Show? Climate and Environmental Justice Policy in California." *Environmental Justice* 2, no. 4 (December 2009): 179–84. https://doi.org/https://doi.org/10.1089/env.2009.0028.

Sze, Julie, and Jonathan K. London. "Environmental Justice at the Crossroads." *Sociology Compass* 2, no. 4 (2008): 1331–54. https://doi.org/10.1111/j.1751-9020.2008.00131.x.

Tangri, Neil. *Waste Incineration: A Dying Technology*. Berkeley, CA: GAIA, 2003.

Taylor, Dorceta E. "The Evolution of Environmental Justice Activism, Research, and Scholarship." *Environmental Practice* 13, no. 4 (2011): 280–301. https://doi.org/10.1017/S1466046611000329.

———. *The Rise of the American Conservation Movement: Power, Privilege, and Environmental Protection*. Durham, NC: Duke University Press, 2016.

———. "The Rise of the Environmental Justice Paradigm: Injustice Framing and the Social Construction of Environmental Discourses." *American Behavioral Scientist* 43, no. 4 (2000): 508–80. https://doi.org/10.1177/0002764200043004003.

———. *Toxic Communities: Environmental Racism, Industrial Pollution, and Residential Mobility*. New York: New York University Press, 2014.

Taylor, Keeanga-Yamahtta. *From #BlackLivesMatter to Black Liberation*. Chicago: Haymarket Books, 2016.

Taylor, Mac. *Cap-and-Trade Extension: Issues for Legislative Oversight*. Sacramento, CA: Legislative Analyst's Office, December 12, 2017.

———. "Letter to Senator Darrell Steinberg and Speaker John A. Perez." Sacramento, CA: Legislative Analyst's Office, June 9, 2011.

Tompkins, Adam. "Cancer Valley, California: Pesticides, Politics, and Childhood Disease in the Central Valley." In *Natural Protest: Essays on the History of American Environmentalism*, edited by Michael Egan and Jeff Crane, 275–99. New York: Routledge, 2009.

"Toxics Activist's Home Is Torched; Despite Setback, Her New Report on Hazards of Incinerators Will Appear." *Rachel's Hazardous Waste News*, no. 233, May 15, 1991. www.ejnet.org/rachel/rhwn233.htm.

US Bureau of the Census. "ACS Demographic and Housing Estimates." 2009–2013 American Community Survey 5-Year Estimates, 2013. http://factfinder .census.gov/faces/nav/jsf/pages/index.xhtml.

———. "Educational Attainment." 2009–2013 American Community Survey 5-Year Estimates, 2013. http://factfinder.census.gov/faces/nav/jsf/pages /index.xhtml.

———. "Selected Economic Characteristics." 2009–2013 American Community Survey 5-Year Estimates, 2013. http://factfinder.census.gov/faces/nav/jsf /pages/index.xhtml.

US Commission on Civil Rights. *Environmental Justice: Examining the Environmental Protection Agency's Compliance and Enforcement of Title VI and Executive Order 12,898*. Washington, DC, September 2016.

US Energy Information Administration. "California: State Profile and Energy Estimates." Accessed May 22, 2019. www.eia.gov/state/?sid=CA.

US Environmental Protection Agency. "Current Nonattainment Counties for All Criteria Pollutants." 2019. www3.epa.gov/airquality/greenbook/ancl.html.

———. *Kettleman City Residential Sampling*. San Francisco, CA, November 2011. https://19january2017snapshot.epa.gov/www3/region9/kettleman/docs /kettleman-pesticides-factsheet-eng.pdf.

———. "Penny Newman: Leading Community Organizer—Stringfellow Superfund Site." Superfund 25th Anniversary: Transcripts of Oral History Interviews, Riverside, CA, October 24, 2005. https://semspub.epa.gov/work/HQ /100000103.pdf.

———. *Toolkit for Assessing Potential Allegations of Environmental Injustice*. Washington, DC, 2004. www.epa.gov/sites/production/files/2015-02 /documents/ej-toolkit.pdf.

US General Accounting Office. *How to Dispose of Hazardous Waste—A Serious Question That Needs to Be Resolved: Report to the Congress*. Washington, DC, 1978.

———. *Siting of Hazardous Landfills and Their Correlation with Racial and Economic Status of Surrounding Communities*. Washington, DC, June 1, 1983. http://archive.gao.gov/d48t13/121648.pdf.

Vickery, Jamie, and Lori Hunter. "Native Americans: Where in Environmental Justice Research?" *Society & Natural Resources* 29, no. 1 (2016): 36–52. ttps://doi.org/10.1080/08941920.2015.1045644.

Vogel, David. *California Greenin': How the Golden State Became an Environmental Leader*. Princeton, NJ: Princeton University Press, 2018.

Walker, Edward T., Michael McQuarrie, and Caroline W. Lee. "Rising Participation and Declining Democracy." In *Democratizing Inequality: Dilemmas of New Public Participation*, edited by Caroline W. Lee, Michael McQuarrie, and Edward T. Walker, 3–23. New York: New York University Press, 2015.

Wall, Michael E., Miriam Rotkin-Ellman, and Gina Solomon. *An Uneven Shield: The Record of Enforcement and Violations under California's Environmental, Health, and Workplace Safety Laws*. New York: Natural Resources Defense Council, 2008.

Wang, Xiao, George Deltas, Madhu Khanna, and Xiang Bi. "Community Pressure and the Spatial Redistribution of Pollution: The Relocation of Toxic Releasing Facilities." *Journal of the Association of Environmental and Resource Economists* 8, no. 3 (2021): 577–616. https://doi.org/10.1086/711656.

Wara, Michael W., and David G. Victor. "A Realistic Policy on International Carbon Offsets." Program on Energy and Sustainable Development, Working Paper no. 74, Stanford University, Palo Alto, CA, April 18, 2008.

Washington, Sylvia. "Ball of Confusion." In *Natural Protest: Essays on the History of American Environmentalism*, edited by Michael Egan and Jeff Crane, 205–21. New York: Routledge, 2009.

Wells, C., ed. *Environmental Justice in Postwar America: A Documentary Reader*. Seattle: University of Washington Press.

Westervelt, Eric. "Off-Duty Police Officers Investigated, Charged with Participating In Capitol Riot." NPR, January 15, 2021. www.npr.org/2021/01/15/956896923/police-officers-across-nation-face-federal-charges-for-involvement-in-capitol-ri.

White, Harvey. "Hazardous Waste Incineration and Minority Communities." In *Race and the Incidence of Environmental Hazards: A Time for Discourse*, edited by Bunyan Bryant and Paul Mohai, 126–39. Boulder, CO: Westview Press, 1992.

White, Monica. *Freedom Farmers: Agricultural Resistance and the Black Freedom Movement*. Chapel Hill: University of North Carolina Press, 2018.

Whitman, Christine Todd. "EPA's Commitment to Environmental Justice." Washington, DC, August 9, 2001.

Wiltz, Teresa. "Racial Generation Gap Looms Large for States." *Stateline*, January 16, 2015. www.pewtrusts.org/pl/research-and-analysis/blogs/stateline/2015/1/16/racial-generation-gap-looms-large-for-states.

Winton, Sonya. "Concerned Citizens: Environmental (In)Justice in Black Los Angeles." In *Black Los Angeles: American Dreams and Racial Realities*, edited by Darnell Hunt and Ana-Christina Ramon, 343–59. New York: New York University Press, 2010.

Wolf, Shaye, and Kassie Siegel. *Oil Stain: How Dirty Crude Undercuts California's Climate Progress*. Tucson, AZ: Center for Biological Diversity, 2017. www.biologicaldiversity.org/programs/climate_law_institute/energy_and_global_warming/pdfs/Oil_Stain.pdf.

Yoder, Traci. "A Tale of Two (Occupied) Cities: Policing Strategies at Occupy Wall Street and Occupy Philadelphia." *University of Pennsylvania Journal of Law and Social Change* 15, no. 4 (2012): 593–615.

Zagofsky, Tara. "Process Evaluation: California Air Resources Board Environmental Justice Advisory Committee (EJAC)." University of California, Davis Extension Collaboration Center, 2014.

Zelko, Frank. *Make It a Green Peace! The Rise of Countercultural Environmentalism.* New York: Oxford University Press, 2013.

Index